BOSTON BOUND

MW00823953

David Venable

© 2011 David Venable
All rights reserved

All rights reserved. This book, or parts thereof, may not be reproduced in any form without permission from the publisher; exceptions may be made for brief excerpts used in published reviews. The information presented in this publication has been compiled from personal knowledge and research from published texts or periodicals. Where such direct excerpts or quotations were incorporated, credit from the source(s) has been provided accordingly. The use of any direct quotes, written reference text, tables, graphics, or photographs not directly credited herein was not intentional. As such, the author, publisher, and editors release themselves from any legal implications with inadvertent re-use of copyright material in any form within this publication. The author does not hold a medical degree or certification of medical knowledge to provide medical diagnosis. The intent of addressing any medical ailments or injuries herein was to provide a personal opinion or advice. Where advice or opinion was provided for medical issues herein, professional medical consultation is recommended. Please consult with a doctor before attempting any exercises or training plans provided in this publication. The content of the book was not written for personal financial gain, as profits will benefit (through donation) the American Cancer Society or an organization(s) dedicated to the battle against cancer. These donations will be managed through the direction of Goals That Give Inc. This is in honor of my mother and all others who have battled cancer.

Published by
Dog Ear Publishing
4010 W. 86th Street, Ste H
Indianapolis, IN 46268
www.dogearpublishing.net

ISBN: 978-145750-139-5

This book is printed on acid-free paper.

ACKNOWLEDGEMENTS

To my parents, *Clinton and Betty*

May God bless you both

And

Special thanks to the hundreds of thousands of volunteers worldwide who make running events happen, from a 5K to the Boston Marathon. Without your support, we would have no events and thus no opportunity to achieve our life goals.

INTRODUCTION

The marathon running boom has fully emerged, and each year more and more runners venture into this unknown and somewhat ominous territory. But even with the marathon's popularity on the rise, less than 1% of the population of North America have run a full marathon, and only a small fraction of that number have run the streets of Boston. Attempting to qualify for the Boston Marathon is a feat not to be taken lightly and, if not approached properly, the training process can actually inflict damage to your body. Boston is considered by many as the pinnacle of marathons, and those who make it there are the elite of the marathon athletes, as runners must first qualify. Getting to Boston is the challenge, but once there you'll find the experience itself is the reward for your hard work.

This book focuses on proven training techniques, tips, and watch-outs that will improve your chances to qualify for the Boston Marathon and run your best at similar distance races. In addition to the core focus of a marathon training schedule, this book provides valuable advice on proper clothing, nutrition, injury prevention, preparation, the selection of the qualifying venue itself, and much more. These are a few of the factors that can influence your qualifying success. Even if you are not planning to run Boston, or you may have already had the privilege, you may still find sections of this book that will complement elements of your existing training program.

Like you, I dreamed of running at Boston and searched for ways to get there. My quest to qualify for Boston forced me to learn much along the way. This text represents the lessons, setbacks, and successes that led me to six Boston Marathons and immeasurable enjoyment in the sport of running.

Along my road to Boston, I researched many sources on how to improve my performance and found that authors were mixed on some key approaches to training and nutrition. Some texts were highly technical, and others were too general, and I became confused regarding what was applicable to my goal of qualifying for Boston. This book is a balanced mix of technical approach and applicable experience. I am neither an elite athlete nor an Olympic medalist. Unlike the majority of running-focused authors, I have no significant claim to fame within the running community. I trained my way to many successful Boston's and numerous other marathons and offer the perspective of an amateur runner who has struggled with the same challenges that you may be facing.

This book is intended for all runners who have the vision and the desire to go to Boston and are searching for guidance to improve their performance in hopes of qualifying for the most prestigious marathon in the world...
The Boston Marathon!

PREFACE

As a fellow runner, I, too, have experienced the dream of someday running in what many say is the most coveted of marathons, the Boston Marathon. My journey to Boston started the year of my fortieth birthday when I decided to run a local half marathon with the sole purpose of surviving. Perhaps this desire was somewhat driven by a slight infection of mid-life crisis or just the reality of the need to give the sofa a rest. Regardless of the motivating circumstance, I entered the sport of distance running as a true novice. So when race day arrived, I was filled with nervous energy and began to question my training approach. I even doubted that my gluttonous intake of spaghetti the previous night would be sufficient to carry me through the event.

Seeded appropriately for my expected finish of two hours, I started in the middle corral among a sea of 40,000 running shoes attached to people of all fitness levels. After the race start countdown reached zero, I was soon on my way to completing the longest running event of my life. One hour and fifty-four minutes later, I crossed the finish line and was given a medal and the obligatory congratulations by the volunteers. Surprisingly, I had survived the challenge.

Sometimes even the smallest bit of success in life encourages us to pursue further improvement in ourselves. Upon crossing the finish line in my first ½ marathon, I transitioned from a person who wanted to complete a bucket list goal in life, into a runner. The running bug had bit, and this ½ marathon was the catalyst that awakened a previously dormant part of my soul. I *needed* to run a full marathon. I soon learned of a local fall marathon, and thought that if I was able to stay in shape, just maybe I could complete a full marathon. Twenty-six miles and 385 yards of challenge lay ahead. I began to share my marathon goal with my peers who unexpectedly asked if I was going to run Boston. Naively, I responded, "Perhaps someday." Then as I started to consider Boston seriously, I was surprised to learn that I had to qualify. After some brief research of the qualifying requirement time for my age group, I realized that my then-current level of fitness was clearly inadequate. To qualify for Boston, I'd have to run a pace for a full marathon nearly equal to my fastest mile time. Yeah, when pigs fly, I said to myself. Then I focused on my fall marathon and trained only with the goal of respectable completion. But my dream of Boston grew.

Still a novice runner and unsure about many things regarding training, I purchased a few books to help answer questions. With surprise, I read that to train for a marathon the term "long run" was re-defined as a staggering 20 miles! So after months—and miles—of training, race day again arrived. It was a brisk fall morning as I walked toward my starting position among a thousand other runners. Pressure began to build. Stay on goal pace, I thought. Then thoughts of the infamous "wall" where runners are mystically drained of strength near the 20-mile point fueled the nervousness that race day brings upon runners. Minutes prior to the start, these anxious thoughts blurred my race strategy, and again I questioned my preparedness for the ominous hurdle that lay before me. But once the event started, I focused on the task. Three hours and forty-three minutes later, I realized that my training plan had worked, and I had run and completed my first marathon. Although I was sore in unexpected places and hobbling for days, my accomplishment more than offset my discomfort. On that day I learned that I could run 26.2 miles. But this sense of accomplishment was short-lived. I was no longer satisfied with just a marathon. I wanted Boston and needed to be faster.

The intrigue of Boston had found a new haunt. For the next year or so, I was on a mission: Boston or Bust! I purchased books and periodicals, went to websites, and sought out faster runners who would entertain my questions, which ranged from how to reduce lactic acid to how to improve my speed. The list of questions seemed endless. No single book focused on qualifying for the Boston Marathon. Nor did any one book provide a condensed summary of a runner's "Lessons Learned" along the road to Boston. So I began to pull together all of the related aspects into my personal Boston training plan.

Boston Bound

Two years after my first marathon, I qualified for Boston at Grandma's in Duluth, Minnesota. However, my success was ugly. I was plagued with nasty hamstring cramps that stopped me within sight of the finish line. While spectators urged me on to finish, I grimaced in pain and frustration. Other runners passed me as my shoes felt locked with the ground. What a nightmare! The finish line clock read 3:19, and I needed a 3:20 to qualify for Boston for my age group. My goal was slowly slipping away. When the race officials came to help me off the course because I was blocking the path for other runners, I quickly woke up. First I managed a slow walk. Then I jogged the last hundred yards to the finish. When I looked at my watch and realized I'd finished in just under 3:19, the grimace on my face turned into a proud smile. I'd just qualified for Boston! I'd made it! I was going to Boston! Since that race, I've shaved off a few more minutes, but the feeling of qualifying that first time was an experience of a lifetime and something that I'll never forget.

There are few who understand the dedication, passion, and personal motivation that this event instills in runners. In the post-finish area, runners are either elated or on the brink of tears due to their qualifying attempt. A marathon is a physically and emotionally draining experience, but it can also be one of your greatest life and fitness achievements. It is truly a motivational experience to position yourself at the 26-mile mark and watch the runners' faces as they near the finish line. Most are pushing themselves to new limits, struggling to sprint those final few feet. Some runners are completing their 50th marathon, while others are seeing the finish line for the very first time. All finishers share the look of determination in these final steps. As a runner, I respect any runner of any ability, regardless of his or her finishing time. A marathon is a great accomplishment deserving respect. Most runners are unique in their form, stride, strengths, weaknesses, injuries, or genetic ability, but if they have the motivation and vision for Boston, I put them all on equal ground to qualify.

I consider myself a typical runner with average running ability. Like most, I've got a 40-hour work week and a family, either of which will limit the amount of training time to pursue running goals. However, my desire to reach Boston, my research, and my training approach enabled me to improve my performance to the level necessary while keeping my training time to a minimum.

I'd be remiss in my duties as a running mentor if I didn't say that the passion for Boston does not come without compromise. Training for Boston takes time and dedication. For some, this goal may rise at a time when such a unique and challenging goal can bring vision to an otherwise clouded life. Boston may keep you from falling at a time when you need the sense of accomplishment, self-fulfillment, or stress relief via the therapeutic endorphins that running provides. Whatever the case, **when you make it**, the road to Boston is an unforgettable experience.

Study this book it in its entirety. The tools provided here—plus your motivation and vision—should bring you what Boston has brought me: the fulfillment of a life dream and an accomplishment that will last a lifetime.

Life is a balance of priorities, but if you want to run at Boston,
it must first become a priority in your life.

Table of Contents

Chapter 1
Boston...Why the Allure?

"The Boston Marathon produces what I feel is the best in American sports. Both small town America and big city America come together in this race as in no other."
- Bill Rodgers, four-Time Boston Marathon Winner (Tom Derderian)

Photo 1.1 History in the making at Boston.

It is a common occurrence for a runner to compete in a half or full marathon and hear the word Boston mentioned or see someone wearing the coveted shirt or jacket indicating their year of duty. From the pre-race conversations among strangers in the staging corral to the post finish area you can count on hearing at least a few personal stories or goals of running at Boston. These runners join the multitude of others worldwide for whom Boston looms in their thoughts, but when the running shoes are laced up, these thoughts give purpose to each stride.

To those who aren't impassioned by running, Boston may be most well known for its many historic events or landmarks, many of which can be viewed if you walk the Freedom Trail. To others, Boston's famous "chowda," baked beans, world champion teams (Red Sox and Celtics), and even a bar named Cheers may be their first association with this impressive city and its people. But to a marathon runner, Boston means the Boston Marathon, and on the third Monday in April, Boston becomes their personal Mecca.

The Marathon

The origin of the marathon dates back to the Battle of Marathon in 490 B.C. when a Greek warrior named Pheidippides ran to Athens (from Marathon, Greece) to bestow the news of the Greek victory over the Persians. Unfortunately, he died a short time after delivering the message. All modern marathons originated from this single event in history. Since that era, the marathon has become one of the most prominent tests of human endurance. In 1894, it was suggested that a "Marathon Race" of 40 kilometers (25 miles) be held to commemorate the Battle of Marathon. Shortly thereafter, a Marathon event was held at the first modern Olympic Games in 1896. Following the lead of the Olympics, the Boston Athletic Association (B.A.A.) organized the first Boston Marathon in 1897, and the race continues to make history to this day.

Why Boston?

The Boston Marathon is the world's oldest annual marathon and ranks as one of the world's most prestigious road racing events. The B.A.A. manages this iconic event, which has been run over roughly the same course since its inception in 1897. Throughout this long tradition, it has been held on Patriots Day (a Monday) and a holiday for Bostonians to commemorate the Battle of Lexington on April 19, 1775.

With runners competing and representing states, countries, and provinces throughout the world, the Boston Marathon draws diversity in competition similar to that of an Olympic event. Since participating in an Olympic event is out of reach for all but a few elite runners, Boston provides a more feasible reality and has become the dream race for most serious non-elite distance runners. From the 15 male entrants in 1897 to the record 37,000 in 1996, the Boston Marathon has grown immensely in both popularity and desire of runners to participate in this "pinnacle of Marathons." Due to its popularity, the B.A.A. has been forced to impose limitations on the number of entrants accepted. In fact, Boston is one, if not the only, open marathon that also requires qualification for entry by meeting stringent qualifying times at certified marathons.

The history, the qualifying time requirement, and the caliber of entrants are the key reasons that thousands, if not millions, of runners throughout the world desire the opportunity to run at Boston. Each year, hundreds of thousands of spectators line the route into Boston to watch and support each of the entrants who have worked hard and sacrificed much just to be there. The caliber and dedication of the race field is mirrored by the quality in the organization of this world-class event. The B.A.A. and the volunteers truly bring to fruition all participant expectations for a great and memorable event.

As a runner, the initial reason that I wanted to run at Boston was the prestige that the event held among my running peers. As I heard their stories of both success and failure to qualify for Boston, I wanted to be there and witness Heartbreak Hill, Boylston Street, and the roars of Wellesley College students. As I learned more about the history and tradition associated with this event, my desire and motivation to qualify increased exponentially, and this was reflected in my focus toward training. I quickly found myself wanting to learn more about how to improve my marathon times. The required age group qualification times are a significant challenge for many novice, as well as experienced, runners. However, the vision of someday running the same route from rural Hopkinton to Boston soon became additional motivation. I was inspired by legends, such as Bill Rogers (four-time Boston winner), Clarence de Mar (seven-time Boston winner), Rosa Mota (two-time Boston winner and 1984 Olympic winner), and Uta Pippig (two-time Boston winner and 1988 Olympic winner).

In addition, Boston is the backdrop for endless stories of sheer dominance, determination, and running longevity, such as the story of three-time winner John A. Kelley. His unprecedented 64-year span of participation in the Boston Marathon is truly astonishing. Another notable marathon was the 1982 battle between Dick Beardsley and Alberto Salazar. Some say the most memorable marathon battle in history, as a mere two seconds separated these finishers. As we transition into the 21st century, the dominance of the Kenyans and Ethiopians is displayed in nearly every major marathon, including Boston. Their performances have become the new benchmarks in world marathons.

Many runners seek out Boston like a beacon, the weekend road warriors, those running for a cause, celebrities, and runners who inspire others. Dick Hoyt is one runner who has inspired many at Boston and throughout the running community. For years Dick has pushed his son Rick, who is challenged with cerebral palsy, to many a strong finish at Boston. This display of strength and courage by both Hoyts is an inspiration to the hundreds of thousands who cheer them on and to others who know their story. At the 2008 Boston Marathon, I had the honor and privilege of conveying my admiration to Dick in person. For someone who has inspired millions with his love for his son while displaying unyielding tenacity, his humble demeanor was genuine and pleasantly unexpected.

These are only a fraction of the stories, the history, and the perseverance that have been demonstrated to the millions of followers worldwide throughout Boston's long tradition. If and when you make it to Boston, running among the world's fastest (past and present) is a profound privilege and a rare opportunity that the average runner will cherish for a lifetime. Boston truly brings out the best in each person who strives to excel in running, and a life achievement that can't be equaled by another marathon.

Photo 1.2 On fresh legs, runners make their way from Hopkinton to Ashland.

The Course

The course offers unique elevation challenges and requires a strategic approach for most runners. The first half of the course is predominantly downhill, and each runner's adrenalin peaks due to the thousands of cheering spectators along the way. Runners will soon find that they need this energy boost as they prepare themselves for the challenges of the second half of the course including the infamous Heartbreak Hill. Thus, running a smart race (an even pace) is a factor to enjoying the experience at Boston, especially if you are considering a Personal Record (P.R.). This legendary course of 26 miles and 385 yards is certified per the International Association of Athletics Federation and USA Track and Field organizations. It starts in the center of the rural New England town of Hopkinton. With a population of just over 13,000, Hopkinton swells to well over 30,000 on race morning but welcomes the runners and the starting festivities with open arms, and has done so since 1924. From Hopkinton, the course follows along Route 135 through the town of Ashland.

From 1897-1923, Ashland served as the race start from various locations; however, during those years the course did not span the length of a full marathon as we know it today. From Ashland, the course continues through the bustling town of Framingham. Just prior to transitioning onto Route 16, runners continue through Wellesley, a small college town. Wellesley may be small in population, but is not in volume, as thousands of female students provide a deafening and inspiring roar as runners pass by the college just prior to mile 13. After Wellesley, runners experience the Newton hills along Route 30 and the well-known Heartbreak Hill near mile 21. After passing through Newton and on to Chestnut Hill Avenue, the route turns onto Beacon Street, where the runners pass the famous CITGO sign and continue to Kenmore Square. From Kenmore Square it follows Commonwealth, passes through a series of streets, and eventually turns onto Boylston. There runners are welcomed by tens of thousands of people cheering them to the finish near the John Hancock Tower in Copley Square. This course is unlike any other, and the B.A.A. lines the route with 24 fluid stations of both water and sports drinks to ensure runners have proper hydration.

Photo 1.3   Runners approach the final landmark of the course.   Just one mile to go!

Course Elevation

As the grade indicates in Figure1.4, the Boston Marathon is predominately a downhill event until mile 16, where it enters into the Newton hills. The most significant challenge occurs at mile 20 and is known as Heartbreak Hill. It ascends to a peak of 250 feet above sea level and unfortunately occurs at a mentally difficult part of the course, but the supportive spectators keep runners motivated. *Boston Globe* reporter Jerry Nason named Heartbreak Hill whom he reported on the 1936 Boston Marathon, in which John A. Kelley passed fellow runner Ellison "Tarzan" Brown. Kelley patted Brown on the shoulder as they both ascended the last and most significant hill on the course. However, that tap on the shoulder motivated Brown to pass Kelley back, and he went on to win the 1936 Boston Marathon. The name Heartbreak Hill has stuck from that day on. Once runners have made it to mile 21, the finish is downhill from there, and thousands of Boston fans line the streets to support runners in these final miles.

Putting the challenges of the Boston course aside, qualifying is the major portion of the "battle." Once runners come to realize that Boston is the prize, they enjoy the ride.

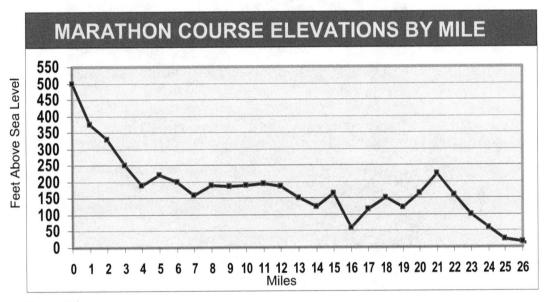

Figure 1.4

Amenities

As usual with most marathon events, there is a pre-race pasta party, a race program, and a results booklet. Again, the B.A.A. and the volunteers do an outstanding job with each. In addition, each participant receives a Boston Marathon long-sleeved t-shirt (to wear proudly) and the all-important finisher medallion. A race expo offers other official amenities such as jackets, shirts, mugs, and most anything a runner could want to celebrate and advertise his/her achievement. I mentioned to my wife multiple times for my first Boston that we needed to clear out our credit card balance just for the expo purchases...and the worst part was that she knew I was serious. Reward yourself with amenities, as you worked hard to be there.

Photo 1.5   Isaac Willett proudly wears his 2010 Boston jacket outside of the Expo Hall, a well-deserved addition to his running wardrobe.

If you can picture yourself proudly wearing one of these... read on!

Chapter 2
Qualification Requirements

"This is not a jogging race"
>   -Boston Marathon entry blank, 1970

Boston is one of the few marathons that requires runners to meet qualification times by age group. These age group requirements are balanced equitably and allow runners of all ages a fair chance to qualify. The Boston Athletic Association (B.A.A.) relaxed the qualification times in 2003. However, due to its tremendous popularity in recent years, the B.A.A. has lowered the required qualifying times by five minutes for each age group (men and women). Additionally, the B.A.A. has implemented a rolling admission to ensure the fastest qualifiers are allowed to enter earlier than slower qualifying runners.

The rolling admission allows runners that have met the qualification standard by 20 minutes or more to enter on the first day of registration. The third day allows qualifiers that have met the standard by 10 minutes or more, and the fifth day allows all runners that have met the age group qualifying standard (see Table 2.2) to register. If the field size (maximum) is not reached the first week, a second week will allow for all qualifiers to register that have met the standards, until the field size is met. This second week will remain subject to selection of the fastest qualifiers registering that week. In short, now simply meeting the qualification standard is not enough, and each potential Boston qualifier will need to train harder to run faster than others in their age group.

These new qualification requirements are effective for the 2013 event and are subject to future revisions. Further detail is on the official Boston Marathon website, www.baa.org.

Photo 2.1   Runners push forward in the final stages of a marathon...possibly seeking a BQ !

For qualification to run the Boston Marathon, entrants must run a certified marathon course. Qualifying times are determined by your age on the date of the Boston Marathon in which you will be participating. All participants must adhere to the guidelines set forth by the Boston Athletic Association (B.A.A.), USA Track & Field (USATF) or equivalent, Wheelchair Athletics USA, and the International Stoke-Mandeville Wheelchair Sports Federation and must meet the standards for eligibility as outlined by these organizations. Participants must be 18 years or older on race day.

Qualification Standards – All Categories

Table 2.2 Qualifying Standards for the 2013 Boston Marathon

QUALIFYING STANDARDS FOR THE BOSTON MARATHON		
Age Group	**Men**	**Women**
18-34	3hrs 05min 00sec	3hrs 35min 00sec
35-39	3hrs 10min 00sec	3hrs 40min 00sec
40-44	3hrs 15min 00sec	3hrs 45min 00sec
45-49	3hrs 25min 00sec	3hrs 55min 00sec
50-54	3hrs 30min 00sec	4hrs 00min 00sec
55-59	3hrs 40min 00sec	4hrs 10min 00sec
60-64	3hrs 55min 00sec	4hrs 25min 00sec
65-69	4hrs 10min 00sec	4hrs 40min 00sec
70-74	4hrs 25min 00sec	4hrs 55min 00sec
75-79	4hrs 40min 00sec	5hrs 10min 00sec
80 and over	4hrs 55min 00sec	5hrs 25min 00sec

Note: These standards are subject to change, please go to www.baa.org to confirm the latest requirements.

Table 2.3 Qualifying Standards Wheelchair Division for the Boston Marathon

WHEELCHAIR DIVISION QUALIFYING TIMES			
Class	**Age Group**	**Men**	**Women**
Open (Classes 3 & 4)	18-39	2hrs 00min 00sec	2hrs 25min 00sec
Open (Classes 3 & 4)	40-49	2hrs 15min 00sec	2hrs 40min 00sec
Open (Classes 3 & 4)	50-Over	2hrs 30min 00sec	2hrs 55min 00sec
Quad (Classes 1 & 2)	18-39	2hrs 45min 00sec	3hrs 10min 00sec
Quad (Classes 1 & 2)	40-49	3hrs 00min 00sec	3hrs 25min 00sec
Quad (Classes 1 & 2)	50-Over	3hrs 15min 00sec	3hrs 40min 00sec

Note: The standards are subject to change, please go to www.baa.org to confirm the latest requirements.

The B.A.A. accepts times from non-timing chip events; however, a copy of your finish certificate or results listing (non-returnable) must accompany your entry. Qualifying times attained at marathons using the Champion Chip timing and scoring device do not require submission of proof.

Photo 2.4   Surrounded by cheering spectators, determined wheelchair participants head to a finish at Boston.

Team Qualification

The Boston Marathon website also provides information regarding team competition. If you prefer to participate in a team, you may consider this avenue for an opportunity to run at Boston. There is no qualifying time applicable to the team competition; however, there are many stipulations that apply including the following. Teams must have current membership to USA Track & Field, the Road Runners Club of America (RRCA) or American Association of Running Clubs (AARC), or to an equivalent foreign national athletics organization, and an individual may not be the only runner on the team. Review _www.baa.org_ for further details and requirements for team participation.

Qualification through Charitable Organizations

If you are unable to qualify via your age group, you may still be able to participate in the Boston Marathon by assisting a charitable organization. The B.A.A. is committed to encouraging and promoting fitness through athletics, and has developed a program with the Boston Marathon and charitable organizations in the Massachusetts area. The B.A.A. assists these charitable organizations by providing guaranteed entries for their organization's fundraising purposes and, in the spirit of charity, encourages all qualified runners to aid in these efforts. Please refer to _www.baa.org_ for a list of organizations that apply or are of interest to your personal charitable efforts.

Having participated in charitable runs, I can say there is both challenge and reward in raising donations for charities that are of personal interest to you or your family. Taking the time to seek out donors while training for a race can be a difficult balance, but you will find it is tremendously rewarding. After all, without challenge, where is reward? Boston is the perfect venue for participating as a charity runner, but plan to sign up early due to the popularity.

Chapter 3
Ten Keys to Qualification Success

"Every truly great accomplishment is at first impossible."
  - Confucius

Photo 3.1 Jubilant runners starting off at Hopkinton know too well the challenge of qualifying.

Okay, enough about the hype of Boston. Chapter 3 is where the shoes hit the road. Before we get started, there is one key point to mention just to make sure you have realistic expectations about what it takes to get to Boston. ***Qualifying is not an overnight process*** and may even take six months to a year or more. But if you enjoy running, the time will pass quickly, and your efforts should be rewarded by numerous sequential personal bests to keep your motivation high and your goal(s) in focus.

How Long Do I Need to Train?

As shown in Figure 3.2, I required roughly 18 months of on/off training to reach my goal of a 200 minute marathon time. This was the qualifying time for my age/gender group for Boston. (Please refer back to Chapter 2 for your required marathon qualifying times.) During this 18-month period, my performance improved at all distances from the mile and above. Remarkably, the body can continue to improve in performance for runners/athletes over a period of up to seven or more years with regular and focused training efforts. Your motivation is a deciding factor in how quickly you improve during those months or years. This data (Figure 3.2) also provides the rate of my personal performance improvement, roughly a 15% improvement per year. Depending upon your effort and focus, you should expect similar results in improvement if you follow the success factors and training plan outlined herein.

Each runner's results will vary, but statistically this graph correlates the relationship of time (in months) expended for training versus the resultant marathon time (in minutes). Numerous factors can influence ones marathon time, however this data shows there is a significant correlation to continued time training at a constant effort and achieving results. To clarify, training at the same pace and distance constantly will not get the results you need. You will not become faster by running a speed you are comfortable with. The suggested approach is to apply continuous and gradual increases in both distance and speed training to achieve the necessary cardiovascular efficiency and strength improvements. Conditioning your body to withstand the rigors of a marathon is a challenge itself. However, to run a marathon for a qualification time requires a methodical approach to training, nutrition, and various other factors. Remember you aren't training to *just* finish, you're training to finish with your personal best!

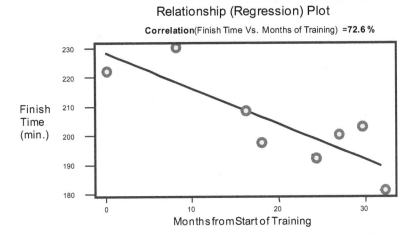

Figure 3.2

While training, be patient with the results and remember that you must push yourself and desire improvement. During training, your body will often tell you that you've had enough, while your mind will remind you those two laps still remain. Training for a marathon is much like the race itself, as your mind will become both friend and enemy. Ultimately you will depend upon your own determination as the deciding factor. The mental training to push further when your body says no was an aspect of training that I personally didn't expect would be such a challenge.

To run a Boston Marathon qualifying time, you will need to condition yourself both mentally and physically. This mental training starts first by envisioning success of short-term goals and completing them. You will subconsciously condition your mind by setting goals for the day, week, or a specific race and focusing on accomplishing those specific goals. Building up these successes and mental accomplishments conditions your mind to accept that what lies ahead will be difficult, but that you've succeeded before. This mental toughness will be necessary during the most challenging portions of your training—intervals and your longest training runs.

Increasing your physical condition for running, as for any sport, takes time and a structured approach. Your approach to meeting your training goals may tell you a lot about yourself. It is important to remember that there is no short cut to Boston unless you enter on a doctor's exemption or are running / volunteering for charitable organizations (both of which are very deserving of the experience). But if you choose the qualifying time route, it will take time, dedication, and hard work.

Key Factors to Qualification

The keys to success in qualifying for Boston come down to a list of Top 10 Factors. Because runners have different limitations (medical, physiological, genetic, nutritional, etc.), this list of factors assumes that physical limitations or injuries do not apply or limit performance or progression through training. Of these Top 10 Factors, you have some control over most, with the obvious exception of weather. Numerous other factors don't appear on this list due their reduced significance on your performance. The intent of this chapter is to provide an overview of some the key areas that should have the greatest impact upon your success as a Boston qualifier.

Key Factors to Successful Qualification

Top Ten Factors	Potential Impact to Finish Time
#1 - **Motivation** - (Desire & mental preparation)	**Up to 30 minutes**
#2 - **Proper Training, and Genetics**	**Up to 30 minutes**
#3 - **Hydration and Energy Replenishment**	**Up to 10 minutes**
#4 - **Proper Nutrition** (prior to event)	**Up to 10 minutes**
#5 - **Race Profile** (assumes non-mountainous venues)	**Up to 10 minutes**
#6 - **Weather** (cold, rain, heat)	**Up to 10 minutes***
#7 - **Running a smart Race** (pace monitoring/race plan)	**Up to 10 minutes**
#8 - **Running Attire and Essentials**	**Up to 5 minutes**
#9 - **Rest, Travel, and Time of event**	**Up to 5 minutes**
#10 - **Coaching**	**Up to 5 minutes****

*Extreme conditions of heat/cold can exceed 20 minutes.
** Assumes that runner has done some research regarding the basics to train and qualify

Every experienced runner or coach will debate the order or significance of these factors, but in reality any one of these factors can drastically impact your performance on race day. The purpose of this ranking is to highlight the fact that you must be motivated to succeed. If you don't have a strong desire to make it to Boston or any other marathon, you will find that you will end up compromising your training and conditioning. If so, your performance on race day will suffer. Only you can decide how much you desire to be included in the fraction of the runners who have concluded a marathon on historic Boylston St.

For each runner, the road to Boston will come with sacrifices involving family, work, and social opportunities/commitments. I guarantee that each will be compromised at various points in your training. If you are an early riser, you may be able to offset some of these compromises by running in the early morning hours. If you are an after work/school exercise enthusiast, then your evening priorities will require adjustment.

The remainder of this chapter provides detail that supports the ranking of these critical factors. In reality, if any become an uncontrollable extreme, it will impact your performance, both physically or mentally. You can, however, minimize your risk by doing research and determining your susceptibly to each of these factors.

#1. Motivation

Photo 3.3   Athlete redefining both motivation and dedication.

Motivation is *the key* to making it to Boston. You can read every book and every magazine and feed your body with all of the right nutrients, but unless you are motivated, it is doubtful that you will run in Boston on Patriots' Day. If you are fortunate to currently be running at your goal pace, you may not need a great deal of motivation to complete the necessary training. However, for the typical distance runner without the motivation and competitive drive to improve, achieving the goal of qualifying for Boston may be challenging. I've met many runners who want to run at Boston, but they clearly don't exhibit the desire it takes to go beyond a half marathon or marathon, even though they possess the aptitude. In some cases, a lack of understanding of the training needs may discourage some runners from going the extra step. Many people can log 20 miles a week; however, reaching 40 to 50 more miles per week and doing speed work is where the motivational division resides.

On your first marathon, you should set realistic goals based upon your fitness level and aerobic capacity (see Table 4.16). If you fail in qualifying, that experience should position you better for subsequent attempts. Each qualifying attempt will propel you closer to your goal as you subsequently focus more on the right training and nutrition. In fact, many runners do not make the qualifying time at their first marathon and may lose confidence. They should be content with the fact that they tried their best and even more so satisfied that completing any marathon is a significant accomplishment in itself. It is usually after this first marathon when the motivation to continue on for a Boston qualification is put to the test.

I recommend the following methods as ways to help stay motivated through the challenging training period.

First, keep track of your personal bests and highlight them in your training log, as shown in Figure 3.4. A training log is a critical tool in managing your training plan, highlighting weekly mileage, and tracking your overall progress versus your plan. After all, progress feeds motivation!

Second, do to not attempt a full marathon without first completing one or more half marathons. This approach aligns your goals on a less demanding event to build confidence. Biting off a full marathon as your first race may result in it being your last race.

Third, have fun with your training by entering 5K, 10K, or half marathons as part of your training. Entering these events will keep you actively engaged with your need to train.

Training Log (Example)

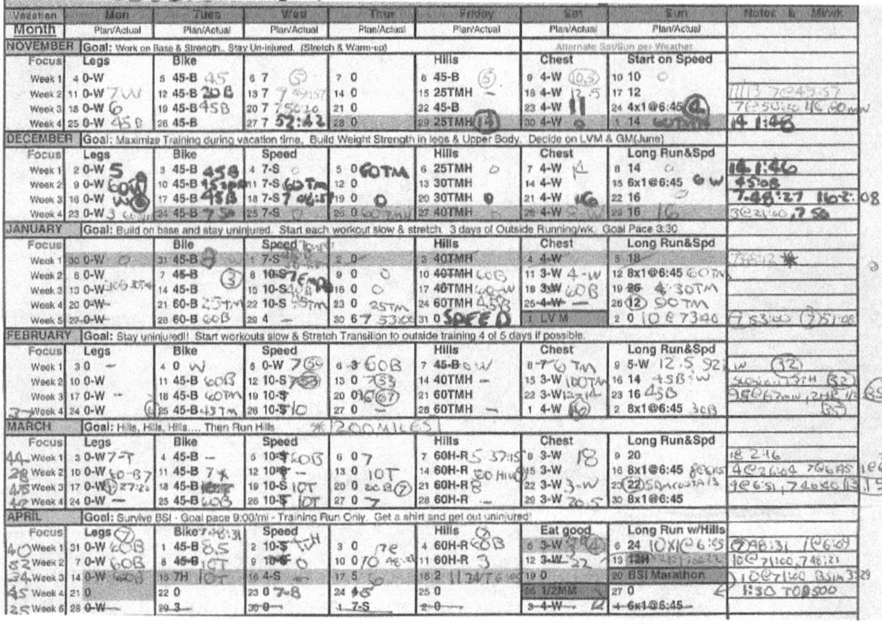

Vacation Month	Mon Plan/Actual	Tues Plan/Actual	Wed Plan/Actual	Thur Plan/Actual	Friday Plan/Actual	Sat Plan/Actual	Sun Plan/Actual	Notes & Mi/wk
NOVEMBER	Goal: Work on Base & Strength. Stay Un-Injured. (Stretch & Warm-up)					Alternate Sat/Sun per Weather		
Focus	Legs	Bike			Hills	Chest	Start on Speed	
Week 1	4 0-W	5 45-B	6 7	7 0	8 45-B	9 4-W	10 10	
Week 2	11 0-W	12 45-B	13 7	14 0	15 25TMH	16 4-W	17 12	
Week 3	18 0-W	19 45-B	20 7	21 0	22 45-B	23 4-W	24 4x1@6:45	
Week 4	25 0-W	26 45-B	27 7	28 0	29 25TMH	30 4-W	1 14	
DECEMBER	Goal: Maximize Training during vacation time. Build Weight Strength in legs & Upper Body. Decide on LVM & GM(June)							
Focus	Legs	Bike	Speed		Hills	Chest	Long Run&Spd	
Week 1	2 0-W	3 45-B	4 7-S	5 0	6 25TMH	7 4-W	8 14	
Week 2	9 0-W	10 45-B	11 7-S	12 0	13 30TMH	14 4-W	15 6x1@6:45	
Week 3	16 0-W	17 45-B	18 7-S	19 0	20 30TMH	21 4-W	22 16	
Week 4	23 0-W	24 45-B	25 7-S	26 0	27 40TMH	28 4-W	29 16	
JANUARY	Goal: Build on base and stay uninjured. Start each workout slow & stretch. 3 days of Outside Running/wk. Goal Pace 3:30							
Focus		Bile	Speed		Hills	Chest	Long Run&Spd	
Week 1	30 0-W	31 45-B	1 7-S	2 0	3 40TMH	4 4-W	5 18	
Week 2	6 0-W	7 45-B	8 10-S	9 0	10 40TMH	11 3-W	12 8x1@6:45	
Week 3	13 0-W	14 45-B	15 10-S	16 0	17 40TMH	18 3-W	19 25	
Week 4	20 0-W	21 60-B	22 10-S	23 0	24 60TMH	25 4-W	26 12	
Week 5	27 0-W	28 60-B	29 4	30 6	31 0	1 LVM	2 0	
FEBRUARY	Goal: Stay uninjured!! Start workouts slow & Stretch Transition to outside training 4 of 5 days if possible.							
Focus	Legs	Bike	Speed		Hills	Chest	Long Run&Spd	
Week 1	3 0	4 0	5 0-W	6 3	7 45-B	8 7	9 5-W	
Week 2	10 0-W	11 45-B	12 10-S	13 0	14 40TMH	15 3-W	16 14	
Week 3	17 0-W	18 45-B	19 10-S	20 0	21 60TMH	22 3-W	23 16	
Week 4	24 0-W	25 45-B	26 10-S	27 0	28 60TMH	1 4-W	2 8x1@6:45	
MARCH	Goal: Hills, Hills, Hills.... Then Run Hills							
Focus	Legs	Bike	Speed		Hills	Chest	Long Run&Spd	
Week 1	3 0-W	4 45-B	5 10-S	6 0	7 60H-R	8 3-W	9 20	
Week 2	10 0-W	11 45-B	12 10-S	13 0	14 60H-R	15 3-W	16 8x1@6:45	
Week 3	17 0-W	18 45-B	19 10-S	20 0	21 60H-R	22 3-W	23 22	
Week 4	24 0-W	25 45-B	26 10-S	27 0	28 60H-R	29 3-W	30 8x1@6:45	
APRIL	Goal: Survive BSI - Goal pace 9:00/mi - Training Run Only. Get a shirt and get out uninjured!							
Focus	Legs	Bike	Speed		Hills	Eat good	Long Run w/Hills	
Week 1	31 0-W	1 45-B	2 10-S	3 0	4 60H-R	5 3-W	6 24	
Week 2	7 0-W	8 45-B	9 10-S	10 0	11 60H-R	12 3-W	13 12H	
Week 3	14 0-W	15 7H	16 4-S	17 5	18 2	19 0	20 BSI Marathon	
Week 4	21 0	22 0	23 0	24 4	25 0	26 1/2MM	27 0	
Week 5	28 0-W	29 3	30 0	1 7-S	2 0	3 4-W	4 6x1@6:45	

Figure 3.4

Every runner has different abilities or strengths. The key is to be rational with your goals and to be 100% motivated to achieve them. If you are unsure of your level of motivation, you should determine if you fit the mold for someone who truly wants Boston. Obviously this test is not scientific, but I believe it is a fair approach to determine your Boston Motivation Level (BML):

Boston Motivation Level (BML) Test

1. Are you willing to run in the dark, in the cold, in the rain, in the snow?
2. Are you willing to run with blisters, with bugs on your face, in the heat of day?
3. Are you willing to run on a treadmill for two hours?
4. Can you force yourself to run intervals to complete 48 laps on a 400m track?
5. Are you willing to put in one to two extra miles to cool down after a hard workout?
6. Are you willing to sacrifice family time and limit social activities during key training?
7. Do you struggle to let kids pass you on their bicycles when on a training run?

If you answered "yes" to at least five of these questions, then you have the motivation necessary to make it to Boston.

However, there is a limit to what is ***reasonable*** when it comes to training, and unfortunately this point highlights a personal story about the extremes some runners may take just to train. I had elected to undergo corrective eye surgery. Thus I had to leave my maintenance running schedule until I was given the all clear from my doctor—also a runner—who understood my need to train. His only requirement was that I wear eye protection to avoid the likely occurrence of a bug in the eye. After receiving the go-ahead from my doctor, I decided to venture out at night with marginal vision due to the healing process. However, my only available eye protection was a pair of sunglasses. I knew my intended route well (location of curbs, potholes, etc.) and could clearly see headlights, but my unexpected nemesis that evening was avoiding parked cars. After three or four near misses due to limited vision, I decided to call it a night. Sometimes there is a fine line among motivation, perseverance, and stupidity, and you may not know it until you get there…or bump into it, in this case.

However, if you find yourself needing a boost in motivation, consider these goals:

- To become the fittest/healthiest you've been in your life
- To achieve a life-long goal
- To accomplish something that so few people do
- For the medal, the shirt, or the coveted jacket
- Because you know someone who has done it
- To prove to yourself that you still have it
- To travel to Boston and other enjoyable marathon cities

Prior to qualifying for Boston, I found myself at venues where I would pick out runners in Boston Marathon shirts to pace with and see how I compared from a fitness standpoint. Perhaps there was some fashion-envy involved, but I found that I wasn't just competing against the clock, and I wanted to compete at a higher level. This informal competition drove my motivation. If you can relate to these comments and have the desire to improve, you will make it to Boston.

A final note regarding motivation is to train your mind by setting goals and rewarding yourself when you accomplish them. Rewards can be as simple as self-recognition for the task completed, acknowledgement of improved physical condition, logging a Personal Record in your training log, or something more tangible like a steak dinner or a favorite beverage after a marathon.

#2. Proper Training and Genetics

Chapter 4 focuses specifically on the aspects of a training plan to qualify for Boston. However, the amount of required training for each athlete is clearly a variable that depends upon starting fitness level, time/days to the event, and the necessary goal pace. A measure of training readiness can be determined by running a race and knowing that you couldn't have pushed harder. If you achieve your goal, then you are usually satisfied. However, if you don't achieve your goal(s), either the goal was too aggressive, you've fallen victim to deficiencies in your training regimen, or you are undertraining. Undertraining may be the preferred failure mode versus over-training as in most cases it only leaves you winded and perhaps with a little less pride than when you started. These failures are a valuable way of learning the importance of what is required to achieve your goal and provide a measure from a preparation/conditioning standpoint.

Undertraining

The typical result from undertraining at a marathon occurs around the three-quarter distance point or beyond when the runner will begin to mechanically and/or chemically break down from an endurance standpoint. Unfortunately, I have firsthand marathon experience with this. Basically, my body began to quit at the 20-mile mark. From that point on, I experienced lactic acid build-up, fatigue, and finally hamstring cramping. In short, I "hit the wall" and jogged or walked the final 10K. After this event, I went to the books and my running peers to find out why and concluded that I wasn't training hard enough to allow me to run an even or negative split (where the second half of the race is run faster than the first). Negative splits are usually the most enjoyable way to run a race, since you pass other runners throughout the second half of the race and finish strong.

Having learned a valuable lesson, I trained for a fall marathon (Chicago) and added distance and speed work into the final miles of my long runs. For an 18-mile long run, I would run the first 16 miles at my goal training pace, then run an accelerated pace for the final 2 miles (at 1/2 Marathon Pace or 1/2 M.P.). This training simulated a negative split in a race/qualifying condition. I also extended my longest run to 24 miles (22mi +2mi @1/2M.P.) to test my fitness and to build my lactate threshold. This training strategy worked great and resulted in a personal record and a very enjoyable marathon. The feeling of running past the 25-mile marker without cramps and being capable of sprinting to the finish for the last mile was worth the extra effort in training.

That experience is one of the primary reasons I wanted to write this book, as I learned that if conditioned properly, my body can perform to the limit that I wanted. Enhancing focused elements of my training plan clearly improved my overall performance.

Overtraining

Overtraining can result in damaged muscle tissue and poor performance, especially if you try to stack two major training or racing events within a short time period. The impact of overtraining can appear to be manageable for the first few miles of the second event, but soon after, your muscles —still under repair—will begin to ache and slow your pace until you reach a sustainable pace. At that point, you will most likely get passed by the people you had passed in the first few miles. Overtraining will also have the same effect if an aggressive or long run is done too late in your training schedule. As stated, your muscles will not be 100% repaired and will not perform at the level you expect. Additionally, if you don't ramp down (taper) mileage and speed work appropriately, your muscles will be fatigued when you need them to be at peak ability.

Overtraining on a macro-level such as too many marathons or miles in one year (or years) can also wear down your body. Overtraining can lead to increased cartilage wear on knees/joints, frequent swelling, bone bruises, and increase your susceptibility to stress fractures. Genetics has some impact on offsetting these potential disabling issues. However, runners need to be aware that sheer miles and the resulting wear and tear can bring your training and running goals to an immediate stop. Train wisely and apply cross-training into your plan to stay healthy as a runner. Cross-training through the use of an elliptical, road bike, stationary bike, etc is an excellent means of keeping you from overtraining. The stress on joints as you build your mileage and especially during peak training weeks will take a toll on your body and ability to run. Cross-training must be part of your weekly training plan.

However, as will be discussed in Chapter 4, a proper taper is also a critical element to your plan and is even more critical when exerting yourself beyond the typical 20-mile run. A 20-24 mile training run should be incorporated into your plan a minimum of three to four weeks before you make an attempt to qualify for Boston. If you are incorporating a marathon into your training plan, it should be no closer than six weeks prior to a qualifying attempt. Some elite runners may train up to 100 miles/wk, which nearly incorporates a marathon into their daily training runs. This training capability has taken them years to develop and is a key enabler to allow for top performance, but this approach greatly increases susceptibility to injury. The key is to increase at a controlled rate (no more than 10% per week) so that you can build muscle, stamina, tolerance to lactic acid, and still allow ample time for muscles to heal for subsequent training or the race itself.

The overall key to training/conditioning and tapering is that you must adhere to the recommended plan and, again, not exceed the 10% increase in weekly mileage rule. Generally, **more miles does not equal better performance** unless applied methodically and gradually. An excellent training effort mixed with a poor taper can result in less than desired results. Both are critical aspects to qualifying success. Chapter 4 will further explain each in further detail and how they complement one another.

Ability/Genetics

From a capability standpoint, genetics does play a role in the limitations that may present themselves during training. For example, the elite distance athletes typically fit a genetic or physical muscular build, bone structure, lung capacity, and even slow twitch muscular composition compared to others. Running weight and leg length are two factors that can impact one's running performance. However, runners challenged in both areas have passed me during various marathons. This is one reason why I personally do not value genetics or running weight specifically as attributes that act as significant detriments to qualifying for Boston. I attribute strong performances by these challenged runners to motivation and cardiovascular conditioning. Some venues classify weight-challenged runners as Clydesdales, and many outperform the thousands of runners of lower weight. As you may already know, a key benefit of running/training is weight loss due to caloric/fat consumption, and the result is muscle tone. A few weeks into training, you will notice muscle tone that you may not have witnessed in the past. Over time, you will eventually find your ideal running weight as you seek the balance of carbohydrate consumption versus your training usage needs.

One has to work with what God and genetics has given them. Although the qualifying times required by the B.A.A. are challenging, they are definitely not insurmountable for novice or runners with less-than non-optimal genetics. If your legs, knees, and feet will allow you to train, then you will need to look elsewhere for excuses.

#3. Hydration and Energy Replenishment

Hydration During the Race

Approximately 2/3 of your body weight is comprised of water, and roughly 75% of your brain, heart, and muscles consist of water. Proper re-hydration during a marathon is critical to ensure these primary functions of your body are maintained at proper levels. I once met a runner that would drink 36-48 oz. of water within moments of the start of the race. His reasoning was that although he sloshed for the first few miles, it would save him time at the water stops for the first six miles. I don't support this approach and wouldn't have taken this approach seriously had he not been a top 50 finisher in a marathon with over 10,000 participants. Many venues will provide only water stops for the first five to seven miles in a marathon and then provide energy drinks in the later miles such as PowerAde® or Gatorade®, to replenish electrolytes. Your body will need added energy and chemicals later in the race so, be sure to switch from water to an electrolyte fluid early during the race. Also, take advantage of each water stop along the route, and try to take on about three to four ounces of water or electrolyte fluid at each stop. These drink stops are usually spaced out every one or two miles. However, taking on any liquid is a challenge for most runners while running hard. Unfortunately, labored breathing is not conducive for easy drinking, and many runners have to slow to a walk to avoid "drowning" in the water stop areas.

Methods for Drinking while Maintaining Pace

- **When grasping the cup, squeeze the cup so that it is closed and makes a smaller opening at the bottom and then drink (See Photo 3.5)**

- **Bring a 5-in. straw with you (tucked under a watch), and pull it out as you approach the fluid stops. You can run much easier while drinking.**

- **Slow to a jog while drinking, but stay clear of other runners passing through.**

Photo 3.5 Runner demonstrating how to run and drink by pinching the cup.

Elite runners have plastic containers located at pre-determined water stops along the way with squeeze bottles or spouts that allow them to get all of the fluid in. A straw will allow non-elite runners that same luxury. Some elite runners will walk through a few water stops to drink and then make up lost time by increasing their pace. As a runner, you will determine what works best for you under these circumstances.

There are rare occasions where you can over hydrate. Over-hydration can cause serious consequences such as hyponatremia (low blood sodium). The odds of encountering this issue are extremely low, and slower runners or walkers may be more susceptible. Drink what you can from one cup as you are <u>running</u> through the water stations. One cup of three to four ounces should suffice until the next stop, typically one or two miles away. Some studies indicate that drinking when thirsty is appropriate, where others say that you should stay ahead of being thirsty which is why many runners are confused with recommended intake. Temperature, rate of energy consumption, and perspiration are three variables that influence the appropriate consumption level. If you are thirsty, it is wise to drink.

Be aware that even when it is cold, your body will require fluid replenishment, even if you aren't thirsty. On warm days, your body will perspire much more to cool itself, and water/fluid intake will be even more important. Drinking fluids in moderation, with three to four ounces for every two miles, is the general rule for avoiding dehydration. Adding more is only required as the temperature rises to offset your hydration losses.

I've seen runners with water packs on their backs and have never understood why they opt to carry an extra four to seven pounds of weight with them just to avoid the water stops and congestion. Water packs are fine for training runs, where water stops are not frequently available; however, the added weight during a race will slow your performance. In addition, the added insulation may increase your body temperature and lead to increased fluid intake or cooling needs and perhaps even chafing issues.

Energy During the Race

Some runners mix their energy drinks and strap them to a running belt. The elite runners have their energy drinks at pre-determined tables along the course. However, the majority of runners resort to energy gel packs and the race-provided energy drinks. At marathons, I personally carry four gel packs to provide the added electrolytes and carbohydrates needed.

Photo 3.6 A runner with a gel energy pack approaching a mile 20 water stop. This is typically the last time during the race that an energy pack will offer adequate energy benefit.

It can take the body up to 20 minutes to process the energy pack into usable glycogen for muscles. Therefore, any supplements consumed as you are reaching the conclusion of the event will only aid in your recovery.

Your body can store as much as 1500 to 2500 calories of glycogen and will require roughly 100 calories per mile. Once you have depleted your glycogen stores, your body starts to consume fat for energy. Unfortunately, fat stores are not as high in energy content, and without efficient calories available, your body will slow. It is critical to replenish lost calories with some form of energy. Energy packs (Powergel®, GU®, etc.) and sports drinks are the select choice of most runners. A recommended consumption of energy packs is at miles 5, 10, 15, and 20. However, runners vary in their consumption needs. Most events provide an energy pack at mile 17 if you wish to carry fewer. This strategy should keep you energized for the duration of the marathon. If it is a cold day the energy packs may be thick and hard to swallow. You should try to take them just prior to the water stop so that you can wash down the gel easier.

Typical Contents for Gel Energy Packs

Sodium	45 mg
Potassium	45 mg
Carbohydrates	26 gm
Calories	120

If you assume that you have stored 2000 calories of glycogen, your body will require another 600 calories from supplements during the race. This equates to roughly five energy packs. Again, most events provide one pack at mile 17. However, this may not be adequate to replenish your lost electrolytes and the carbohydrates needed for energy. The energy packs are designed to provide carbohydrates in the form of sugar and, thus, are easily digested. Energy packs are an effective source of carbohydrates and electrolyte replenishment and are recommended for training runs and marathons.

One final consideration regarding electrolyte replenishment; solids (bananas, apples, etc.) will typically not digest well during a race because the digestion process is greatly slowed to conserve the body's valuable energy. Because your body adjusts for the required energy needs, only fluids or sugars (no solids) should be ingested during the event.

#4. Proper Nutrition

3-5 Days Prior to Race

Starting three to five days prior to the marathon, you should eat a high-carbohydrate diet. Now that you are running less mileage, your body will begin to store reserves of glycogen from the surplus of carbohydrates. This storage of glycogen is due to fact that you are now consuming fewer calories than your body was demanding just days/weeks earlier for the long runs. Rice, pasta, bread, potatoes, pancakes, and corn are all excellent sources of carbohydrates.

Pre-Race Meals

Since the body requires 24 to 48 hours to convert complex carbohydrates into energy, a pre-race pasta dinner the night before will do little to benefit your performance. A heavy pre-race dinner is not a good idea. This type of meal only adds weight and will not be beneficial until the recovery stage of the race.

A high-carbohydrate pasta dinner is recommended two nights before the event or perhaps for lunch the day prior.

Pre-Race (Race Day)

Most events typically start in the early morning hours between 6:30 a.m. and 8:00 a.m. It is advised to eat a light to average breakfast consisting of juice, bread (bagel or roll), banana, and/or cereal. Each of these options is high in carbohydrates and easily digestible. If you walk or ride out to the starting line, it is advisable to take an energy drink or water with you and an additional energy bar. The energy bar is typically fully absorbed in advance of the race if consumed at least 30 minutes prior to the start. The morning of the race you should consume between 200 and 500 calories from carbohydrates. It is advisable to eat at least three hours before race time to ensure that the meal does not adversely impact your performance and to provide ample time for conversion of simple carbohydrates.

Typical Contents of a Pre-Race or Workout Energy Bar

Sodium	95 mg
Potassium	200 mg
Carbohydrates	45 gm
Protein	10 gm
Electrolytes	320 mg
Calories	230

#5. Race Profile

The race profile should not be taken lightly, as major elevation increases can result in a much slower pace for a portion of the event. Most runners can pick up the pace on the downside of a hill. However, attempting to make up for lost time by sprinting downhill is not wise. Working muscles differently and at increased speeds may make you more susceptible to injury. If an event includes a major change in elevation (anything over 200 ft), you should plan your pace accordingly. Expect slower pace times and perhaps a slower overall time. A hill like the one shown in Figure 3.7 may take an additional four to six minutes to climb over two miles, or two to three minutes per mile slower than your goal pace. If an elevation change occurs later in an event (past mile 18), you may have muscle fatigue to deal with in addition to muscle cramps, which may be exacerbated by the obstacle itself. Overall, my advice is to use these hilly events as training runs. Enjoy the run and train for a negative split to gain experience with running the second half faster. You will be surprised how good you feel when passing the many runners that went out too fast or attacked too hard and are now facing lactic acid build-up or fatigue late in the race. You may even choose to use the uphill portions to walk, especially if you are still working towards running your first marathon. Walking or slowing your pace during these uphill sections will help to keep you strong for the last six miles.

A word of caution is that most venues incorporate an uphill section at some point, and it is usually a good idea to do a pre-race walk, jog, or drive through the areas you believe will offer the most challenge. Get out of your car and actually jog or run up the hill at your desired pace. These hills can be very intimidating when you are driving. However, when you are running, they aren't as ominous. An intimidating hill may cause you to overcompensate your pace by running slower at the start of the race to store energy. This will result in a slower overall time. As a suggestion, don't approach a venue too conservatively, but run at a constant effort on uphill and downhill sections of the course.

Example of a Race Profile

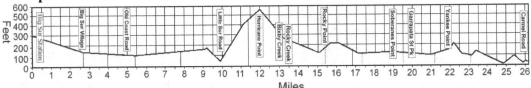

Figure 3.7 Courtesy of Big Sur International Marathon.

#6. Weather Conditions

The morning temperature on race day has a direct impact to your performance. Races that offer a starting temperature in the low 50s(°F) and a finishing temperature in the high 50s/low 60s(°F) will provide the best opportunity for success. Most venues are scheduled in the spring or fall, providing the best opportunity for optimum marathon conditions. Rarely do events occur in the heat of summer.

Cold, wind, rain or extreme heat can be significant determents to running your qualifying race. Unfortunately, poor conditions are usually unpredictable. It is suggested to avoid any event that has a high likelihood of adverse conditions.

Cold

Cold race days will typically require that you dress in layers. Easily removable layers are the secret to running on a cold day. A runner has the option to invest in premium running clothes to be worn throughout the entire race or to wear disposable clothes and shed them once weather conditions improve. Be aware that shedding pants will usually require time to stop. Shirts can easily be discarded while running. The old standby is to wear a garbage bag with holes for your head and arms. Although they aren't flattering to fashion-conscious runners, garbage bags are an efficient insulator from cold and rain and can be an excellent interim addition to your race attire when not sure of conditions for the first few miles of a race.

The basic rule for what to wear for an event is to dress for a temperature 20°F warmer than the actual temperature during the race. As your body heats up and the cardiovascular system is operating at race conditions, your body will generate enough heat to keep you warm. I personally find it extremely difficult to pick out my race clothing prior to an event. A few degrees can mean the difference between long pants versus shorts, and as conditions warm during a long race, you may find yourself overheating, and your pace slows. During many races, runners begin the race physically cold and heat up to race temperature about two to three miles into the event. Windy conditions are even more difficult to dress for. Adding an additional jacket to break a biting cold wind can add weight, bulk, or other discomforts that are not expected. Cold weather can intimidate any runner, especially when the temperature dips into the 30°F range or below.

Running in cold conditions can still be a pleasurable experience, if you are dressed correctly. Avoid cotton sweats and shirts due to their water retention properties and poor wicking capability. There are times when one must make do with what was brought to an event and make the best of it for any unexpected weather change. For this reason, I suggest bringing clothes that bridge a wide range of temperatures and weather conditions.

Photo 3.8 Elite runners know the importance of gloves on cold mornings.

Gloves are a must if there is any chance the starting temperature will be 50°F or below. Gloves are beneficial when race conditions are damp, as moisture cools the body quicker due to wind chill. In these conditions, you will find that cold hands are one of the main contributors to loss of body heat. As much as 30% of body heat escapes through your extremities. Your hands will definitely feel the effects of wind chill and will cool quickly.

Many experienced runners can use their hands similar to a radiator to regulate their body temperature, and when warmed up, they will shed their gloves.

Ear protection and hats are optional depending upon the start temperature. As you run on days of varying weather, you will begin to learn what works best for you. There are obvious downsides to being too warm, as well as too cold. Dressing in disposable layers is always a good back up plan for days when the weather may be unpredictable.

Typically there are three layers important to a runner: (1) the **Base layer** which is critical in keeping moisture away from your body; (2) the **Middle layer** for warmth; and (3) the shielding **Outer layer** to protect you from the wind and rain while utilizing vents, allowing the body to breathe. The outer layer normally consists of a jacket. This layer may be shed when the temperatures rise. Due to the loss of body heat when the body is wet, it is important to stay dry on cold rainy days, as you are much more prone to lose body heat when you are wet.

During the 2007 Boston Marathon, the runners were faced with some of the most challenging weather conditions the event had ever faced. A nor'easter hit Boston the night before the race and brought rain, winds in excess of 45 mph, and temperatures in the high 30s(°F). Many runners (myself included) faced difficult decisions the following day, such as how to dress and even where to put the bib number when layers were shed. Faced with rain and wind and cold at race start, long pants, rain jackets, and gloves were a prerequisite for the day. About 10 miles into the race, I opted to shed my middle layer as the temperatures warmed slightly to the upper 40s(°F). However, a chilling rain with wind continued, so staying dry and warm was my key concern against the wind chill. In preparation for the choice of what to shed, I opted to put my bib number on my pants so that I could shed either top easily. That strategy worked well. When running on a cold day, be sure you have warm dry clothes in your garment check bag at the finish. That preparation can be easily overlooked when considering adverse conditions. In addition, plan the layers you may shed, and place your bib number on clothes you will definitely retain.

Wind

Wind chill can also become a major factor during training runs. Even though the air temperature may be in the 40s(°F), a brisk wind may be all that it takes to keep you inside on the treadmill. Typically, runners rarely train outside when the air temperature drops below 30°F, even on a sunny day. This is due primarily to the amount of additional and constrictive clothing that is necessary to stay warm during long training runs. However, if/when you are forced to train outside when the temperature is low and the wind is high, it is necessary to buy and wear the appropriate clothing designed specifically for such conditions. Cotton sweats are a recipe for disaster, due to their moisture retention and/or lack of wicking capability. In addition, they offer poor wind resistance. I highly recommend purchasing the appropriate running gear for cold weather if you will be forced to train in adverse conditions.

Table 3.9 Wind Chill Chart

Wind Speed (MPH)	Actual Air Temperature in Degrees Fahrenheit						
	50°F	40°F	30°F	20°F	10°F	0°F	-10°F
	Temperature with Wind Chill Applied						
0	50	40	30	20	10	0	-10
5	48	37	27	16	6	-5	-15
10	40	28	16	4	-9	-24	-33
15	36	22	9	-5	-18	-32	-45
20	32	18	4	-10	-25	-39	-53
25	30	16	0	-15	-29	-44	-59
30	28	13	-2	-18	-33	-48	-63
35	27	11	-4	-20	-35	-51	-67

Rain

If the temperature is in the 55°F to 70°F range, a rainy day should not hinder your performance unless you become waterlogged and shoes and socks become noticeably heavier due to the added water weight. For this reason, it is recommended, if running in wet conditions, that you wear thin socks or mesh socks. These options do not retain much water. In addition to the appropriate socks, you should wear shoes that have a vented sole. The weight of water from waterlogged shoes and socks will noticeably slow down your pace. For cooler days when you expect to run in the rain, you may want to consider going to a rain-repellent material like Gortex. However, on warmer days you may choose not to repel the rain, to stay cool.

When faced with a light rain condition on a warm day, you may find that performance is better due to retained external water, which maintains a lower body temperature. Heavy rains and/or lightning at the start of a race will typically mean that the race will have a delayed start or be postponed completely. One suggestion that will benefit you when a chance of rain is in the forecast is to bring a full-size trash bag with you to the start of the race. Having a sudden burst of rain prior to the start of a race causes people to scramble for shelter, and typically there is never enough to go around. At this point, people may even start to envy your trash bag attire…probably one of the few times in life when this is the case.

Heat, Humidity and Sun

When running an event where heat and humidity are factors, both oxygen intake and breathing become more difficult. As air temperature rises, the density of the air decreases, and each breath taken provides less oxygen to the lungs and muscles.

This combination of humidity and heat is a runner's worst opponent in a race or training run. A loss in performance due to heat and humidity can be most noticeable during an interval training workout. These workouts are when the body is demanding the highest oxygen flow to muscles. This reduced oxygen intake leads you toward an anaerobic condition more quickly. Anaerobic is defined as performing at a level above the oxygen requirement to support sustained exercise. To compensate for the reduced oxygen due to the heat and humidity, your breathing rate increases, and thus you become more easily fatigued.

The body dissipates heat by varying the flow of blood that circulates through the body. Sweating also helps to cool the body, when evaporation of sweat occurs. However, high relative humidity reduces the body's ability to cool by evaporation. When the heat gain to the body exceeds what the body can cool, heat-related illness can occur, such as sunstroke, heat cramps, and heat exhaustion. One other factor to account for regarding heat is body fat percentage. Each percentage increase in total body fat will cause the body to feel the effects of heat and humidity sooner.

Suggestions for Running/Training in Hot Weather (Day Time)

- Run in the morning or evening
- If you opt to wear a hat, soak it with water to keep you cool
- Wear mesh-type clothes that don't hold moisture
- Pour water on your head, neck, and arms whenever possible
- When training, use walk breaks to help to cool you off
- Drink cold water to help in keeping your body temperature down
- Use sprinklers and available water fountains/faucets to drink/soak
- Eat lightly before running on hot days
- Light rain showers may be refreshing to train in (without the threat of lightning)

The effects of heat will definitely slow you down during a marathon. If at all possible, schedule a qualifying event that has an optimum starting temperature of approximately 50°-55°F and a finishing temperature not much over 60°F. However, if you are faced with competing in an event where the temperature is 70°F or 80°F, you will see in Table 3.10 that your running times will increase by approximately one minute per hour of running at 70°F and two minutes per hour at 80°F. For example, if you are a 4-hour marathon runner, on a 70°F day you will finish around 4 hours 4 minutes, and on an 80°F day approximately 4 hours 8 minutes. If you are running above 80F, just enjoy the run and don't push it. This table is not exact, but provides an estimate of the impact of heat to your qualifying attempt. Note: this does not include reference to humidity or sun, which, as explained previously, will add further performance loss.

Table 3.10 Approximate Impact of Heat on Finishing Time for a Marathon

Temperature		3:00 marathon	4:00 marathon
60°F		0 min	0 min
70°F 21°C	(Add 1 minute/hr)	+3 min	+4 min
80°F 26°C	(Add 2 minutes/hr)	+6 min	+8 min
90°F	(Add 3-4 minutes/hr)	+9–12 min	+12–16 min

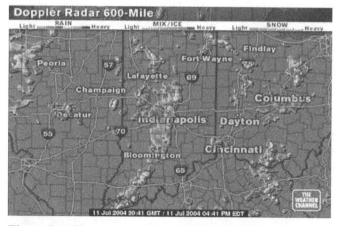

Figure 3.11 Picture courtesy of The Weather Channel

If your training plan requires that you run long runs or intervals during the heat of summer, you may want to wait for a time when a cooling summer rain shower is available. You can choose to run either during the light showers or shortly after the rain.

In some cases, such as shown in Figure 3.11, you may only have a few hours when the glaring sun and heat are suppressed. Watch the weather channels or go online to view weather. The Weather Channel or local news stations are good choices to view weather.

If you are faced with a hot and humid qualifying race day, it is advisable not to seek out your qualifying time, but rather enjoy the race. Make sure you visit each water stop for fluids and electrolytes that will definitely be lost during the race.

According to the National Weather Service National Oceanic and Atmospheric Administration, direct sun exposure can increase the Heat Index by 15°F. Due to the risk of heat exposure, move your training time to morning or evening, or just slow down due to these factors. It is most important that you don't expect to perform to your training goal for the day. Training in heat should be avoided, as approximately 200 Americans succumb to heat-related deaths every year.

Table 3.12 Heat Index

Temperature (°F) versus Relative Humidity (%)

°F	90%	80%	70%	60%	50%	40%
80	85	84	82	81	80	79
85	101	96	92	90	86	84
90	121	113	105	99	94	90
95		133	122	113	105	98
100			142	129	118	109
105				148	133	121
110						135

The Heat Index is the temperature that the body experiences when both heat (actual air temperature) and the relative humidity are combined. Table 3.12 is based upon shady and light wind conditions.

Exposure to direct sunlight can increase these Heat Index values up to an additional 15°F. This is a major contributor to heat-related illnesses. Overcast days may shield the sunlight and make it more tolerable to train. However, mix direct sunlight with heat and humidity, and the recommendation is to wait for a better time or conditions to train.

Below are some tips for how to dress on race day. Each of these recommendations will change with the influence of direct sunlight, humidity, etc., and are only baseline recommendations. Personal preference, venue, wind, and other factors will modify these suggestions.

Temp	Suggested Running Attire Based upon Temperature
20-29°F	Long thermal running pants (polypropylene tights recommended), warm socks, long-sleeved running shirt with wicking capability (inner layer) with long-sleeved thermal polypropylene (outer layer), optional fleece or warm shirt for middle layer, hat (knit-type) with wicking preferred, and gloves for extremity protection.
30-39°F	Long running pants or tights, warm socks, long-sleeved running shirt with vest or second shirt for added warmth, hat (knit-type), gloves.
40-49°F	Shorts or lighter weight tights, preferred running socks, long-sleeved shirt or short sleeve running shirt with vest, gloves (disposable), and optional knit-type hat. Arm warmers are also a good option for the 40-49°F range due to their flexibility when encountering winds or variations in temperature during a race.
50-59°F	Running shorts, preferred running socks, short-sleeved shirt, optional warm-up shirt (disposable), optional gloves.
60°F or above	Lightweight shorts, preferred running socks, mesh shirt or singlet.

As previously stated, cotton should always be avoided due to the water retention properties and poor wicking capability. Polypropylene is a necessity for any dedicated runner. This material keeps the runner warm while allowing for perspiration to escape. It is important to purchase running attire of high quality for flexibility, water wicking, and warmth when running in cold climates. A few of the many companies that offer premium running clothes are www.nationalrunningcenter.com, www.roadrunnersports.com, www.sporthill.com, and www.asics.com.

#7. Running a Smart Race

Running a smart race should be the objective of any serious marathoner. Going into a qualifying event without a race plan, without reviewing the race profile, without driving the course, or without thinking of your time splits can be a recipe for disaster. Without a plan, you should still finish the event, but will lose valuable minutes when qualifying time is valuable. A smart race is measured by many factors. These include meeting your goal time and finishing strong, but not too strong. For example, if you are sprinting at the end, you may not have used your reserves or spread them out over the final miles adequately.

In my opinion, when running a marathon for a specific time goal, a pacing band or the use of a pace group should be used to help you track your actual time versus desired time splits per mile. Going into a critical qualifying attempt without either of these valuable tools is like flying a plane in the fog without instruments.

Pace Group
Most major events offer the benefit of official pace groups where runners can sign up to run as a group with the intent of finishing at the time they select. Each of the runners that sign up will be wearing bibs on their back that indicate their pace time (for example: 3:00, 3:15, 3:30, 4:00, 4:30, 5:00, etc.). The leader of the group is a volunteer who is typically an accomplished runner capable of easily meeting the pace. These groups can and should be used if you need support and motivation while running or need to passively monitor your time. Some groups will go out slightly faster than goal pace and may do so to account for slower second-half splits. Also, there may be a group of runners that has dropped back in pace from the actual lead group, and is no longer part of the true pace group. Therefore it is important to start out with a clear understanding of the pace group leader. Introduce yourself prior to the start, as it may be helpful to establish rapport with the pace leader to get insight to his/her pace plan.

Pacing Band
Photo 3.13 is an example of a pacing band, which provides goal times at each mile split to achieve the target time of a Marathon. In this example, the pacing band provides even mile splits for an overall 3:30 time.

A pacing band can keep you focused on your task and provide acceptable feedback on your ongoing performance. The key with these tools is that you know where you are and can somewhat control your destiny. Going out too fast or too slow early in a race can drastically impact your performance.

Until you are comfortable with monitoring your pace without these tools, use them. If a pacing band is not available, you can make your own or write your 5, 10, 15, 20, and 25 mile goal splits on your arm. If you decide to make a home-made pacing band, be aware that sweat or spillage from drinks may reduce the clarity of the numbers. Many marathon expo events offer pacing bands free of charge or for a minimal charge.

Photo 3.13 An example of a pacing band.

#8. Running Attire and Essentials

In addition to the selection of clothes to match the elements listed previously, there are a few not-so-obvious items that will help your performance under varying conditions. The base or inner layers may be the most critical.

Men will find that some running shorts include integrated support and may opt not to wear additional underwear. If you have experience with this, by all means use what works for you. However, if you are not sure, stay away from cotton briefs, as they do not provide moisture wicking capability and can be abrasive to the skin in the areas that are subjected to movement. Typically, after a 7- to 10-mile run, you will wish that you had selected a Lycra® or microfiber-equivalent soft material. Also, if your upper legs are subject to rubbing while running, it is highly recommended to add the longer leg design (Photo 3.14a) under your shorts or utilize spandex fitness shorts, made of Lycra®. This material also helps to prevent chafing by reducing moisture. Women have different fit challenges than men. However comfort, support, and a selection that reduces abrasion are key elements of the base/underwear.

The recommended essential attire for variable temperature range conditions are below.

Base/Underwear (Men)

Photo 3.14a

Base/Underwear (Women)

Photo 3.14b   Photo 3.14c

Warm Wear (60°F and Above)

Men's running shorts and singlet
Photo 3.15a-3.15b

Women's compression shorts and shirt
Photo 3.16a-3.16b

Cooler Wear and Layers (40°F to 60°F)

Long-sleeved running shirt   Running vest   Arm warmer(s)   Running pants/tights
Photo 3.17   Photo 3.18   Photo 3.19   Photo 3.20a-3.20b

Photos provided by and copyrighted by ASICS America Corporation

Cold Conditions (Below 40°F)

Thermal tights/pants   Windproof insulated jacket(s)   Wool hat or skullcap   Gloves
Photo 3.21   **Photo 3.22a-3.22b**   **Photo 3.23**   **Photo 3.24**

Photos provided by and copyrighted by ASICS America Corporation

Shirts/T-Shirts

Shirts are typically made of 100% cotton. I would discourage cotton shirts for any event greater than 10K. Although cotton is soft when dry, when mixed with moisture from rain or sweat it can be abrasive on the chest and lead to irritation or bleeding due to continuous rubbing across the nipples. Use cotton t-shirts for training runs or short distance races. Shirts made of Coolmax® or comparable material offer excellent moisture wicking capability. You should be able to find any style, from singlets to thick long-sleeved designs, that will fit every weather element you may encounter. One excellent feature found in cold weather shirts is a thumb hole to keep your hands warm due to wind exposure on cold days. Remember, the cotton race shirts provided with the venue should be used for the trip home and definitely not the race itself.

Tights

Full-length tights can be an excellent selection for a venue with a start temperature of 35°F-45°F. Tights offer good protection against the wind and cold and are available in various material choices for temperature extremes. I recommend at least two pair of tights. One lightweight pair of tights can be a great selection for temperatures between 35°F and 45°F. A heavier and insulated pair may be used for temperatures below 35°F. Both may not be necessary based upon your regional climate, but polypropylene materials are recommended for wicking capability and resistance to the cold. Tights or close-fitting (wicking) sweats are used by runners because they are lightweight and are less restrictive.

Shorts

As typical with other running attire, there is a wide variety of running shorts, from compression type to the typical split-side running shorts (as shown in Photo 3.15). Lycra is a typical material for shorts because it stays relatively dry. Some shorts offer pockets, while others offer zippered pouches for keys or gel packs. Some shorts have built-in briefs and eliminate the need for wearing underwear. As mentioned previously, cotton briefs should be avoided for any run. Women have been wearing compression shorts (of spandex or polyester blend) for years, and the trend is starting with men due to the advantages. Many running attire companies offer both compression shorts as well as the traditional split-side shorts with added mesh pockets. Many distance runners and tri-athletes use compression shorts with integrated back pockets due to the ease of carrying energy gel for the duration of a long event. A few months into running, I developed a preference for compression shorts to eliminate chafing issues on my inner thighs. Personal preference and running comfort are paramount in your specific selection of shorts.

Sweats

Sweat pants (made of cotton) are not recommended for distance running. They offer warmth, but if you plan on running any distance, they will retain sweat and add weight to your run. Cotton sweats are best left in the garment check bag for pre-race warm-up and post-race change of clothes.

Sports Bras/Support Tops

These garments are designed for women to provide support during exercise. In some cases, runners may choose to wear two sport tops or wear a sports bra under a shirt, depending upon the weather. As with most running attire, it is important to have a sports bra for support, but you will also need to ensure that it has the capability to wick moisture to keep you relatively dry. It is suggested to purchase a higher quality bra that combines moisture management and support. There are many to select from and ASICS, Nike, Champion, New Balance, and Under Armour are a few key suppliers.

Photo 3.25   Sports bras are a vital garment of many female runners.

Shoes

Possibly the most important element in your running gear and the primary inhibitor of running injuries are shoes. There are many different types of running shoes on the market. For a new runner, it can be very confusing. Shoes for distance running should be purchased at a specialty running shoe store. Some stores will prefer certain brands over others. Talk with the salesperson about how long they've been running or have worked there to get an understanding of their level of experience. If you are not comfortable with their knowledge, then there is always another shop. I highly recommend staying away from the typical shoe stores in the shopping mall unless they carry the brand that you have pre-selected and have worn with success.

Specialty running stores are worth the initial extra effort to select proper shoes as you enter into distance running. You may have to try a few pairs of shoes or brands until you find a good match for your needs. In addition, most specialty shoe stores request that you run in the shoe first to evaluate your specific running shoe needs. Don't get discouraged if the shoe brand and style selected are not the same as a running peer, as what works best for someone else does not mean that will be a good match for you.

· Breaking in Running Shoes

Running shoes typically do not need to be broken in and, unlike dress shoes, they do not stretch. **Never run a long distance race in new shoes.**

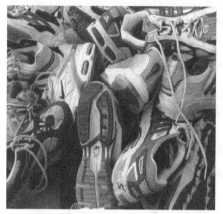

New shoes are typically defined as shoes with less than 25 miles logged on them. Even if the shoes are the same brand you have used for years, slight differences in the insert, stitching, or other abnormalities may lead to blisters.

Although maximum cushioning occurs when shoes are new, some runners use the first 25 miles as a break-in period prior to a race. A best practice for shoe selection used for a marathon is to ensure that you have at least one long run completed with the shoes. Some runners keep a set of good-fitting shoes separated from their training shoes to keep the miles low and only use them for critical races.

Photo 3.26 Shoes ready for donation.

Training for a marathon will require that you wear out a few pairs of shoes. Remember to donate your slightly worn shoes to charity. Many running stores offer donation service.

· Shoe Size

It is highly recommended to buy running shoes at least one size above the size you wear in a casual or dress shoe. Toes require room to move, and as you run your feet tend to swell slightly. A common foot injury that many runners experience is damaged or lost toenails from shoes that are too small (Photo 3.27). This injury can become painful during the run as well. Always get fitted for shoes while wearing the socks that you plan to wear while running.

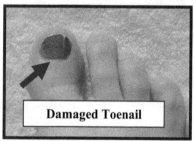

Damaged Toenail

Thick socks can make a big difference in fit. Runners that run with additional gel pads, sole inserts, or extra socks due to foot injuries should be aware that these items will constrict the foot area of the shoe. For these cases, it is recommended to move up one and a half sizes to accommodate the added items surrounding your foot/feet.

Photo 3.27 Toenail damage/loss due to the lack of room in the toe area of a runner's shoe.

Also be aware that different brands of shoes will fit differently, and sizing up for one brand may not equal the other. If you find that you happen to have a loose-fitting shoe, you can remedy the situation by wearing thicker socks, or tightening the laces. Additional insoles may be used. However, when two insoles are used within one shoe, the stability of your foot in the shoe is greatly compromised.

· Shoe Pronation

As a runner, you will undoubtedly hear the term pronation while visiting a running store. Pronation is the term used to describe the type of movement that your foot experiences during a running stride. The duration of this movement is from the time your heel contacts the ground to the time you push off for another stride. It is defined as the normal rolling movement of the foot when it lands on the outside of the heel and then rolls inward as you push off. Normal pronation depicts a foot with straight alignment and even distribution of force as you push against the running surface. Overpronation occurs when the foot continues to roll toward the inside of your foot as you push off. It is determined by excessive wear on the inside of the shoe. Underpronation occurs with the runner who tends to run on the outside of their feet. It is determined by excessive wear on the outside of the shoe.

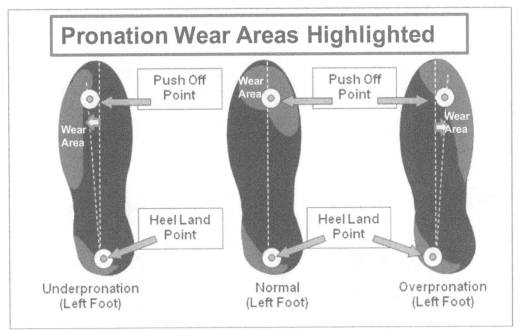

Figure 3.28 Comparison of running pronation types (By wear on left foot).

So you may ask yourself, what does this mean to me as a runner? Understanding the type of running movement by the wear on your shoe is important for avoiding injury. Having a running shoe (expert) salesperson or even a podiatrist watch you run is essential to avoiding injuries to the foot and or leg joints. By understanding this terminology, you can then match your foot with the type of shoe that meets your running needs. There are three types of shoes for runners: **motion control, stability,** and **cushion**.

- **Motion control shoes** are used for overpronators. These overpronators typically have flat feet (low arches), which provides for good shock load distribution across the foot. However, overpronators will require additional motion control of the foot, and their feet typically have excessive roll inward.

- **Stability shoes** are for a neutral (normal) foot. A neutral foot has a medium arch. Stability shoes will provide good distribution of force across the foot for impact.

- **Cushion shoes** are built for the underpronators. These underpronators have high arches, and the load from impact is distributed on a smaller area of contact on the foot (outside of the foot). Therefore, added cushion is needed to even the load or supply cushion throughout the foot. Cushioned shoes are also important to runners who are recovering from impact- or stress-related injuries (tendonitis, shin splints, stress fracture, runner's knee, etc.) and are in need of extra cushion to reduce the impact force on their joints and tendons. Also, if you are faced with predominately running on concrete or asphalt, it may be wise to purchase cushioned shoes to reduce the chance for possible injuries. Masters division runners (over 40 year olds) may consider this as a conservative strategy to reduce the risk of injury due to reduced bone density associated with increasing age.

Each type of shoe has specific applications depending upon your weight, the pronation of your feet, and your arch height. Therefore, it is critical to select the right shoe for you. As previously mentioned, it is highly recommended that you consult a shoe specialist at your local running shop until you have found a shoe that matches your running and performance needs. A common error for first-time marathoners (including myself) is to find a shoe that looks fast, is lightweight, and a preferred brand or price range. I quickly learned the value of the right shoe after a stress fracture and tendonitis brought my running to a stop due to the wrong shoe type.

· Shoe Rotation

Anyone training for a marathon will require more than one pair of shoes. Typically, a shoe's maximum life is between 400 to 500 miles. Running in a shoe that has passed its maximum life can cause injuries due to the reduction of cushioning. To help with this problem, it is suggested to rotate between two pairs of shoes once you've put about 200 miles on the first pair. At this point, add a second pair into your training, and label your shoes with some permanent marking (i.e. #1/#2, A/B, Old/New, etc.) to keep them separate (Photo 3.29).

Photo 3.29 Labeling shoes is beneficial when rotating pairs.

You should always use your newest shoes for your longer training runs, as they will have the maximum cushioning. Save the older shoes for the short distance or off-road training. Conversely, you can always just replace your shoes with new ones at 400+ miles, but keep in mind the cushioning capability is compromised as you get higher mileage on the shoes.

Socks

Unlike shoes, it is okay (even recommended) to run a race with new socks. They are more comfortable and may even provide slightly more cushion than broken in-socks. Some runners utilize two socks per foot when running for added cushion. Unless you have tried this on training runs, you may not want to attempt two socks during a marathon due to the potential for a friction blister from the rubbing of socks. Another injury could come from damaged toenails, as the second sock reduces the space for toe movement or foot expansion. As a rule of thumb, distance runners wear socks with good cushioning ability, and sprinters wear thin socks for speed. Whichever the case, make sure that your socks are not bunched up anywhere inside your shoe on a long run or race, as this may lead to blisters.

Petroleum Jelly

The value and use of petroleum jelly was unfortunately something that I learned by trial and error. Since everyone has a different physique as well as running style, chafing during long races or training runs may or may not occur. If it does, the friction can lead to a serious rash, discomfort, or in some cases, bleeding. One key to reducing this discomfort is to wear Lycra® or microfiber underwear. Definitely avoid cotton underwear. In some cases, the material may not completely eliminate discomfort with long runs, and petroleum jelly in these friction-prone locations (toes, inner thighs, groin, inside of upper arms, etc.) will ensure you can focus on the run and not discomfort.

Nipple Protection

Photo 3.30

This was an issue that I thought was for other runners, and that I really didn't need to guard against nipple injuries. Like this person in Photo 3.30, it can happen if you are not prepared.

For men, running in cotton shirts during training runs of five miles or more may start to rub the ends of the nipples to the point where they are tender and may potentially bleed. Obviously, this is only applicable to men, as most women wear support bras/tops and don't need to be concerned about this type of issue. I've personally seen dozens of cases in various events. Male runners should take notice of this and take necessary precautions so that you don't end up as shown in Photo 3.30.

Running Watch

The most important feature of a running watch is visibility in day and night conditions. The running watch is the primary component of any serious runners' attire. Typically a digital face with a lighted display for night runs is the choice of most runners. More sophisticated versions include a heart rate monitor.

Easy access of start/stop and reset or lap functions are key even when you are wearing gloves. I highly recommend that a runner be very selective about the watch that they choose, as it will become both your friend and enemy on runs as you race against the clock.

Photo 3.31

Heart Rate Monitors

Personally, I believe heart rate monitors (HRMs) have value in training, especially interval running. A runner should use one on all runs until they've become accustomed to the capabilities of their heart/body and their performing heart rate under various training stress. As you continue to train, you will start to push yourself harder, and your performance and volumetric efficiency will improve. Your maximum HR does not increase, but you ability to run faster by increasing your margin (beats/minute) to your maximum HR is your enabler to run faster through training. This margin signifies improvement in your cardiovascular efficiency.

Long runs and even tempo runs are designed to allow margin in your HR levels, and an HRM is not required. However, intervals or other speed workouts will definitely push the limit of your maximum HR. Since it is not recommended to exceed your maximum HR, you should wear a monitor for the more stressful workouts. Many publications recommend a calculated maximum heart rate of **[Maximum HR = 220 – age]**. However, this has been noted to be too conservative for people over 40 and overestimates capability for people under 40. The October 2007 issue of *Runner's World* has an alternative formula **[Maximum HR= 208 - 0.7 X age]**. To start out, use the most conservative formula, and work toward the higher value (of the two formulas) as you improve your cardiovascular capabilities.

Another use of an HRM can be applied to constant speed workouts. As your body starts to fatigue (or overheat), your heart rate will increase to provide more oxygen or blood flow for cooling. This heart rate measure will provide you with a baseline of your physical condition, and this fatigue point should increase as you build your cardiovascular system. A good application for constant speed HRM is on a stationary bike, as you have an easily controlled environment and intensity.

Many successful runners and tri-athletes train specifically at target heart rates and utilize monitors during training and competition. If you would like to measure your heart rate maximum, it can be determined by running a mile at your fastest pace. Near the final quarter mile or so, take the highest reading on your heart rate monitor.

Global Position Satellite (GPS) Running Tool

With the introduction of GPS into running in recent years, the level of data analysis to improve performance has increased significantly. These tools can provide excellent real-time data on instantaneous speed in miles per hour or miles per minute. They can determine your total distance run within a few feet and also provide timing for the race or workout. Other features of a GPS that are applicable to runners, such as one offered by Garmin (see Photo 3.32), include precise elevation information; amount of calories burned; lap history (distance, time, average pace); and a pacing alarm when you drop below a desired pace in your workout. One of the more interesting features is the capability to download software to generate a map of your running routes, such as the one shown in Figure 3.33. All of the data for your routes can be stored and compared against your times for the same route or different routes. This tool will make the traditional running watch obsolete, due to the wealth of information it can provide in a relatively small package.

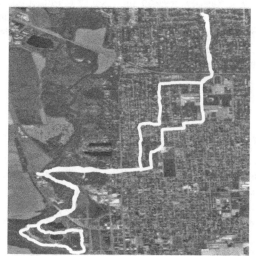

Photo 3.32 Photo courtesy of Garmin

Figure 3.33 Use of a GPS can provide your route details.

Hats

Baseball-style hats are a valuable piece of running gear, especially on nightly training runs to avoid the glare of headlights from oncoming traffic. Without a hat, you're forced to hold your hands up to your eyes to shield them. With the distraction of the headlights, you may not be watching where you are stepping and are more susceptible to an injury. Hats are also helpful on mild or cold temperature training runs or races. They help to shield heat loss through your head and allow you to conserve energy that normally would be used to keep you warm. Since up to 40-50% of your body heat can be lost through your head, wearing a hat on cold training days is a must. However, stay away from hats during warm temperature events due to the additional heat retention (insulation) that a hat provides. Heating the body on an already warm day may cause additional water loss due to sweat and may potentially raise your body temperature, which may lead to elevated heart rate and premature fatigue.

If you do prefer to wear a hat to keep the sun out of your eyes, a visor or a thin white mesh hat are both excellent choices.

Photo 3.34 White hats are a popular selection on a warm sunny day.

Sunglasses

Find sunglasses that don't fog up and are designed to fit close to your eyebrows, as they will be prone to sweat drops on the lens. If your lenses start to fog up or have sweat runs about three miles into a race, you'll wish you had left them at home. Suppliers of fog-free and vented sunglasses are at the running expos prior to many events.

Many different styles are offered in running catalogs or online. If you are set on running in sunglasses, start with inexpensive glasses to find a pair or a style that works. Since exposure to ultraviolet rays from the sun can lead to glaucoma and cataracts, you should ensure that the sunglasses you select filter out UVA and UVB rays.

Some suppliers of contact lenses offer sunglass equivalents in contact lens form with UV protection. This is a great feature for runners and eliminates the fogging issues while protecting your eyes and reducing the opportunity for a sun-associated headache.

Photo 3.35 Sunglass style is obviously in the eyes of the beholder.

Running Belts

Both runners and tri-athletes often use running belts designed to hold three or four small bottles for energy drinks. These can be helpful supplements to re-charge you with electrolytes; however, there is some added weight, and the bottles tend to bounce (and distract you) as you run. Carrying a running belt is purely optional, as almost every event has water stops with sports drinks that serve the same purpose. If you find that running belts are too cumbersome, pouches can be clipped onto your running pants to store energy packs, keys, or other items needed during a training run or a race. The runners in

Photo 3.36 are using the typical application of running belts, and the woman to the far left is using a larger water pack typically fitted with a straw in the front for hydration. If you do select a belt, the items you carry and fluid containers should not impede your movement. In most cases, running belts are an unnecessary added weight and should be left at home, unless you require a specific form of energy drink due to stomach issues. Iron Man events, which incorporate a 2.4 mile swim and 112 mile bike ride prior to a full marathon, are much more draining to your energy levels, and hydration belts are more of a requirement for replenishing depleted energy stores in those events.

Photo 3.36 Running belts or fluid packs are unnecessary items for a marathon.

#9 Rest, Travel, and Time of Event

Rest

Chapter 7 contains a section specifically devoted to evaluating the impact of rest and travel upon performance. For obvious reasons, the more rest you get prior to any major or strenuous event, the better you should perform. Do not travel by air the day before a marathon qualifying attempt due to the resulting exhaustion it can create because of the stress of travel, packet/bib pick up, rushed meals, and logistics. The day prior to a qualifying attempt should be as stress-free as possible. In addition, it is most critical to get a full night's sleep two nights prior to the day of the race. For example, if the race is Sunday, then the amount of sleep Friday night is more important than the amount of sleep you achieve on Saturday night. Ultimately, resting fully both nights is optimum. Conserving energy in the final 48 hours is highly recommended, so plan accordingly.

Travel

Time changes due to race location are also a major consideration. If traveling east or west or crossing multiple time zones, you should account for this in your daily activities and sleep schedule. There have been times when I needed to get to sleep earlier than usual due to time zone changes and unfortunately was not successful. As these nights progressed, I stressed more about my lack of sleep and focused on getting to sleep rather than relaxing. In some cases, the hotel or location you selected for lodging/sleep may become an issue. Late-night door slams, elevators, noisy hallway conversations, etc., can be annoying and keep you awake. A recommendation to thwart the noise is to request the quietest room available and bring ear plugs and loud alarm clock(s). Two alarm sources (clocks or cell phone) may psychologically allow for better rest, knowing your chances of sleeping through redundant alarms is unlikely.

Time of Event

The majority of marathons will start in the morning to avoid peak traffic times and thus provide minimal impact to the non-running community. In addition, for warmer venues an early start is a necessity, as the heat of day becomes a factor as you approach mid-day. For those venues, I don't mind getting up at 4:00 a.m. to avoid the heat. However, when heat is not in the forecast, a chilly dark morning can deplete you of energy while trying to stay warm. It is imperative to stay warm to conserve energy for the race, so make sure you wear sweats and utilize the clothing check service, if provided. If the race is without this service, bring one or two large trash bags and enclose yourself to shield or cocoon your body from the cold while you enjoy pre-race snacks or rest.

If shuttles are offered, they will tend to get you there much earlier than needed, so expect to have a long pre-race morning. The combination of an early start with cold temperatures will take a toll on your energy level and may cause you to have a sluggish start. In addition, these early races may involve a start when it is still dark outside. In most cases there will be lighting, but don't count on it for the entire portion of the course prior to sunrise. Potholes or other road obstacles will be a concern in pre-dawn conditions.

Also, consider what your body clock is accustomed to doing in the morning. As an evening runner, I believe I run quicker at night than in the morning, and I am probably at optimum speed at mid-day. One recommendation is to try to get in your last few training runs, and especially your long runs, at a time that is similar to the marathon start time. Be sure to watch your time splits for the first few miles to see if you are significantly slower as your body adjusts to the demand for energy. Again, the first few miles should be slightly slower as you warm up cold muscles, but by mile three you should be on pace. Another recommendation is to run at an easy pace at least one-quarter to one-half mile prior to the start. My best marathon time occurred when I was late for the start and ran at an easy pace just over a mile to get to the start.

Combining an early start with a shivering cold body when you are already sleep deficient is a recipe for a slow start. It may only be worth a few minutes over the course of the entire marathon, but when Boston qualification is involved, every second counts.

#10 Coaching (Providing a Path to Success)

If you include the benefits of reading and learning better techniques from books, periodicals, and videos on enhancing your performance, this could be defined as coaching. Elite runners will typically hire a coach. However, we don't all have the luxury to hire a coach and thus lean on texts and video tutorials. In my quest for Boston, I didn't know specifically how to improve my running ability to take it to that next level, so I turned to numerous books and periodicals and talked with my running peers.

If you are able to hire a coach, you may find that the value of a coach can be two-fold. Not only do they provide you with a training schedule with the intent of meeting your objectives, but they also act as a motivator to keep you focused on your goal. Coaches are also helpful to ensure that you train smart and minimize your risk of injury. As previously mentioned, more miles are not always better, and training smart is vital to staying healthy. Check local high schools, charitable organizations which sponsor marathon events, or go online to find a coach who can meet your needs.

If you are unable to find a coach, seek out guidance from a fellow runner who has more experience in running, marathons, nutrition, and the other factors important for success. Make sure you take that advice for what it is—advice. Not all runners are specialists who can help you specifically, but they can clearly offer input to your training and running endeavors based upon their personal experience.

An Optimum Age to Qualify?

If you have focused on these ten areas in your efforts to qualify for Boston, then you have positioned yourself well for a Boston Qualification (BQ). However, after reviewing the new 2013 B.A.A. qualification standards by age group, I became curious about the possibility of some age brackets being more advantageous than others. Therefore, I compared the age bracket qualification times versus the age group world record times for both men and women. Admittedly, I was somewhat surprised with the results. The findings indicate that there are, in fact, some ages where it may be "easier" to qualify for Boston when considering the performance of the world's best performances within the same B.A.A. age group.

Figure 3.37   Comparison of 2013 BQ Time Requirements vs. World Records

World Record Marathon Times in BQ Age Groups (Men and Women)

	BQ Age Group	18-34	35-39	40-44	45-49	50-54	55-59	60-64	65-69	70-74	80-over
Women	Women: WR Age	29	35	42	NA (est)	50	55	63	69	72	80
	World Record (min.)	135	141	146	148.5	151	172	194	215	226	276
	BQ Requirement (min.)	215	220	225	235	240	250	265	280	295	325
	Best chance for BQ	37%	36%	35%	37%	37%	31%	27%	23%	23%	15%
Men	BQ Age Group	18-34	35-39	40-44	45-49	50-54	55-59	60-64	65-69	70-74	80-over
	Men: WR Age	30	35	40	45	50	55	60	65	73	80
	World Record (min.)	125	123	128	134	139	145	158	161	174	223
	BQ Requirement (min.)	185	190	195	205	210	220	235	250	265	295
	Best chance for BQ	32%	35%	34%	35%	34%	34%	33%	36%	34%	24%

Legend: WR: World Record time for marathon. Source: *Runners World* magazine (Feb. '09) - minutes
BQ Requirement: Boston Qualification time per B.A.A. age group - minutes
Best chance for BQ: The percentage of margin between world record time Vs BQ age group

The data in Figure 3.37 reveals that there are a few age groups more advantageous when trying to qualify for Boston versus the optimum capability (see row: Best chance for BQ).

For women: All age groups from 18 to 54 over offered the best chance to qualify. The 2013 BQ age group standards continue to be much more challenging for women 55 years and over.

For men: The B.A.A. appears to have weighted the qualification times more evenly based upon male capability, as most age groups appear to be equally challenging. However, a few age groups offer a slight margin in your chance for a BQ. These are age groups 35-39, 45-49, and 65-79.

As indicated previously, the B.A.A. standards for qualification are subject to change, and these comparisons (based upon 2013 qualification requirements) may not be applicable to future Boston Marathon events.

Chapter 4
Training

"To run faster, you must train faster"
- Jeff Galloway, *Marathon*

Photo 4.1   Speed training is the best tool a runner has to improve marathon pace, but it can be the most challenging part of your training plan.

Most anyone can complete a marathon if they put in the minimum required training runs. However, the key to qualify for Boston is to focus your training on the basics (speed and distance) and go beyond what it takes to *just* complete a marathon. Typically, whether you achieve or fail to meet your goal time is determined by how you perform in the final 10K of the event. But first, you must get into marathon condition and then focus your training for a strong completion of those final 6.2 miles.

This chapter provides specific training elements to improve your physical and cardiovascular condition. Each of the key basic elements of marathon training is covered in the first section **(1)** of this chapter, **The Basics of Marathon Training**. The second section, **(2) Running Strong the Final 6.2 Miles**, focuses on how to enhance your performance to run on pace during those final grueling miles.   The third and final section, **(3) Training Aids**, provides a few methods to help you to stay focused on your training and keep you motivated.

1 The Basics of Marathon Training

A marathon is an event *not* to be taken lightly. If you are not physically and mentally prepared, the experience can be so devastating that you never attempt another. You can't cram for a marathon like you would for a test, as your efforts in endurance training are clearly shown on race day. In addition, your muscles will be painfully sore for days if you've undertrained. Training is the **only** way you can improve your performance. Luckily, one of the amazing attributes of your body is that it is designed to improve in both performance (speed) and endurance when taken through a repetition of training cycles with gradual increases in intensity. These training patterns are highlighted in almost every running book, and each has preferences in their suggested approach. However, they employ the common theme of speed work and increased distance through a disciplined approach.

Before we get started on the specific elements of training, there is an aspect of training that parallels life. *You will have good days and bad days*. Not every day will show improvement. Just because you took longer to run a set route this week than the previous week doesn't mean that training isn't working. It may mean that you are slightly fatigued from a previous workout, you haven't been eating right, you are low on rest, the weather is uncooperative, your body is fighting a cold, or you just aren't motivated. Your muscles may be telling you they are tired, and you need to allow them time to heal. If you experience pain, fatigue, extended soreness, or other discomforts, you should listen to your body and adjust or delay training. Pushing through physical injuries as a runner is not advised.

Figure 3.2 in Chapter 3 illustrated the point that improvement is not continuous from day to day or race to race. Temperature, injuries, and fatigue were all factors that affected why I did not have a straight line of continuous improvement. Your daily runs will have the same variation, but the overall result should show improvement over time if you are training properly. Genetics, age, motivation, and nutrition are keys to determine how much you can improve. So if you can accept the good training days with the bad training days, then you are ready to get started.

Building a Base Fitness Level

If you are new to running, you may not know your base capabilities. From a base fitness level, you are essentially starting at low endurance and poor volumetric efficiency, sometimes referred to as VO2 max. VO2 max is expressed as a numerical value given to determine how efficiently your body can transport oxygen to your muscles when under demand. Simply stated, VO2 is your aerobic capacity. Understandably, with a low VO2, you will struggle the first few times out for a run around the block or to complete a mile. As a new runner, you may find it easy to throw in the towel… but don't. This start-up period is one of the most significant hurdles you'll encounter on your way to Boston. You will likely experience training days where you cough, have shortness of breath, and your legs feel heavy. This is your body telling you that your cardiovascular system is not built up. **Do not push hard during this start-up training period.** You will be mentally and physically challenged to complete each workout, and jogging and or walking to complete the distance is acceptable. The key is to continue to work toward running your target distance without taking breaks or walking.

As you complete the initial three or four weeks, where you are building a cardiovascular *Base* with a weekly average of up to 20 miles per week, you should notice that your breathing is becoming more consistent, and your cardiovascular system is more efficient at sending oxygen to your muscles (VO2 max). In order to improve fitness, you need to run at least three times per week and slowly increase your mileage by a maximum of 10% each week. As a general guideline, a minimum of training twice per week will roughly maintain your fitness level, unless you are running at significant mileage or adding cross training. Table 4.2 provides a basic schedule for building a base for marathon training.

Table 4.2 Building a Base for Marathon Training

M	T	W	TH	F	S	S	Total Miles
Rest	Run 2-4 miles	**Rest**	Run 2-4 miles	**Rest**	Run 5-8 miles	Cross train by elliptical or bike 40 minutes (4 equivalent miles)	**13-20**

Once able to complete the base fitness training easily, you should be ready to start into a First Marathon Training plan. This plan only provides you with the basics to complete the marathon with **no specific time goal**. That should be the intent of your first marathon. The major challenge for most first time marathon runners is to complete the marathon. Therefore, training for your first marathon (Table 4.3) focuses only on distance and cross training without focus on speed. This plan provides you with the **minimum** requirements to complete the distance while running (or no significant walking included). The longest distance week (highlighted below) of seven sequential days accounts for 38 equivalent miles when cross training is included. This weekly mileage is well below the recommended level for a Boston qualification attempt. That is not yet the goal, however. First, we must focus on building strength, cardiovascular capability, and confidence in our ability, then focus on a legitimate qualification attempt later.

Table 4.3 Training for First Marathon (Goal of Completion)

Weeks Before Marathon	M	T	W	TH	F	S	S	Total Miles
10 weeks	Rest	Run 3 miles	Rest	Run 4 miles	Rest	Run 10 miles	Cross Train 40 minutes (4 equiv miles)	21
9 weeks	Rest	Run 3 miles	Rest	Run 4 miles	Rest	Run 14 miles	Rest	21
8 weeks	Rest	Run 3 miles	Rest	Run 4 miles	Rest	Run 10 miles	Cross Train 60 minutes (6 equiv miles)	23
7 weeks	Rest	Run 3 miles	Rest	Run 4 miles	Rest	Run 16 miles	Rest	23
6 weeks	Rest	Run 3 miles	Rest	Run 4 miles	Rest	Run 10 miles	Cross Train 60 minutes (6 equiv miles)	23
5 weeks	Rest	Run 5 miles	Rest	Run 4 miles	Rest	Run 18 miles	Rest	27
4 weeks	Rest	Run 5 miles	Rest	Run 7 miles	Rest	Run 10 miles	Cross Train 60 minutes (6 equiv miles)	28
3 weeks (Maximum Distance Week)	Rest	Run 5 miles	Rest	Run 7 miles	Rest	Run 20 miles	Rest	32
2 weeks	Rest	Run 3 miles	Rest	Run 7 miles	Rest	Run 10 miles	Cross Train 40 minutes (4 equiv miles)	24
1 week	Rest	Run 3 miles	Rest	Run 4 miles	Rest	Run 12 miles	Cross Train 40 minutes (4 equiv miles)	23
Marathon Week	Rest	Run 3 miles	Rest	Run 4 miles	Rest	Marathon 26.2 miles	Rest	33.2

Note: Example of equivalent miles: 40 minutes of cardio cross training = 4 equivalent (running) miles.

When the goal is simply finishing, your training pace should be at a pace where you are able to carry on a conversation while running. Running at a quicker pace for the seven mile distances and below is acceptable, but the ten mile and above distances should be run only slightly quicker than a jog where a conversation is easy to maintain. Also, if possible, substitute a half marathon event in place of one or two of the 10-to 14-mile distance runs, as this will provide excellent experience and conditioning for your first marathon.

Advancing Your Fitness Level

Okay, now that you've logged some mileage and perhaps completed a first marathon, you can focus on increasing your speed and endurance. For example, you may be running 20 miles per week and averaging a pace of 8:40 per mile. If you need to run at a pace of 7:30 per mile for a marathon to qualify for Boston, you need to do some major work that may span months prior to the marathon. This involves increasing your weekly mileage, and speed work becomes a must.

As an advanced runner, you will need to add a few new terms to your running vocabulary, such as Tempo, Fartlek, and Interval runs. Each will be discussed in this chapter, and they are keys to improving your speed and maintaining a faster pace. Without incorporating some type of speed work into your training, you will not improve your pace significantly. Raw mileage definitely helps, but *maintaining the same pace during each workout will not make you faster*.

Suggested Stretches

Runners have different opinions regarding when or whether to stretch. As a general rule, you should not stretch a cold muscle. The best approach is to walk or jog for three to five minutes to get your muscles warm. Once you have blood flowing to muscles, work through a few stretches as shown in Photos 4.4-4.7.

After ten to twenty minutes or so into your workout (for distance runs), stop and stretch your muscles further. If something is tight or is in need of stretching, it is usually evident by this time. After this second stretching, continue with your workout at the intended intensity. Once you've completed your work-out, cool down by jogging or walking. After the cool down, stretch and replenish lost fluids with water or a sports drink. This is an excellent way to reduce lactic acid in your muscles and physically cool yourself down after a significant workout.

If you are doing speed work, it is much more critical to include a warm-up and stretching period prior to speed training. If you find that you have kinks or minor points of pain in muscles or joints in the first few minutes into your warm-up, go slower and gradually ease into your training. For example, when doing intervals, first lightly stretch and jog 400 meters. Repeat until you've completed at least 1200 meters to 1600 meters (1 mile) of warm-up, then start your stretching routine. Also, never force your muscles beyond a comfort point. As your muscles warm up, your flexibility increases.

Stretching is a critical component of running and other similar sports where the strongest muscles of your body (legs) require an extra level of attention to ensure that they are at maximum flexibility to reduce chance of injury. Many runners will quickly stretch or spend less than one minute to stretch these critical leg muscles. To ensure proper stretching is achieved, stretches should be held for 30 seconds (each leg) and repeated two or three times. If you are spending 10 to 15 minutes when stretching in preparation for a workout, that should be sufficient.

The following photos illustrate a few of the key stretches important to runners, where the focus is on maximum flexibility for major muscle areas.

Photo 4.4 Hamstring Stretch
Keep back straight when stretching.

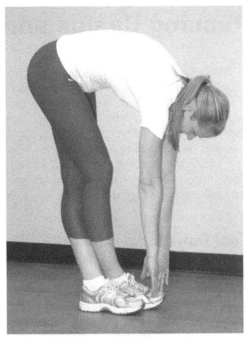

Photo 4.5 Glute Stretch
Cross legs and hold for 15-30 second each side.

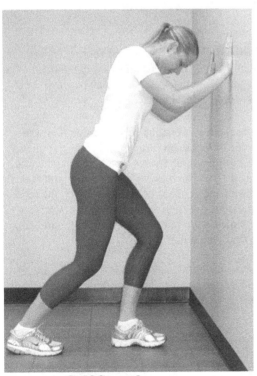

Photo 4.6 Calf Stretch
Bent knee will provide maximum stretch.

Photo 4.7 Quad Stretch
Alternate left hand with right leg.

Running Basics and Form

Warm-Up

A suggested method of starting a workout also applies somewhat to a race: *Go slow to go fast.* In other words, start out slowly and work your way up to workout goal pace. Starting off at full stride without a proper warm-up will lead to injury. Younger athletes may be able to get away with starting out fast, but older runners (30+) are typically less flexible and, thus, more prone to injury. A suggested method starts your workout with a three-to five-minute warm-up of light jogging, then gradually working your way up to a moderate pace. Just remember, a warm-up is required for all workouts, as well as races. Just don't overdo your warm-up! I've seen runners warming up with sprints at a marathon, wasting energy and exposing themselves to a pre-race injury. Warm-ups at goal pace are beneficial, but not sprinting.

Cool-Down

Similar to a warm-up, the cool-down is recommended as a method of protecting the body from cramps or injury caused by sudden stops. A cool-down consists of a slow jog or walk and helps to remove any buildup of lactate acid that may be remaining from a speed workout. After the 5-to 10-minute cool-down, be sure to incorporate at least 5 to 10 minutes of stretching. The post cool-down stretching is the optimum time to increase flexibility for your future training or races.

Running Form

Running form is an often overlooked yet fundamental component of your training. If you train with improper form, you will not perform to your capabilities when running for a goal time. The primary elements of good running form are:

Flat movement   Energy utilized to raise the body while moving forward is wasted energy. Instead, try to keep your head at a stationary distance above the ground. Once you focus on trying to maintain a flat or parallel movement with reference to the ground, you should find that your stride and pace will be smoother, and your leg turnover will be quicker. In other words, don't bounce.

Breathing   The focal point for breathing is usually the frequency of breaths versus strides. This ratio will clearly depend upon your pace. The faster the pace, the more breaths are taken; however, you will find an optimum ratio when you are running. Typically, it will be three strides breathing in and one stride breathing out, or two strides in and one stride out as the pace increases. When running intervals or speed work, it may be a one-to-one ratio. The key with breathing is not to be concerned with the ratio. Your breathing will adjust to the demands on your cardiovascular system for the type of training you are doing. Just keep your torso upright so that you achieve maximum lung capacity and optimum stride length. The breaths per stride will come naturally as you find your pace.

A common challenge a runner faces with breathing is how to deal with a side stitch. Typically, the remedy is to take deep breaths and hold in your breath longer. Obviously, this is difficult when you are in a race. You may need to slow down to hold your breath long enough to help alleviate the pain.

Stride length   Runners may become faster by focusing on increasing the number of strides taken as opposed to only increasing their stride length. Many of the elite runners have very quick strides, approximately 180 per minute. A long stride combined with fast turnover will lead to quicker times if your aerobic capacity can match the demand. Ultimately, your body will determine your stride length, due to your breathing efficiency. The key is to be comfortable in your stride and breathing prior to your qualifying attempt. Most distance runners will typically keep their feet low to the ground to conserve energy and move their arms synchronously with their legs, while holding their forearms parallel to the ground and keeping their hands relaxed.

Running form   The runner in Photo 4.9 demonstrates the sagging posture that plagues runners when core muscles fail to keep them upright or they tire to the point in which they lose focus on running form. This slouching/sagging posture will slow you down, due to a shorter stride length. By maintaining an upright posture, such as demonstrated by the runner in Photo 4.8, this allows for optimum stride length, which results in optimum speed and running economy. A great example of utilizing upright form was Michael Johnson's winning posture in both the 200 meter and 400 meter events in the 1996 Olympics. As a distance sprinter, his running mechanics were a key component to his success. Distance runners, as well as sprinters, can benefit by running upright, with attention to training core muscles being critical to success.

Photo 4.9 This runner struggles with upright form near the 21 mile mark of a marathon. This is a common area for runners to begin to lose focus on form.

Photo 4.8   Stephanie Herbst-Lucke shows great form at the 2008 Olympic Marathon Trials. She continues to be one of the best masters division marathon runners.

Be sure to incorporate core muscle training into your plan to support your torso, and learn to focus on maintaining good posture when you are running/training. Your running economy is critical when looking to shave off valuable seconds or minutes in a qualifying run.

"The Wall"

The Greek warrior Pheidippides ran from the city of Marathon to Athens back in 490 BC, covering the distance of a marathon (thus the origination of the name) and dropped dead shortly thereafter. Unless you plan to end up like him, you may want to consider a gradual approach to building up your physical endurance.

Gradually building up physical endurance is the primary way to prevent becoming totally exhausted, or hitting "the wall" in the late miles of a marathon. There are a number of theories on what causes a runner to hit the wall. Some believe that "the wall" can occur if a runner pushes the body beyond the point of the lactate (acid) threshold. Due to lactic acid build-up in the muscles, the body slows. Others claim a similar result occurs when the carbohydrates stored in the body in the form of glycogen are depleted, and the body starts to burn fat for fuel. Below are two potential causes of hitting "the wall".

· **Lactic acid surplus-** When running or exercising aggressively, glycogen (carbohydrates) is consumed at a faster rate than normal. The byproduct of this energy conversion is lactic acid. When lactic acid builds up in your muscles, the enzyme used to produce energy is turned off, which subsequently reduces your ability to absorb calcium. Calcium is a key element that allows the muscles to contract normally. Without an adequate calcium supply, you are gradually forced to slow down due to cramping. Once you've accumulated lactic acid beyond the limit that your muscles are conditioned to remove, the phenomenon of hitting "the wall" can occur.

· **Glycogen burn to fat burn transition-** When the body's primary fuel source changes from a high percentage of glycogen to consuming of fat, the body slows down, because fat is a less efficient form of energy.

When lactic acid builds up and/or glycogen stores are exhausted, the body is not able to perform to the expected ability. Proper training makes it possible for runners to increase their body's ability to perform for longer periods of time at a high level of efficiency before hitting "the wall."

Regardless of what causes one to hit the wall, you will be forced to slow if you haven't properly trained for the pace you are running. However, when your body operates at lower levels of lactic acid production achieved through conditioning or by reduced running effort, it is effective at generating power/expending energy for prolonged periods without the accumulation of excess lactic acid in the muscles.

As mentioned, lactic acid build-up is normally not a sudden event. However, muscle lock-up due to calcium or electrolyte deficiency can come upon you quickly. In most cases, a runner can sense when muscles are on the verge of cramping or when energy depletion is approaching. To remedy either situation and regain your running economy, you need to add carbohydrates and electrolytes or slow your consumption of energy (i.e., slow your pace). These two elements, the level of lactic acid, and the burning fat instead of glycogen, either alone or in combination are the best-defined contributors to the phenomenon known as "the wall."

Aside from the nutritional factors covered later in Chapter 7, two key training methods should be incorporated into your marathon training plan to reduce your likelihood of meeting "the wall." Training long runs will condition your body to store glycogen in anticipation of more or longer endurance runs, and tempo runs and speed work will gradually raise your lactate (acid) threshold.

The more you train at a pace faster than your lactate (acid) threshold pace (where the lactic generation rate is faster than removal), the greater your margin is of performing without being affected by lactic acid build-up for a marathon. This threshold training, or tempo run should be done at a pace that you can maintain for about an hour. Table 4.23 incorporates the long run and tempo runs as part of the overall recommended training plan prior to a marathon. If you are unsure what your lactate (acid) threshold pace is, typically it occurs at your half marathon pace. Since this event is shorter than a marathon, the buildup of lactic acid, as well as electrolyte deficiencies, usually don't impact runners. However, a marathon will definitely offer the opportunity for these issues to arise. And as a rule, your marathon pace should be at least three to five percent slower than your half marathon pace.

Key Training Methods to Avoid Meeting "The Wall"

- **Go beyond 20 miles -** incorporate a training run of 26 miles at 5-7 weeks prior to your qualifying attempt (run at goal marathon pace (M.P.)+ 30-45 seconds)
- **Use a weekly 50-minute tempo run -** to condition the cardiovascular system and increase your lactate threshold

Improving Running Performance

To improve your performance, you must eat right to give your body the proper fuel. You must also train correctly by increasing the demand on the muscles, while allowing them to recover and build strength. This entire chapter and Chapter 5 are focused on providing you with a proven approach that will increase your running economy and performance.

Improving your performance comes down to these key factors:

- **Building your base fitness level-** This may take months. It is critical once you start to build upon your weekly mileage that you do not exceed increasing it by 10% per week.
- **Work on speed-** This training is a focused approach to allow you to run at your goal pace by training at a pace faster than your goal pace.
- **Work on endurance-** Endurance is improved as you increase the duration (distance) of the distance runs.
- **Increase frequency-** Increase the number of times run per week, not to exceed five runs.
- **Work on strength-** Incorporate hill runs, weight training, and cross training.

Aerobic and Anaerobic Training

Aerobic Training
Exercising or running at a pace that allows oxygen to reach the muscles is called aerobic training. Long runs and tempo runs are definitely intended to be aerobic runs. However, due to their increased pace, tempo runs can approach your aerobic threshold.

Anaerobic Training
Exercising at a pace greater than aerobic training, where sufficient oxygen does not reach the muscles or the level is greatly reduced, is termed anaerobic training. In this situation, there is not an efficient transfer of oxygen from the lungs into the blood stream. This limits the availability of oxygen to fuel the muscles. Interval runs are an effective means of anaerobic training, as they are performed in anaerobic conditions where breathing is typically at or near your maximum rate.

Burning Fat for Fuel

After you have exercised 15 to 45 minutes, your body starts to burn some level of fat as energy. In the first few minutes of a run or race, your body burns oxygen as primary fuel, then quickly shifts to a mix of glycogen and fat. As the glycogen reserves are depleted, the body shifts to burning primarily fat. Once the body transitions to primarily burning fat, your performance is compromised, because fat is an inefficient source of fuel. The end result of this phenomenon is that the runner is forced to slow down.

As mentioned in Chapter 3, fueling the body during a marathon with gel energy packs is critical to avoid burning fat as your primary fuel source. When someone trains at a high level of output (e.g., tempo runs), they use a much higher percentage of glycogen than fat, as the body is demanding premium fuel for peak power. However, when training at a lower exertion rate or walking, the body uses less efficient fuel or fat as primary energy until there is a surge in energy demand.

Build a Mileage Base

Now that you've committed to training for Boston, you may ask yourself how many miles your longest week will require. The mileage alone can be intimidating at first, but as you build mileage through training, the peak mileage week, as well as peak distance day, will only be a slight increase from the previous week(s) levels.

Your first year is the cautious year when it comes to mileage, especially for older runners. Regarding the peak mileage week, you may want to consider the following as a guideline for peak mileage, to reduce the risk of injury. It is also advisable, as you are building up your mileage, to adhere to the 10% per week increase limit.

Guideline: Peak Mileage Week (3 weeks prior to event)

First year running	**38-50 miles per week**
Second year running	**50-65 miles per week**
Third year running	**above 65 miles per week**

Note: Year-round training is beneficial to maintain high mileage.

The key for new runners is, **don't do too much too fast**. Once you have a goal, the temptation is to train as hard and as fast as you can. However, you are more susceptible to injuries if you push too hard. Most experienced runners have learned this the hard way (myself included). Training for a marathon is not like taking a mental test; you can't prepare by cramming the night before. Imagine pulling an all-nighter by running 60 miles the evening before the marathon. Although this analogy is very impractical, it does get the point across. You cannot rush training when endurance and building fitness are involved. From a speed standpoint, **go slow to go fast** and build your endurance and base training before you start to do speed work. Table 4.23 (Recommended Training Schedule for Boston Qualification) starts speed work only after the base training and fitness levels are established.

Selecting Training Routes

When considering training routes, you need to select a route that matches the intended goal for your training plan for that day. For longer runs, you may have the opportunity or need to combine multiple routes to achieve your desired distance.

Intervals

If you are planning to run intervals, a school with a running track is the preferred location. However, if a school track is not available you can measure a one-fourth, one-half, or full mile loop to accomplish your intervals. The key with interval runs is to have an accurate course distance where you can ensure that you are meeting your pace plans with consistency.

Distance Runs

When considering the recommended distances in Table 4.23 for tempo, long runs, and so forth, you should approach each distance with a pre-selected route. For example, the seven-mile tempo run and the three-mile run at marathon pace could be a combination of two individual runs (see Routes A and B in Figure 4.10). Obviously, each route could be approached separately. For a long run, you could use the combination for 10 miles, 13 miles, 16 miles, 17 miles, 19 miles, 20 miles, and so on. Although it may become boring to run the same route numerous times to achieve the distance, this route approach allows you to keep track of your times/pace more accurately and also schedule stops for the necessary water and electrolyte needs. Another option would be an out and back route for your long runs. If you have a way to get fluids and can plan for stops every five miles or so, that is optimum. You may even bring a few dollars with you to purchase drinks at gas stations or convenience stores along your route. If you live in an urban area, the choices are numerous. However, so are the road hazards from cell phone drivers, dogs, and traffic itself.

Training Routes

Route A (3 miles)   Route B (7 miles)

Route A, a short three-mile route around a pond.

Route B, a longer route through urban roads.

Performance Analyzing Tools

Training Tools

Companies such as Garmin®, Polar®, and others continue to offer improvements in the application of GPS technology into running watches. A plethora of data is available from these tools including instantaneous speed, calories, best pace, distance, elevation, and so forth. These tools provide excellent data for the runner and allow PC (data) downloads to easily chart output to measure performance and track improvement. Regardless of how you obtain your performance data, the key is to gather your data and analyze how you are doing compared with your established goals.

Photo 4.11 Garmin® Forerunner 205 offers excellent features for the distance runner.

Post-Event Analyzing Tools

Nearly all venues offer timing clocks along the course of the marathon or half marathon to allow you to determine your actual race time versus your goal time. These results are typically posted on the race website at the following distances; 5K, 10K, 1/2M, 30K, and Finish or other increments accordingly. It is highly recommended that you evaluate how you finish the final 25% of the race. If your times (mile pace) result in a slower pace, then you were not adequately prepared. Another method of tracking your performance is to use your running watch and use the lap button for each mile, then review after you've finished. Again, the key to this data is to take the time to review your performance in increments and not just as the final overall time.

Building Speed

Without question, speed work is **the** most important method to improve your marathon finishing time. Simply putting in the miles will not improve your speed. In the words of Jeff Galloway, a running expert and author of the book *Marathon,* "To run faster you must train faster." As a highly reputable expert in running, he clearly emphasizes the importance of speed work. If you are serious about Boston or just running faster, you must incorporate speed work into your training plan.

Fartlek Training

Fartlek training involves running at 60 to 70% effort pace and maintaining that tempo, mixing faster segments (at 90% of maximum) for short intervals, then going back to the slower pace and repeating. Typical Fartlek training sessions should be 20 to 30 minutes. These sessions will help you condition your cardiovascular system at a more tolerable rate than interval or tempo runs.

Fartlek running is also a fun method of training with a group of two or more runners. One runner leads the single-file pack at a fast pace. He/she then drops back and rests, waiting his/her turn after each of the other runners in the pack has taken their turn at leading and setting the pace. If running a Fartlek workout on your own, pick out light poles, mail boxes, or signs on a loop route, and run your fast pace until you have reached your object, and then slow to a recovery pace. You may even incorporate a track into your Fartlek workouts. Run a lap at 60 to 70% effort, and then add a 220 meter (one-eighth mile) at fast pace, followed by a lap of recovery, and then repeat. Fartlek training allows the runner to be creative with workouts.

Figure 4.12 illustrates an example of a Fartlek route that was developed from personal experience. One evening while on a five mile training run, I passed through a neighborhood and noticed a new running "toy"...a police vehicle speed indicator. What runner can't resist adding a few extra bursts of energy to see how fast they can go, especially if the result is shown in bold, bright lights? Well, the Fartlek challenge was on. I circled the small block numerous times with the intent that the next loop I would try to increase my speed by 1 mph. After a series of 5 loops, and some questionable looks by my neighbors, I finally managed 16 mph. As a car passed shortly thereafter, erasing my temporary accomplishment, my legs reminded me that a 6th lap would have to wait until the next training run. Be creative with your Fartlek training, as the routes and methods are limitless.

Figure 4.12   The ultimate Fartlek route

Interval Training

Interval runs, in my personal opinion, are the most important training tool at your disposal. The runs improve your race time by improving your ability to sustain a fast marathon pace. Interval runs are defined as a predetermined distance run at a goal pace with a short break or rest in between intervals. The rest time is typically two to three minutes, at most. This keeps your heart rate up and continues to build up your lactate (acid) threshold. For marathon training, I recommend one-mile intervals integrated into your training schedule. If you are training for a 10K or even a half marathon, a one-mile interval should be more than adequate for conditioning, and half-mile segments may be more applicable. In addition, interval running should not occur every week. I recommend that distance (long) runs be substituted for interval runs on alternating weeks.

The following plan (Table 4.13) is a proven method for long run and interval run training.

Table 4.13 Alternating Interval and Long Runs Bi-Weekly

Weeks Before Marathon	Training	Pace	Number of Intervals X Distance
10	(Intervals)	M.P. -45 to 60 sec	6 X 1 mile
9	(Long Run)	M.P. +30 sec	16-18 miles
8	(Intervals)	M.P. -45 to 60 sec	8 X 1 mile
7	(Long Run)	M.P. +30 sec	20-26 miles
6	(Intervals)	M.P. -45 to 60 sec	10 X 1 mile
5	(Long Run)	M.P. +30 sec	20-26 miles
4	(Intervals)	M.P. -45 to 60 sec	12 X 1 mile
3	(Long Run)	M.P. +30 sec	20 miles
2	(Intervals)	M.P. -45 to 60 sec	8 X 1 mile
1	(Long Run)	M.P. +30 sec	12 miles
Marathon			

M.P. = (Goal) Marathon Pace
M.P. -45 to 60 seconds = Marathon Pace/mile minus 45 to 60 seconds, or 45 to 60 seconds quicker/mile than (Goal) M.P.
M.P. +30 seconds = Marathon Pace/mile plus 30 seconds/mile Pace

Intervals explained: If your goal M.P. is 8:00/mile, your interval pace should be M.P. – 45 to 60 sec/mile, or 7:00/mile to 7:15/mile. For an 8 x 1 mile interval run @ 7:00, you would run 8 individual miles (at one-mile increments) at your indicated pace, with a short recovery rest (three minutes) between each mile.

Suggested Interval Speeds Compared to the Marathon Goal Time

Marathon Goal	Approx. Goal M.P.	Suggested Interval Pace for Training
4:15	9:45/mile	8:45 – 9:00/mile
4:00	9:10/mile	8:10 – 8:25/mile
3:45	8:35/mile	7:35 – 7:50/mile
3:30	8:00/mile	7:00 – 7:15/mile
3:15	7:28/mile	6:30 – 6:45/mile
3:00	6:52/mile	5:55 – 6:10/mile

M.P. = (Goal) Marathon Pace

For most runners, interval training is mentally the most difficult component of marathon training. Typically, you are running laps and, unfortunately, it is easy to stop short of your goal. Dedication to completing each interval workout is critical because this type of workout has the most tangible impact on improving your race times. As you continue to train and condition, you will find subsequent interval training sessions will become easier and you will start to drop your mile times accordingly. This is a sure sign that the interval training is working and you are improving your speed. As an example, you may drop interval mile times from 7:30 min/mile to 7:00 min/mile over a period of a few months by continuing to incorporate interval training into your bi-weekly workouts. It is acceptable to run intervals slightly quicker than your goal pace, but typically not quicker than 15 sec/mile. Consider adding an additional challenge to run each interval quicker than the previous or set a specific time that you don't want to exceed. I typically saved my fastest interval time for my final interval, as this forced me to manage my energy consumption much like in the marathon itself.

The Secret to a Personal Best (Boston Qualifying) Marathon:

Speed Work..........   **Speed Work ....**   *More* **Speed Work**

Photo 4.14-A    Photo 4.14-B    Photo 4.14-C

Important Rules about Speed Work

- **Don't do speed work (intervals) too often.** Intervals should be done once every two weeks. The body will retain the conditioning from interval training for about two weeks. In the interim, Tempo runs and Fartlek runs will supplement speed work.
- **Always warm up 5 to 10 minutes before speed work.**
- **Allow time for recovery, or incorporate recovery runs, or rest the following day after a hard workout.** It takes runners over 35 years of age twice as long to recover from strenuous speed runs or long runs.
- **Your speed capability is somewhat dependent upon your fast twitch muscle composition.** You may improve your speed by incorporating some high knee running or jumping to improve the response of your fast twitch muscles.

Tempo/Constant Pace Training

A tempo run is an extended constant pace run that is at least 15 seconds slower than your 10K pace (min/mi) and about 30 seconds slower than your 5K pace. Tempo runs are favorites of many runners, and preparation for a Boston qualification attempt should incorporate at least one tempo run per week of 50 minutes, which is slightly longer than the "typically" recommended run of 30-40 minutes. In addition, you should add a one-to three-mile cool-down following the workout. Tempo runs are instrumental in building leg strength, as well as increasing your VO2 max and your lactate (acid) threshold. Tempo running is an effective method of increasing marathon speed, as the runner works at a level of intensity faster than their comfortable training pace.

Just as a reference, your goal Marathon Pace (M.P.) should be about 30 seconds per mile slower than your tempo runs.

Tempo Pace = 10K pace + 15 seconds
Marathon Pace (M.P.) = Tempo Pace + 30 seconds
Long Run Pace = 10% slower than Marathon pace

Building Endurance

Endurance is gained by training at long distance. Running long distance (12 miles or more) is a proven and effective method for improving your capability for maintaining speed for the duration of a marathon. Long runs, much like speed work, are components of your training plan that definitely should not be compromised. When or if conflicts in training time arise, be sure to make time for long runs.

Two Important Rules about Long Runs

1. **Your long run pace should be slower than your marathon goal pace by about 10 percent.**
2. **Do not increase your weekly mileage by more than 10 percent per week.**

For example, an 8:30 M.P. goal would be an approximate 9:15 to 9:30 long run training pace (or +10%). Some texts recommend up to 20% slower, which at this pace equates to around 2 minutes. Ten percent slower should be adequate as you build strength/endurance. You may also incorporate some quicker miles at 5% slower than M.P. on portions of your long runs, but only as you are nearing your longest mileage week.

Long Distance Runs

As mentioned, speed work is a critical element to your training regimen. However, it alone will not round your capability to the point where you can continue at a specific pace for 26.2 miles. Distance runs are a **must** for anyone training for a Boston qualification or any marathon. If you are not capable of putting together a string of long runs that peak at 20 miles or more, you will most likely struggle to make it the full distance of a marathon. Most authors suggest that a runner should run at a pace on these long runs (12 to 20 miles) that is slower than your M.P. goal. As you are starting the early weeks of your training program, I agree with this suggestion. However, as your fitness level improves and you are more able to easily match your pace goal for speed intervals, you should also be capable and comfortable in running long runs at 10% slower than goal M.P.

This approach will provide the psychological benefit of allowing you to run at a level near to the level required on race day. In addition, be sure to focus on your form (upright posture) in your long runs, especially for the last four to six miles, as this will be important come race day. Running at goal M.P. for portions of your long runs is also an excellent way to boost your confidence as you build distance to your long runs.

Many reference books on running and running marathons mention that the long run should be limited to 20 miles, whereas Jeff Galloway recommends 26 or more miles for your longest run. From a personal experience standpoint, I ran a Personal Record (P.R) when my training incorporated a marathon (run at 85 to 90% of my goal M.P.) and followed it with a 20-mile taper training run. This convinced me that a 26-mile training run can help you reach your goal M.P.

Other Endurance (Long Run) Training Hints

- **Select a route that is out and back, as opposed to a series of loops.**
  - Out and back routes feel as if you've accomplished something by traveling to another town or city.
  - Repetitive loops are too easy to cut your run short.
- **Add surges late in your training run to simulate race conditions like hills.**
- **Use the first few miles as warm-up at M.P. + 20%, and then finish the remainder of the run at M.P. + 5 to 10%.**
- **Do not train at M.P.**
  - The best way to train for something is to simulate the event or activity as closely as possible. Unfortunately, long runs at goal M.P. are very hard on the body.
  - The purpose of a (training) long run is to build endurance, and if run at M.P., your extended recovery time will negate the benefits while in your training plan.
- **Use a route with water fountains or gas stations, and bring cash for sports drinks.**
- **During training run(s), practice drinking from a cup with water by placing it on a post or in your mail box as you pass by.**
- **If you can't carry on a conversation during your run, your long run pace is too fast.**
- **Use the day prior to a long run as a short run day and the day following your long run as a rest day or cross training day.**
- **A long run can be considered anything longer than 12 miles.**
- **A runner who completes two or three long runs of 18 to 20+ miles during training will reduce the possibility of hitting the "glycogen" wall.**
- **If you miss a long run, don't try to make it up. If you have a few long runs completed already and still are five or more weeks out from the marathon, you should continue training without missing future long runs.**

Determining Your Fitness Level

How to Gauge Your Fitness Level

Your fitness level can be easily established by entering short distance races. It is recommended to enter a local 5K or preferably a 10K race as you start toward your goal of increasing your fitness level. By doing so, you can predict your expected marathon or half marathon times by referencing Table 4.16. These shorter races/runs are an excellent measure of your ability and will provide you with early racing experience that will aid in launching your marathon endeavors. As indicated, this table represents predicted times, and some may perform better than the chart at shorter or longer distances, based upon multiple factors.

Photo 4.15   Runners push at the start of a 5K race. Due to the short distance, 5K runs usually attract a wide range of participants, from novice to expert. 5K runs are a popular venue for festivals or fund-raisers.

Table 4.16   Estimated Performance at Marathon Compared to Shorter Distances (+/- 5%)

Lactate Threshold Pace Min/Mile (Min/km)		VO2 Max Pace Min/Mile (Min/km)		5K	10K	13.1 Mile	Boston Marathon Qualification Times
6:42	(4:09)	5:54	(3:39)	18:41	39:20	1:26:40	3:05
6:51	(4:15)	6:00	(3:43)	19:00	40:10	1:29:12	3:10
7:00	(4:21)	6:09	(3:49)	19:30	41:00	1:31:30	3:15
7:20	(4:33)	6:25	(3:59)	20:30	43:00	1:36:06	3:25
7:30	(4:39)	6:33	(4:04)	21:00	44:00	1:38:00	3:30
7:44	(4:48)	6:46	(4:12)	21:30	45:06	1:40:42	3:35
7:49	(4:51)	6:51	(4:15)	22:00	46:00	1:42:51	3:40
7:59	(4:57)	6:59	(4:20)	22:30	47:00	1:44:45	3:45
8:22	(5:11)	7:21	(4:34)	23:22	49:12	1:49:30	3:55
8:31	(5:17)	7:30	(4:39)	24:00	50:20	1:51:37	4:00
8:45	(5:26)	7:41	(4:46)	24:50	52:20	1:56:18	4:10
9:13	(5:42)	8:06	(5:00)	26:10	55:20	2:03:40	4:25
9.41	(6:00)	8:32	(5:16)	27:20	58:10	2:10:30	4:40
10:16	(6:21)	9:02	(5:35)	29:30	61:05	2:16:05	4:55
10:49	(6:41)	9:32	(5:54)	31:00	64:00	2:22:48	5:10
11:30	(7:07)	10:08	(6:16)	32:30	67:00	2:29:02	5:25

Note: Marathon times are highlighted for **2013** male and female qualification standards (see Chapter 2).

Lactate Threshold and VO2 Max

As shown in Table 4.16, the lactate threshold is calculated at 85% (or .85) of your VO2 max. These two measures of fitness are determined by your performance (speed) at specific distances.

Lactate Threshold

Lactate threshold is the point at which lactic acid builds up in your muscles quicker than your blood stream can remove it. It occurs when you exceed a level of exertion for a sustained period. For example, from Table 4.16, if you were to run a 7:00 (min/mi) pace in a marathon and are capable of a 1:29:12 half marathon or better, this should allow you to run at an acceptable pace where lactic acid excess will not hinder your performance. This is purely an example of what many authors cite as a factor that can limit your performance. However, after reading segments from the *Lore of Running* by Dr. Tim Noakes, I personally believe that it is a fictitious point. Although he says that lactate levels rise with the level of intensity, there is no such point as an "abrupt threshold" where muscles and muscle performance is impacted. He states, "Lactate is a natural product of carbohydrate metabolism during exercise. As the rate of energy production rises, so more carbohydrate is used…" He also states that there is much hype about lactate testing and the ability to predict performance. However, he concludes that lactate threshold is of little value, and theVO2 Max may be a more suitable indicator.

In summary, I personally believe it is beneficial to understand the physiological phenomenon that occurs when exerting your body to high levels of energy output. However, I would not recommend using "lactate threshold" as an applicable term to your training. As a new runner to marathons, I'll admit I faced some apprehension about the possibility of hitting "the wall" if I exceeded the threshold. The threshold is not a point, but a gradual build-up of lactic acid due to high energy consumption. If you have trained with intervals and tempo runs adequately and have sufficient glycogen stores built up from long runs, you should not hit "the wall." As mentioned previously, the deficiency of calcium may cause muscle cramps and lock up your legs. However, this is not associated with lactate threshold, but can be construed as hitting the wall due to chemical deficiencies during a marathon.

VO2 Max – Aerobic Capacity

VO2 max is a numerical value to equate to your aerobic capability to distance compared to time, such as in Table 4.17. However, the key with exercise is that the faster you run, the more oxygen your body needs. The more you train at speed, the greater your volumetric efficiency (aerobic capacity) becomes to support this higher oxygen flow, and thus your fitness improves. Table 4.17 shows a few examples of your volumetric efficiency/aerobic capacity as it relates to various running distances. If you track your running times and personal bests, there is little need to know about your VO2 or aerobic capability because you cannot measure it (practically), but you can measure your times. VO2 and VO2 Max are referenced throughout this text to be synonymous with aerobic capacity. Otherwise, the numerical aspect of VO2 is nice to know but difficult to apply.

Table 4.17 VO2 Aerobic Capacity

Running Times Expected Compared to Aerobic Limitation (+/- 5%)				
Aerobic Capacity VO2 Max	Mile	10K	Half Marathon	Marathon
41	7:00	47:00	1:44:45	3:45:00
44	6:30	45:00	1:39:30	3:32:30

In summary, VO2 (max) and lactate threshold are both measures that provide insight as you prepare for a qualification marathon. However, both may be viewed as supplemental data where the primary data critical to your performance are your actual times achieved at distance. The key is not to push yourself beyond the level your body is conditioned to perform when running a long distance event.

Winter Training

If you need to drop your marathon time 30 to 45 minutes or more, it may take you over a year to accomplish this, depending upon your initial fitness level. If you are faced with a similar challenge, I suggest looking at your first year to focus on your base fitness, work on your form, and drop any unnecessary weight. You should plan to run a fall marathon as a first attempt (assuming that you start training in the spring) to see how you perform. If you are unsuccessful in qualifying for Boston, you should continue to train through the winter months to hit the spring at nearly 60 to 80% of your goal fitness level (VO2 Max). It is suggested in many publications to take two to three weeks off from running during winter. However, continue to do some type of cardiovascular training like cycling, cross country skiing, and swimming, to maintain your cardio fitness level, but rest your feet, knees, and other stressed areas. Winter maintenance training is critical to keep you focused on the subsequent year goals.

Figure 4.18 is a summary of my first eight marathons. Winter training or year-round training was started after marathon #2, with marathon #3 being an early spring venue. Winter maintenance training continued between marathons #5 (October) and #6 (January). January is not the optimum time for a quick marathon regardless of whether the maintenance training continues. Clearly the January and April marathons (#6 and #7) conditioned my body for a PR in the spring (#8).

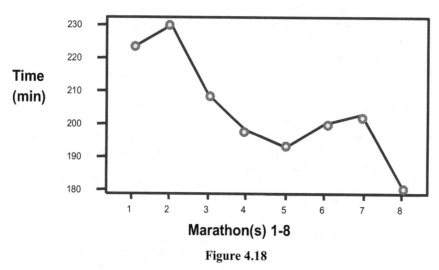

Marathon(s) 1-8

Figure 4.18

Winter Maintenance

Table 4.19 is a typical winter workout schedule to maintain fitness level. If you are lucky enough to live in a region free of winter snow and ice, you may be able to maintain your on-road or trail running year-round. However, if your region is susceptible to the harsh elements of winter (cold weather), you may be wise to invest in a treadmill or join a fitness club that offers treadmills or an indoor running track. In addition, you will notice that the winter plan recommends the use of a stationary bike or elliptical to maintain your cardiovascular system and build leg strength. Elliptical machines offer a close equivalent to running, but without the joint stress or impact and are highly recommended for year-round training.

If you can adhere to this schedule during the winter, you should be conditioned for picking up a spring marathon training schedule 8 to 12 weeks in advance of the marathon event, depending upon your training mileage goals.

Table 4.19 Cold Weather Maintenance Training Schedule

Monday	Tuesday	Wednesday	Thursday	Friday	Saturday	Sunday	Total (equiv.) Miles/wk
Stationary bike or elliptical 60 min. at 80% max heart rate (**6** equiv. miles)	Run **4** miles at (tempo)	**Rest** Weights: legs and upper body (optional)	Run **6** miles at M.P. on treadmill	**Rest**	Run **10** miles at M.P.+30sec (outside if possible or indoor padded track)	**Rest** Weights: legs and core body	**26**

equiv. = equivalent running miles

Treadmill Basics

Cold weather training will help you maintain a fitness level that will keep you in the game for a spring qualifying attempt. Most serious runners who live in areas of adverse winter weather will do best to invest into a treadmill. A plethora of styles and features are available for treadmills. Listed below are a few key features worthy of mention.

Recommended Features for Treadmills

- **Electric motor of 2.5 hp or higher**
- **Speed capability of 10 mph or greater**
- **Grade changing capability to at least 10 degrees**
- **Padded track (some models offer adjustable cushioning)**
- **Drink holder and CD/MP3 holder for long runs**
- **Variable speed programs for speed work or interval running**
- **Cooling fan, a rare feature on most treadmills, is a must where air movement is limited**

Most treadmills provide a display in minutes per mile or miles per hour, and in some cases both. The equivalent paces for each can be easily calculated as the following:

Minutes/Mile (min/mi)	Miles/Hour (mph)
10	6.0
9	6.7
8	7.5
7	8.5
6	10

When running on an angle, there are few, if any, treadmills that provide information on equivalent (level) pace. Since you are consuming more energy or calories when running at an angle, your effective pace is faster. Many runners (including myself) have a difficult time determining their equivalent level running pace (min/mi or mph). Table 4.20 provides an equivalent pace per mile versus the treadmill speed (mph) and at a specific percentage grade or angle. (Note: The higher the angle, the greater the equivalent speed.)

If you use the following example of running at seven miles per hour (7.0Mph) at a 7% grade on the treadmill, this equates to an equivalent (faster) pace of 6:11 minute/mile. Normally, the flat or level pace would be 8.6 minute/mile. Simply said, if you apply a grade or elevation to your treadmill, you are effectively running at a faster pace (typically shown in mph) than what the treadmill indicates. Running at a grade not only allows you to work out slower (speed) to achieve your cardiovascular goals, but it also allows a slightly different angle of contact for your joints, which may be overstressed.

Table 4.20 Determining Actual Pace when Running on an Angle

Mile Pace vs. Treadmill % Grades							
Equivalent Pace (min/mile)	Pace Provided in Miles Per Hour (MPH) by the Treadmill						
	6.0 mph	6.5 mph	7.0 mph	7.5 mph	8.0 mph	8.5 mph	9.0 mph
9:19	2.9% grade	1.9% grade	1.0% grade				
8:15	4.8% grade	3.5% grade	2.5% grade	1.6% grade	1.0% grade		
7:24	6.6% grade	5.2% grade	4.0% grade	3.0% grade	2.2% grade	1.4% grade	
6:44	8.4% grade	6.8% grade	5.5% grade	4.4% grade	3.5% grade	2.6% grade	1.9% grade
6:11	10.2% grade	8.5% grade	7.0% grade	5.8% grade	4.7% grade	3.8% grade	3.0% grade
5:43	12.1% grade	10.1% grade	8.5% grade	7.2% grade	6.0% grade	5.0% grade	4.1% grade

Excerpt from Table 7.1 Daniels Running Formula, Jack Daniels PhD, published by Human Kinetics

Treadmills that offer varying angles of operation are effective for simulating hill runs and can be used for hill training, as well as other components of your training plan. However, one point that is rarely made regarding treadmills is that your energy consumption on a treadmill is less versus actual running, where you are propelling yourself forward. You can train effectively on a treadmill and condition your muscles for the rigors of a marathon. Equivalent treadmill miles, however, do not directly equal road miles. If the conditions allow for running outside, it is much preferred for training effectiveness over a treadmill.

When training on a treadmill at an angle, you are expending more energy than on a level treadmill surface. Be sure to monitor your heart rate to keep it in a safe zone (especially when on a treadmill), as hill simulations on a treadmill can elevate your heart rate quickly.

Photo 4.21 illustrates some of the more popular features for treadmills including built-in television, hand-grip heart rate, and a plethora of programmable training cycles (hills, random, intervals, etc.).

Most public fitness centers offer treadmills with the latest in features. Treadmills are a great way for runners to incorporate variation in running during cold weather months, due to their features.

Photo 4.21

2) <u>Running</u> <u>Strong</u> <u>the</u> <u>Final</u> <u>6.2</u> <u>Miles</u>

The Bermuda 10K

For most seasoned marathon runners, there should be few surprises in Table 4.23. But what may set this approach apart from the multitude of other training plans is the focus on the last 6.2 miles. These are the miles that typically *make or break* a qualifying performance. So how do you focus on the last 6.2 miles? It's easy. Go back to the basics of speed, endurance work, and energy replenishment, but do them at an increased and extended intensity. Various areas in this book detail each of the elements that pertain to the overall race, but the next few topics in this section detail supplemental training that will improve your performance for the most critical zone of the race. I call this portion of the race the Bermuda 10K, because you go into it, but you're not sure if, or when, you'll come out.

Boston Qualification Training Schedule

You'll find that most every book about running will provide a recommended training schedule for specific goal time(s). Not surprisingly, so does this book. However, there are a few key differences in the approach listed in Table 4.23 that can make a difference in your performance and qualification attempt for Boston. Again, since the goal is qualifying for Boston, where a PR is most likely required, I have stepped it up a notch in four critical training areas:

- **Long run distance**
- **Long run pace**
- **Cross training**
- **Hill training**

Long Run Distance

Most authors will stick to the 20-mile maximum for the longest run. However, I have found that running an actual marathon (26.2-mile training run) or at least a 24-mile training long run provides excellent conditioning. But one key difference is the training marathon should be six to seven weeks out prior to your qualifying venue. However, if you don't opt to run a 26.2 mile-training marathon, keep your longest run at the three-week point, but reduce it to 24 miles maximum.

When running the 24-or 26.2-mile training run from your schedule, run the first 20 miles at your M.P. + 30 seconds and the remaining miles as close to your M.P. as you can manage. This approach simulates racing conditions but doesn't totally stress your body, as an actual marathon distance would. During these longest training runs, you should start to feel the lactic acid buildup in your thighs. That is the intention of this specific workout. This longer training run will slightly increase your lactate threshold but will not damage your muscles to the point where they need a long recovery period.

Long Run Pace

I found as I was nearing completion of my training plan (approximately six weeks prior to the marathon), speed work was allowing me to run comfortably at or near my goal M.P. on long training runs. You should not be able to run at M.P. for extended distances early into your training program. But, as your body improves, you need to maintain the intensity necessary to improve further. Running at the same pace for long runs throughout your training plan (i.e., M.P. + 45 seconds) will improve your endurance, but not necessarily to an optimum level. Therefore, you will note in the training schedule

(Table 4.23) that the long run pace varies early in the program and becomes more demanding as you progress in fitness.

In some respects, it is necessary to train beyond your necessary race performance level to ensure a proper margin for success, but you have to do so cautiously. Running long runs at or near M.P. will condition your legs and lactic acid capability for the actual event. However, it is not recommended to run your entire long run at goal M.P. within five weeks of your event. The time to recover will potentially offset the gains made. The only exception is the final long run of 12 miles at M.P.

Cross Training

Although biking and running work the leg muscles differently and can consume calories at different rates, biking and similar cross training exercises build muscles and cardiovascular capability just as running does. For that purpose, I equate six miles of running to 60 minutes on a stationary bike or elliptical. These "miles" can be counted in your weekly total. This approach will help to reduce joint stress while gaining valuable cardiovascular fitness.

With strength training (weights), this rule does not apply. In addition, weight training should cease two weeks prior to the event, as minimal strength benefits will be gained. Working your muscles with weights during this time may start to deplete your glycogen stores. Cycling or elliptical work can be continued to within one week of the event but at a lower energy level, to store glycogen.

Since most non-elite runners are full-time workers, the opportune time to get in a good interval or distance run is on a weekend. These long run days should be followed by a full day of rest or cross training. Recovery, and specifically proper recovery, are as important as training itself. Working the muscles too often or during key repair times can reduce your performance.

Hill Training

There are benefits to running hills (hill-repeats), as they develop strength in the upper and lower leg muscles (quadriceps, hamstrings, calf muscles, and gluteus maximus). Since not every runner has the luxury of hills or trails for training, there are some viable alternatives for vertically challenged regions. Cross training equipment such as an elliptical, stair climber machine, or treadmill may be used to replace hills by varying the equipment inclination.

Using hill-repeats as part of your training involves running up a moderate hill for a distance of 1/8 mile to 1/4 mile on a continuous gradual incline at a 10K or M.P.-30 second pace. Actual pace will depend upon the slope. Once you have reached the peak, turn around and decline at an easy controlled pace. When at the bottom, continue this in a repetitive manner until you have completed approximately 6 miles or 50 to 60 minutes.

Chapters 5 and 6 provide further detail on cross training, strength training, and the use of hills to build strength early in a training program.

The runner in Photo 4.22 has selected a hill that provides an excellent opportunity for a focused hill-repeat training session.

Photo 4.22

Table 4.23 Recommended Training Schedule for a Boston Qualification

Weeks Prior	M	T	W	TH	F	S	S	Total Miles	Notes
Base Training									
14 Weeks	7 miles at MP	60-min bike or elliptical or 6 miles at M.P.	7 miles at M.P.	Rest	5 miles at MP	12-14-miles **long run** at M.P.+45sec	Rest	**37-39**	
13 Weeks	7 miles at MP	60-min bike or elliptical or 6 miles at M.P.	10 miles at M.P.	Rest	5 miles at MP	12-14-miles **long run** at M.P.+45sec	Rest	**40-42**	
Hill-Repeat and Strength Training									
12 Weeks	7 miles at MP	60-min bike or elliptical and strength exercises	7 miles at **tempo** + 3 miles at M.P.+30 sec	Rest	5 miles at MP	60-min **hill-repeat** at M.P.-30sec (or 6 miles)	4-6 EP **(recovery)** or 60 min elliptical and strength exercises	**38-40**	Focus on Hill training for strength
11 Weeks	11 miles at MP	60-min bike or elliptical and strength exercises	7 mile at **tempo** + 3 miles at M.P.+30 sec	Rest	5 miles at MP	14-Miles **long run** at M.P.+40sec	Rest	**46**	Use a local half marathon race, if available
10 Weeks	7 miles at MP	60-min bike or elliptical and strength exercises	7 mile at **tempo** + 3 miles at M.P.+30 sec	Rest	5 miles at MP	60-min **hill-repeat** at M.P.-30sec (or 6 miles)	6-8 EP **(recovery)** or 60 min elliptical and strength exercises	**40-42**	Focus on hill training for strength
9 Weeks	11 miles at MP	60-min bike or elliptical and strength exercises	7 mile at **tempo** + 3 miles at M.P.+30 sec	Rest	5 miles at MP	18-miles **long run** at M.P.+30sec	Rest	**50**	First significant long run

(Continued)

Table 4.23 Recommended Training Schedule for a Boston Qualification (continued)

Speed Work and Long Runs – Serious Training

Weeks Prior	M	T	W	TH	F	S	S	Total Miles	Notes
8 Weeks	7 mile at M.P.	60-min bike or elliptical or 6 mile at M.P. + strength exercises	7 mile at **tempo** + 3 mile at M.P.+30 sec	Rest	5 mile at M.P.	8 X 1 mile **interval** at M.P.-60sec	8-10 mile EP **(recovery)** or 60 min elliptical. + strength exercises	44-46	Focus on speed work complete all 8 intervals
7 Weeks	11 mile at M.P.	60-min bike or elliptical or 6 mile at M.P. + strength exercises	7 mile at **tempo** + 3 mile at M.P.+30 sec	Rest	5 mile at MP -- or -- *Rest*	20-mile **long run** at M.P.+30sec. ----- or ----- *Training Marathon at M.P. + 30-45sec.*	Rest	52 --- or ---- 53.2	First 20 mile run stay on pace ------ or -------- *Note – if full marathon training run, adjust on these days*
6 Weeks	7 mile at M.P. -- or -- *Rest*	60-min bike or elliptical or 6 mile at M..P. -- or -- *Rest*	7 mile at **tempo** + 3 mile at M.P.+30 sec -- or -- *Rest*	Rest	5 mile at M.P.	10 X 1 mile **interval** at M.P.-45sec ----- or ----- *If marathon 1 wk prior, 4X1 interval at M.P.- 60sec/mile*	8-10 mile EP **(recovery)** --- or ---- *If marathon 1 wk prior, 60 min elliptical*	46-48 ----- or ---- 15	*Note – if full marathon training run, adjust on these days*
5 Weeks	11 mile at M.P.	60-min bike or elliptical or 6 mile at M.P. + strength exercises	7 mile at **tempo** + 3 mile at M.P.+30 sec	7 mile at M.P.	5 mile at EP	22-mile **long run** at M.P.+30 ---- or ---- *If marathon prior, 16 at M.P.+ 60sec/mile*	Rest	61 --- or ---- 55	Break in new shoes this week <u>at the latest</u>
4 Weeks	7 mile at M.P.	60-min bike or elliptical or 6 mile at M.P.. + strength exercises	7 mile at **tempo** + 3 mile at M.P.+30 sec	5 mile at M.P.	Rest	12 X 1mile **interval** at M.P.– 60sec/mile --- or ---- **Half Marathon** training run at M.P. - 15sec/mile	8-10 mile EP **(recovery)** --- or ---- if **Half Marathon**, make this a rest day	48-50 --- or ---- 41	Use a local Half Marathon race, if available, as replacement for intervals
3 Weeks	11 mile at M.P.	60-min bike or elliptical or 6 mile at M.P. + strength exercises	7 mile at **tempo** + 3 mile at M.P.+30 sec	7 mile at M.P.	4 mile at EP	22-24-mile **long run** at MP+30 with last 4 miles at M.P. ----- or ----- *If Marathon run at Wk6 or Wk7, reduce mileage to 20 max at M.P.+30*	Rest	60-62 --- or ---- 58	Use race shoes and race attire to verify chafing/issues

(Continued)

Table 4.23 Recommended Training Schedule for a Boston Qualification (continued)

THE TAPER									
Weeks Prior	M	T	W	TH	F	S	S	Total Miles	Notes
2 Weeks	5 mile at M.P.	60-min bike or elliptical or 6 mile at M.P.	7 mile at **tempo +** 3Mile at M.P.+30sec	Rest or 3-5 mile at EP	5 mile at M.P.	8 X 1 mile **interval** at M.P.–45sec /mile	Rest or 60 min elliptical	**34-39**	Interval run should be even-paced
1 Week	11 mile at M.P.	3 mile at M.P.+30	7 mile at **tempo +** 3Mile at M.P.+30sec	7 mile at M.P.	5 mile at EP	12-mile **long run** at M.P.	Rest	48	Eliminate cross training and weight training
Race Week	7 mile at M.P.	5 mile at M.P.	3 mile at EP	Rest	Rest	**Boston Qualifying Marathon**	Rest	15+26.2	Carbohydrate loading all week

* For all long runs it is acceptable to have drink stops for fluid replacement at convenience stores, gas stations, etc. Understanding that this will add to your overall time, you can use this time for stretching, bathroom, drinking and gel/carbohydrate and electrolyte replacement. Also, add a second strength training day/week when appropriate.
* Denotes revisions to plan if Marathon was run at wk6 or wk7 prior to BQ Marathon attempt

Legend
EP = Easy Pace (easy talking pace) or roughly M.P. + 1 min/mi.
MP = Marathon Pace (review your Boston qualifying pace for this)
MP – 45 sec = Marathon Pace less 45 seconds/mi.
MP + 30 sec = Marathon pace plus 30 seconds/mi.
(Recovery) = Recovery run after a hard workout at slower pace
Tempo = Goal Marathon Pace – 30 sec, or approx 10K Pace + 15 sec/mi.

Final Note on Your Training Schedule

You will need to plan ahead to ensure that you focus on speed work and long runs on alternating weekends. Again, a longest run of 22 to 24 miles should be run 20 or 21 days prior to your event, or if you have incorporated a training marathon (at M.P. + 30 to + 45 seconds) into your training, it should be completed around six to seven weeks prior to your qualifying race. Finally, this is a recommended plan. As such, it is not critical that you hold to this exact plan, but for best results please try to maintain the key elements required during each weekend/Saturday. If you find that it is too aggressive for your current fitness level, revert back to the first marathon plan until you have improved capability.

Mileage

Building Fitness with Mileage

From a fitness standpoint, the last 6.2 miles of the marathon are about mental and physical endurance as well as managing and replenishing your energy sources. Assuming you keep your body temperature cool and your body hydrated, you need the necessary stamina to keep pace or even accelerate these last few critical miles. This endurance is accomplished by putting in extra miles that include multiple long runs of 20 to 24 miles staggered over the weeks prior to the marathon, or incorporating a training marathon approximately six to seven weeks prior to the race.

You can also build conditioning and endurance by utilizing multiple qualifying attempts as training runs. A person serious about qualifying for Boston should enter at least two marathon events during the year and possibly three events (for early season training or actual marathon experience). Figure 4.24 illustrates a real example of the mileage run over a 250-day period that included three marathons with two serious attempts at qualification. The initial attempt in April involved a course with significant hills, so the average course time was a few minutes slower than most flat marathons. The April event was approached with the intent of gaining experience with running a negative split (second half of the race run quicker than the first half), as well as building up the base endurance for the June event. Each marathon you complete will provide personal lessons learned for subsequent marathons, especially regarding clothes, nutrition, hydration, shoes, or just general mental preparation.

As you can see from Figure 4.24, the long runs show a continued distance increase on alternating weeks and numerous runs in the 10-mile range that include tempo training. With an overall average of 5.5 miles per day, this is a fair example of the training required for a serious attempt at Boston.

My mile interval time improvements during this training period started at 6:50 per mile (spring) to sub 6:30 per mile (fall). One other change from the spring to the summer/fall training was the addition of a 24 mile training run to increase the lactate threshold and to strengthen leg muscles. The result was a P.R. and another Boston qualification time in October. The key point from this graphic is that getting to Boston may take multiple attempts and a continuous training approach.

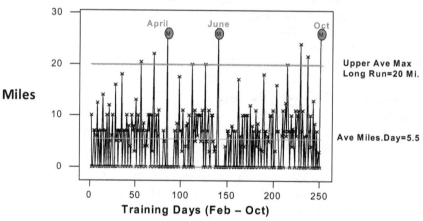

Figure 4.24

Note: Actual times for each attempt were as follows: April = 3:29, June = 3:18, Oct = 3:13.

Ramping Up and Ramping Down (Taper)

Figure 4.25 illustrates the ramp-up mileage required for a marathon over a typical three-month training period. As you ramp up in distance with long runs, your body builds muscle and cardiovascular endurance. These long runs are followed by a very critical part of training, the taper. The taper, or reduction in mileage, should start at three weeks prior to the marathon. The taper allows for optimum performance while maintaining some level of quality-focused training.

As stated previously, long runs are the key to improving your endurance. As a general rule, you should not increase your long run mileage by more than two miles each run (on alternating weeks); however, you may have to run only when time permits. If you find you have to adjust your training schedule around conflicts, be sure to continue your training, but don't try to make up for lost miles all at one time. Simply adjust your training schedule to something you can manage, and always ramp down as the race approaches. Your final long run should be three weeks prior to the marathon.

Note in Figure 4.25 the runner (me) missed the opportunity to stay on schedule with a long run around the middle (see between days 55 to 35) of the training plan. An illness, work, weather, travel, or other factors may prohibit you from getting in a full long run on the specific day you had planned. This is okay. Long runs and interval runs do not have to be completed on the exact alternating weekends. If you deviate by a few days, you will still be okay, but your training schedule may be thrown off until you can match up or come close to alternating weekends. Again, the key is to do the distance when you can. The high mileage runs in this training plan were 12, 13, 15, 17, 20, 22 (start of the 3-week taper), and the marathon.

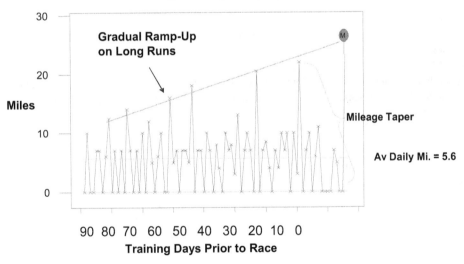

Figure 4.25

Average Weekly Mileage

A successful combination of any marathon schedule is alternating high mileage weeks with speed/interval weeks that result in lower mileage. In Figure 4.26, you will see that on alternating weeks, the long run weeks account for approximately 60 miles per week, whereas the total mileage during the speed work weeks drops to approximately 40 miles. Again, these distances will vary, depending upon the experience and conditioning of the runner.

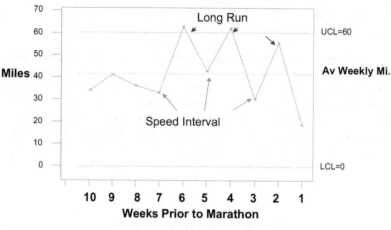

Figure 4.26

Highest Mileage Week

In order to build the strength and endurance required for a marathon, most training schedules incorporate one week that yields the highest mileage, typically the same week of the longest run. Figure 4.27 illustrates a high mileage week of 63 miles. Rest days came both before and after each of the 20-mile long runs. Typically, your highest mileage week should be the third full week prior to your event. After you have peaked from a total distance week, you must taper down with reduced mileage and rest to recover.

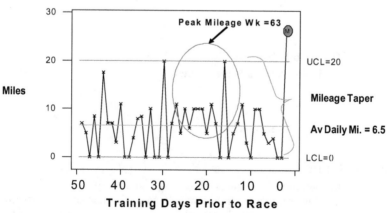

Figure 4.27

Quality Long Runs: Going Beyond 20 Miles

The transition from a novice marathoner to a Boston qualifier is accentuated by the desire to improve both endurance and speed. This can be accomplished by adding long runs that exceed 20 miles and a training plan that incorporates running speed at M.P. at the conclusion of the long run. This effort simulates racing conditions. For example, run the final two to four miles of your longest run at goal M.P. As you can see from Figure 4.28, I combined consecutive long runs at four weeks prior and three weeks prior to the event. This strategy goes against the guideline of alternating speed work and long runs; however, I wanted to ensure that I optimized my glycogen and lactic acid capabilities to offset the potential hamstring cramps that plagued me in previous attempts. This approach worked, and I set a personal best while still providing a taper to both mileage and effort.

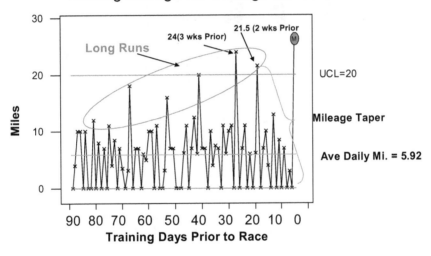

Figure 4.28

Training with Races

Many running experts cite the benefit of races intermixed with a marathon training schedule. The addition of 5K, 10K, or half marathon event(s) inside of your training schedule are valuable in gauging your fitness level and specifically speed preparation. The 5K and 10K events can be interchanged in place of the normal interval speed work training session. In addition, these shorter distance races are excellent confidence builders.

Whether you choose to be part of a team triathlon, a biathlon, or a running venue, the competition and conditioning gains are valid substitutes for interval or tempo training.

Long Runs and Racing = Success

During my most focused year of training, I incorporated a system or sequence of running events that provided outstanding results. This approach may be on the aggressive side for novice runners, as it incorporates long distance events (including a marathon) into your training schedule with enough time to recover prior to the qualifying attempt.

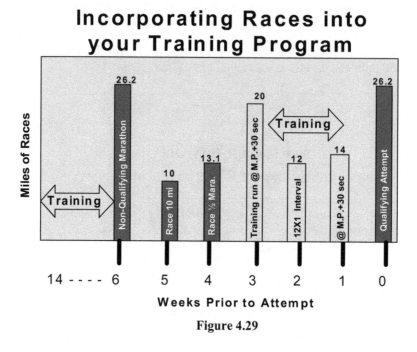

Figure 4.29

Figure 4.29 provides a synopsis of the races that were incorporated into my regular training schedule that led up to a personal overall best marathon (shown at week 0) at the age of 43.

Using Races as Part of Training

Running a race during your training schedule requires that the runner put forth a sustained effort at a level that is more intense than normal training levels. When combined with ample recovery, this effort can yield excellent results.

Many authors preach that a runner should not participate in marathons when they are too close together. Doing a marathon six to seven weeks prior to a qualifying attempt when you are not running at 100 percent effort, however, is an excellent way to build speed and endurance. Again, I must stress the point that the training marathon be slower than your goal M.P. I highly recommend going beyond the typical 20 miles for training and incorporating actual races prior to your qualifying attempt. If you have the opportunity to incorporate shorter events or even a marathon into your training schedule, plan for them while you are developing your training plan. Actual races are a good way to practice drinking on the run, as well as testing out all other applicable items that will be part of your qualifying attempt.

"Those who increase their longest run from 20 to 26 miles show a range of improvement from 10 to 20 minutes…in their marathon time"

Jeff Galloway

As shown in Figure 4.29, improving your performance for the overall marathon (including the final 6.2 miles) requires going beyond the typical 20-mile long run. Incorporating extra miles into your long runs and the addition of a few strategically placed races into your training plan can help you avoid the Bermuda 10K. This strategy will prepare you for the final 6.2 miles.

Running Surfaces

Because you are putting in the extra effort to qualify for Boston, this requires you to put in more miles than the typical marathoner. In addition, those miles could lead to injury unless you mix your running surfaces periodically. Running continuously on asphalt or concrete for all of your miles is not recommended. Wherever you have other training surfaces available, you should try to incorporate them during a portion of your weekly training regimen.

Rubberized running tracks at a local school will provide the needed distance for interval running. It is suggested that you find a school with a padded track for your speed work. The added cushion will help to minimize susceptibility to injuries. Typically, these tracks are asphalt with an added rubberized surface. Long runs can also be completed on a circular soft running surface. It may become monotonous, however, and difficult to track your lap number and mileage when running in circles.

Photo 4.30
High school tracks are perfect for intervals or speed work.

Photo 4.31
Rubberized surfaces offer excellent cushioning.

Asphalt or black top surfaces are only slightly softer than concrete and do provide some flexibility when the surface is warm. When running on a hot day, however, be prepared for added heat convection from the black surface.

When running on black top or country roads, you may opt for the cinder-like gravel and dirt mix on the side of the road for additional cushion.

Switching between the asphalt and the gravel surface periodically will provide a welcomed change to loading on your feet and joints. This approach will not slow your pace much, but you will still need to be cautious of road hazards, such as debris, puddles, potholes, and uneven surfaces. It is easy to sprain an ankle on uneven pavement which, unfortunately, is common with asphalt surfaces.

Photo 4.32 Running on the soft (gravel) shoulder periodically will offer a good mix of cushion when running distance on asphalt.

Concrete is better for hot day runs, as the temperature of the surface will stay cooler than asphalt, but it is the worst surface for joints, due to its lack of energy absorption. Whenever I have to run on a concrete surface for extended miles, I try to add some grass or asphalt during the run to protect my joints from the surface hardness.

Sand is a *very* effective surface for training and will most likely result in your highest heart rate, as opposed to any other surface, due to the rolling resistance of sand.

Photo 4.33 Sand running

Sand running is the most difficult surface to maintain speed, due to the varying surfaces such as wet sand, loose sand, and running through water. In addition, it can be very challenging even if only at sea level because of the added heat and humidity. If you are included in the lucky few who have a running route or access to a lake or seashore, you are envied by many runners and non-runners. However, there is one downside to running on sand. It is difficult to correlate the distance on sand as compared to roads and other hard surfaces, since the rolling resistance is much higher. Look to sand running as a perk for vacation exercise or an enjoyable replacement for tempo runs.

Recent studies have indicated that barefoot running may be more beneficial in preventing knee or foot injuries due to the change in foot/stride to account for the impact. Sand running should be an excellent surface to test this theory, as shoes are optional and the impact is lessened.

Grass is also an effective surface for long runs when you need a softer surface due to non-serious injuries like shin splints, tendonitis, recently healed stress fractures, or sore joints. I trained 100 percent for a marathon on grass by running on the soccer and football fields at a local high school while in the latter stages of a healing stress fracture. I was able to put in my mileage, but training on grass allowed virtually no speed work. Although it was a weak performance, I was able to finish the event, which was the ultimate goal at the time.

Dirt trails are perfect to use for long runs. Trails work great to minimize the stress on joints and the soft surface is a welcome change when training on hard pavement. However, running with nature brings with it various trail hazards such as logs, rocks, steep grades, and so on. Be cautious about the time you run on the trail as daylight is much preferred.

3) <u>Training Aids</u>

Overcoming the Challenges of Training

Training on Your Own
Training in a group is much more motivational, but groups may not push you to the level necessary for speed work. It is recommended to train on your own for interval runs. Tempo or long runs, however, may be more enjoyable to train with a partner assuming you are both capable of the speed required.

Completing Speed Workouts
The temptation to stop short of your interval mileage is sometimes difficult to overcome. For example, if you are planning to run eight one-mile intervals (8 X 1mi) intervals and you are running on a circular track, stay focused on completing all eight miles. Your body will tell you that six miles is enough; don't listen to it. You may want to reward yourself with a sports drink or snack as an incentive to complete the entire workout. This is when it helps to incorporate local 5K or 10K events into your training schedule to break up the monotony of a circular loop associated with intervals.

Completing Long Runs
When doing long runs, try **not** to have circular routes that go by your home more than once. Again, the temptation will be to cut it short due to convenience. Remember, this strategy will not help you on race day. Long runs are easier to complete if you plan to go out a certain distance and back, as opposed to multiple circular routes. In addition, these shorter circular routes can be monotonous, especially if just a few miles long.

Time
Work, family, and other commitments aren't always as flexible as runners would like. If you have to bring running clothes and shoes with you on business trips, do so, but try to stay at a hotel with a treadmill or run in safely lighted streets. Even if it is three to four miles, you will feel better than doing nothing at all. Also, involve your family in running to allow you to share a common interest, live healthier, and also accomplish your training goals by structuring them as family events and vacations.

Maintaining Hydration
Plan your long run route so you can stop briefly for water and/or electrolyte replenishment. Good examples are gas stations or convenience stores spaced around five miles apart.

Weather
Winter training is nearly impossible for runners living in the northern states or colder climates unless you are willing to don snow shoes. A treadmill is worth the investment, especially when the mercury

drops below freezing. The added weight of the winter clothes alone adds to your body mass and places more stress on your feet and knees. Another negative to training during winter is the shorter days, when darkness sets in around five to six in the evening, which offers little time to run in the daylight. This is when it pays to have good winter training clothes, where the inner layer allows your skin to breath and the outer layer insulates. Remember to always wear reflective outerwear on the evening training runs.

Running with Others or Music

Training with Other runners

Many people opt to train with another runner or a running group. Carrying on conversations can be an excellent way to pass the time and share the experience of the day. It is suggested that when you are choosing to run with a partner(s), you determine what you want from the workout, especially if the training partner is a slower runner than yourself. You may opt to run with your partner(s) at the beginning of your workout to loosen up and then separate to run at goal pace and re-group later.

From a family standpoint, you may opt to run while a child or spouse rides a bike alongside of you. It is a good way to share family time and accomplish your training workout. Bicycles offer various methods to allow adults and children to ride together with the runner alongside. A tandem child seat can be added to most adult bikes, which can add to some family fun (or competition) during a training run.

Photo 4.34 Out to race daddy

Running with Music

Some prefer hearing the sounds of their surroundings while running instead of listening to music. Others seem glued to their IPODs or digital players while exercising. There are advantages to each, but music is purely an individual preference while running, as well as the music selections. Some songs provide high energy and help immensely with keeping a fast pace while training or during speed runs. You can even be creative in arranging the mood of your digital selections. For example, the first song may be high energy to get the adrenaline going for stretching and getting pumped for the event or training run.

Follow the stretching selection(s) with songs that are at a slower pace as you start your run. Pick some personal favorites to help you relax for the first few miles. This sounds counterproductive to the purpose of the training. It is an excellent way, however, to mentally remind yourself not to start out too quickly. After a few slow/easy tempo songs, then follow with high energy songs to focus on your workout while you enjoy pushing yourself.

Run without music for your actual races, to allow for full concentration on the task. However, music for training runs is a good way to pass the time, keep the momentum going, and even boost the adrenaline for those challenging interval runs. A word of caution regarding music while running—your hearing ability will obviously be reduced for hearing sounds like cars and dogs. You will need to stay even more aware of these and other road hazards while running with music. Trails or tracks are more suitable if running with music. Use your judgment as to what is appropriate or safe while running with music.

As shown in Photos 4.35 and 4.36 some runners prefer to run with music and don't mind the added wires and headphones. Some running events prohibit runners from wearing headphones, due to safety concerns.

Photo 4.35 Armband IPOD   **Photo 4.36** Clipped to shorts

Everyone has their favorite music for inspiration or motivation. Here are a few personal favorite songs that may give you an idea what to add to your CD/MP3/IPOD player, if you choose to run or train with music.

- Boston (for obvious reasons) – *Don't Look Back*
- Vangelis – *Chariots of Fire*
- Lenny Kravits – *Dig In, Where Are We Running*
- Bon Jovi – *It's My Life/Now or Never*
- Survivor – *Eye of the Tiger*
- Rocky – *Gonna Fly Now (Theme from Rocky)*
- AC/DC – *Thunderstruck*

Other Training Benefits

Health Benefits

Health itself is a motivator to stay healthy. Running and training are great ways to improve or maintain your health. Through your continued training, you will develop a much stronger heart and increased lung capacity that promotes your cardiovascular fitness. When running a marathon, the blood flow through your body is roughly 16 times the flow when at rest. This higher blood velocity works to clean out veins and arteries of plaque or fatty buildup. This cleaning action leads to improved circulation, as well as blood pressure reduction. Your heart rate (or pulse) will drop, as well as your blood pressure due to your heart's ability to more effectively flow blood through your body.

Running and exercising in general have been found to reduce cancer risk, prevent diabetes, reduce heart disease, strengthen bones, decrease blood pressure, boost your libido, raise your good cholesterol (HDL), as well as improve your general mood. Many also find that good workouts will help you to get better sleep. When combining improved health and fitness with the accomplishment of a marathon, you will no doubt exude pride and self-esteem. You may also find that you start to eat healthier to fuel your fitness.

Amazingly, your body knows what is good for it and uses its energy supply to support running and will start to shut down unnecessary functions, such as digestion, to ensure more blood—and the oxygen and glucose within it—goes to the working muscles. This phenomenon allows your body to use energy where it can best support your body, based upon the needs. In essence, your body helps itself to become more fit. How can you argue with that logic? Your body needs fitness.

Psychological Benefits

As you are training for Boston or any other marathon, your health will improve, and your energy and endurance will be higher than ever. In addition, many publications cite the fact that runners become more outgoing and "extravertish." Not only does their fitness level make them feel better about their physical condition, they also become proud of their accomplishments among their peers. In a sense, it is a way for adults to experience the same type of competitive atmosphere children experience in organized sports. Some publications have even documented that running is a form of organized playtime for adults. From my own personal experience, I'm guessing they weren't including intervals as playtime. Regardless, the rewards and self-satisfaction that running brings can change one's attitude on the importance of a mentally and physically healthy lifestyle.

Running has also been proven to reduce stress levels in adults, and many seek these natural morphine-like hormones to achieve a sense of well-being. Perhaps this is why the majority of marathon runners today are over 40 years of age. The baby boomers need help to cope with the ever-competitive business world, getting gray, and other challenges that forty years will bring. Thankfully there is an outlet... running.

It has also been concluded that runners will better manage companies. A Ball State University study concluded that entrepreneurs who run as a part of their fitness regimen have companies with better sales compared to businesses owned by non-runners. Researchers looked at 366 small business owners and concluded that when incorporating running into their lifestyle, they lead more successful companies. Who knows, running may inspire you to... become President?

Photo 4.37

Chapter 5
Cross Training

"Not only in running, but in much of life is a sense of balance and proportion necessary"
- Clarence DeMar, seven-time Boston Marathon winner

Photo 5.1 Cross-training will properly condition you for the challenges on race day.

While running serves as an excellent and necessary means of training for a fast marathon or a Boston qualification, the constant pavement pounding from marathon training will eventually take a toll on your feet and knees and can lead to muscle imbalances or potentially reduced flexibility. However, you can best extend your longevity as a runner and improve your chances for a Boston qualification by incorporating cross training into your training program.

Cross training provides the needed muscular balance that promotes proper running mechanics. It also relieves pressure on joints and muscles while allowing you to train aggressively. Besides improving muscular balance, cross training may be best known for its benefits in enhancing cardiovascular system fitness.

Unfortunately, for most marathoners, the need for cross training may not become obvious until they have been injured and are then forced to use other training methods. This is due to the fact that most runners don't realize that muscle imbalance and reduced flexibility can contribute to injury susceptibility, even though their training regimen has conditioned them well to run a marathon quickly.

As a marathoner, don't underestimate the value-added benefits of cross training—it will be a major mistake if you do. Remember, you will go beyond the typical marathon training requirements to qualify for Boston; therefore, you will place more stress on your body than the typical novice marathoner. Don't wait to find this out when it's too late! Even if you don't plan to qualify for Boston, however, incorporating cross training into your regular training plan will be a beneficial necessity that will keep you running longer and healthier.

The contents of this chapter briefly describe a few of the various types of cross training and the benefits provided. Understandably, your access to the type of equipment necessary to cross train may dictate what you can economically select (i.e., stationary equipment, pool, bike, etc.). Joining a local gym, however, may be the most suitable option.

Cross Training Basics

Swimming, water running, cycling, elliptical training, stair climbing, power walking and other similar types of cardio-based activities are all excellent cross training methods. I don't advocate counting weight training as a source of your cross training, because strength training provides minimal cardiovascular benefits. Many runners select cycling because they experience a similar sensation of speed and a similar rush of endorphins that they would get from running. Whichever the preferred cross training method, I strongly advise incorporating a minimum of one day (two is recommended) per week into your marathon training schedule, as shown in Table 5.2. The best days for cross training are the first two days following the most strenuous run for the week. If you opt for a second cross training day in your training week, it may be combined with a short distance running day. During the off days I recommend cross training for a minimum of 60 minutes. This strategy will allow you to rest core running muscles for recovery while you continue to train other muscles required for physical balance. A mix of 30 minutes on stationary/bike and 30 minutes of elliptical is an excellent choice for balancing muscle structure when complementing running.

Cross training not only helps to prevent injury, but it also effectively reduces performance recovery time after an injury. If an injury happens during your quest for Boston qualification, seriously consider increasing cross training (with doctor's approval) to keep your motivation high and performance loss minimized as you heal. You can even track your cross training progress (in calories/hour) as you would with your running personal bests. Sure, this isn't running, but it will still work toward your marathon qualification goal while maintaining cardio fitness. Substantial running fitness loss takes a month or more to significantly diminish, and continued cross training will keep you in the game, from a cardiovascular standpoint. Much like running a smartly paced marathon, cross training keeps your training plan on pace by keeping you conditioned to run.

As noted in Chapter 4, Table 4.23, the training schedule should incorporate at least one or two days per week devoted to cross training/strength building.

Table 5.2 Training Schedule (with cross training included)

		HILLS & STRENGTH TRAINING							
12 weeks	7 mile at MP	**60 min bike or elliptical** (Equiv 6 mi.) **and strength exercises**	7 mile at Tempo + 3 at MP+30	Rest	5 mile at MP	6 X 1 mile Hill Run @ MP-30 min/mile	4-6 EP (recovery) **or** **60 min elliptical** (Equiv 6 mi.) **and strength exercises**	38-40	Focus on Hill training for strength
11 weeks	11 mile at MP	**60 min bike or elliptical** (Equiv 6 mi.) **and strength exercises**	7 mile at Tempo + 3 at MP+30	Rest	5 mile at MP	12-14 mile Long Run at MP+30-40sec with drin	Rest	44-46	Use a local ½ marathon race if available
10 weeks	7 mile at MP	**60 min bike or elliptical** (Equiv 6 mi.) **and strength exercises**	7 mile at Tempo + 3 at MP+30	Rest	5 mile at MP	6 X 1 mile Hill Run @ MP-30 min/mile	6-8 EP (recovery) **or** **60 min elliptical** (Equiv 6 mi.) **and strength exercises**	40-42	Focus on Hill training for strength
9 weeks	11 mile at MP	**60 min bike or elliptical** (Equiv 6 mi.) **and strength exercises**	7 mile at Tempo + 3 at MP+30	Rest	5 mile at MP	16-18 mile Long Run at MP+30sec with drink stops	Rest	48-50	First significant long run.

Note: Cross training days are highlighted.

Cycling

Road Cycling

Cycling is an excellent method of cross training when your core focus is running. It puts less stress on your impact joints (feet, knees, etc.) and offers the opportunity to build and balance leg strength. Cycling will further improve your aerobic capability and overall cardiovascular fitness. However, because it typically takes more time to burn an equivalent amount of calories than running (at roughly a 2:1 ratio), this could be a potential challenge to road cycling and its effectiveness as cross training.

Another challenge to road cycling may be the weather and other variable factors. Because you will be dependent on weather, light, and perhaps the time required for suiting/airing up tires, it may be difficult to fit road cycling into your schedule. Therefore, training time, or more appropriately, cross training time, may not be a luxury at hand. A stationary bike may serve as the most convenient and optimum selection.

Photo 5.3 Road bike cyclist.

Stationary Bikes

Most stationary bikes, road bikes, and mountain bikes offer shoe straps or shoe clips that allow the cyclist to provide propulsion on both the downward "push" and the upward "pull." This complete power stroke builds the thigh muscles and hamstrings to further compliment your conditioning gains from running.

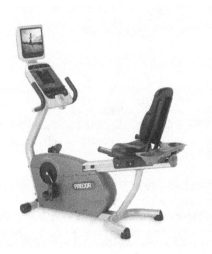

A stationary bike features variable load capability, which allows you to train yourself appropriately within the optimum workout time allotted. Because of the risk of training over-aggressively, I recommend using an HRM for training with a stationary bike or other cross training machines. They can easily elevate your heart rate above normal or target levels.

Road bikes can also offer a great workout by varying the gear selection, terrain, or how hard you want to push yourself. Either selection of cycling (road or stationary) will contribute to your muscular balance and fitness. Some premium stationary training machines (elliptical or bike) offer TV or video upgrades (see Photo 5.4). This capability will make the hours seem shorter, and watching inspirational videos (i.e., marathons, triathlons, etc.) will definitely fuel your motivation.

Photo 5.4 Stationary bikes provide excellent variable resistance capabilities. Be sure to use a heart rate monitor for heart rate control.
Photo from www.precor.com

Cycling Trainers

If you don't have room for a stationary bike or the luxury of $800-plus for a good road bike, you may opt for a device called a trainer.

Cycling trainers are stationary rollers that mount to the rear wheel of your existing bike and provide variable resistance through magnetic, viscous/fluid, or air. They offer a compact design and are much less expensive compared to a stationary bike. However, you will still need a road or trail bike to train, as shown in Photo 5.5.

Photo 5.5 A cycling trainer can be used almost anywhere; inside or outside.

Spinning

If you don't have a stationary bike or access to a road bike/trail bike and wish to cycle for cross training, you may want to consider joining a gym that has stationary bikes or offers a spinning class. Spinning classes often provide an excellent aerobic workout where the course instructor will often change the pace and position of the rider to work various muscle groups.

Cycling Shorts

If you are a novice to cycling, you will find that there are shorts specifically designed for over-the-road cyclists that incorporate additional padding for added comfort. Typical workout shorts can be used for stationary bikes, but again be aware that because cycling involves a significant amount of leg movement, chafing can occur. As with running, application of Vaseline or other petroleum gels may inhibit chafing.

Water Training

Swimming

As an alternative to running, swimming strengthens the cardiovascular system, builds lung capacity, and eases the stress on joints. Even though it does little to build the runner's strength, it still provides an acceptable method of cross training. In fact, swimming is one of the best exercise activities (if not *the* best) to relieve stress on joints while providing an excellent cardio workout.

For the runners who wish to utilize swimming for a significant portion of their cross training or perhaps broaden their competitive endeavors by entering a triathlon, there are a few factors to consider. Since a triathlon utilizes a balanced mix of swimming, biking, and running, it usually meshes well with the training plan of a runner. If the triathlon goal is a half Ironman distance or greater, however, the focus on running-training and time to effectively train for running may be diminished.

If the triathlon event is kept to a sprint triathlon where the swimming requirement is typically around 400 to 800 yards, the number of hours required in a pool would be much more tolerable than training for a 1.2 mile swim (half Ironman) or 2.4 mile swim (full Ironman). These endurance events will require a significant amount of pool time and will take away from running time and your marathon speed.

Photo 5.6 Tri-athletes set out on an early am swim. Many distance runners supplement their running with competing in sprint or longer distance triathlons.

Water Running

For non-swimmers or injured runners, water running provides the opportunity to use running muscles and the same mechanical motion without the impact. This process speeds recovery from injuries while keeping your cardiovascular system in good aerobic condition. Its popularity has grown as an excellent therapeutic tool for ailing running injuries. All you need is a pool and some type of flotation device to keep you afloat while "running," such as a ski belt or floatation vest. Due to the resistance of the water, you can simply change the intensity of the workout by increasing your leg speed. You'll find that this type of workout is just as hard, if not harder, than running. However, the cool water temperature will keep you refreshed.

Stair Climbers and Elliptical Trainers

Stair Climbers

A stair climber will reduce stress on joints due to reduced impact. Some stair climbing machines offer continuous contact between the feet and stair, while others require separation as the stairs rotate. The power that you deliver through your thigh, quadriceps, and glutes as you climb will build your running strength. As with stationary biking, you should monitor your heart rate and train within your target zone.

A good target zone is to train at 70 percent of your Maximum Heart Rate (see the Heart Rate Monitor in Chapter 3 to calculate maximum heart rate). Stair climbers offer sufficient cross training conditioning; however, due to the joint impact with some models, I would not recommend that they be 100 percent of your cross training choice.

Elliptical Trainers

An elliptical machine provides the opportunity for an excellent cardiovascular workout. Elliptical trainers are offered in models that train upper and lower body (both arm/chest), as well as leg exercises. Some elliptical trainers focus specifically on leg exercise (as shown in Figure 5.7 and Figure 5.8). Either model will offer varying inclines to increase your cardio demand. The elliptical is an excellent choice for cross training because it provides a low impact alternative to running, aids the training process during periods of injury recovery, and enhances strength conditioning. Elliptical motion best duplicates the running motion by utilizing more running muscles than most other cross training exercises.

Choosing the elliptical for the majority of your cross training is recommended due to the benefits provided in developing leg strength, low impact approach, and cardiovascular training. It is also a personal favorite of mine for those same reasons.

Photo 5.7 The elliptical, an excellent cross trainer.

Photo 5.8 *Photo from www.precor.com*

Walking

To the "die hard" runners, walking for exercise isn't even in their vocabulary. Understandably, some runners will prefer not to walk during an event just from a pure pace standpoint or perhaps even pride. However, walking briskly offers training benefits, just as in running. Since the impact on joints is substantially lower than running, walking provides a good way to cool down or warm up. It can also be done with a non-runner companion who seeks to be supportive in your efforts. Incorporating walks into your training schedule is definitely a viable method to increase your endurance and cardiovascular limits.

In addition, some runners may choose to incorporate walking as an integral component of their marathon(s) and even their qualification run. I have personally witnessed the benefits of mixing running and walking during a marathon. At my first Grandma's Marathon, I noticed a woman who was repeatedly passing me as she ran. I was returning the pass at every mile or so, obviously passing her during the walking portion of her marathon effort. Her running pace was faster than mine, but by walking, she was able to maintain an average pace faster than mine, which was potentially fast enough to qualify her for Boston. That was enough proof for me.

Walking can be successfully incorporated into a marathon. In some cases, runners can improve their overall time by mixing a pre-determined walking time for the first 18 to 20 miles and running on "rested" muscles for the remaining 10K.

Most runners will walk a short span of the race during the water stops. These short breaks can periodically give your body time to recover, thus allowing you to sustain your desired performance level.

Photo 5.9 Walking can be incorporated into any race.

Suggested below in Table 5.10 are a few examples of ways to incorporate walking "breaks" into your marathon. Bill Rogers (four-time Boston winner) even walked during two occasions on his P.R. at Boston. And although I am *clearly* no Bill Rogers, I too, walked for a few minutes during my P.R. Sometimes your body will be able to sustain a higher level of performance with just a small break in the demand on your running muscles, so that oxygen and glycogen can find their way back into them. Walking also helps prevent the onset of leg cramps brought on by fatigue, or the lack of oxygen and electrolytes, or both. Late in a marathon is not the time to walk, due to the temptation to continue longer than planned. Be sure to be disciplined in your time allotment for walking and do so early in the marathon (up to mile 22). After mile 22, let your adrenalin take over and run the remainder.

Table 5.10 Incorporating Walking Breaks Into Your Marathon

Marathon Pace	Time Walking	Per Interval of Running
3:00	15 seconds	Every 2-3 miles
3:30	30-60 seconds	1-2 miles
4:00	1 minute	Every 8-10 minutes
4:30	1 minute	Every 6-7 minutes
5:00	1 minute	Every 5-6 minutes

Closing Comments

Beyond What Is Normal

For Boston, you will be required to go beyond the novice marathon training plan, which necessitates incorporating cross training to allow you to go that extra distance. Since you are adding miles and perhaps running more miles per/week than ever before, the need for a balanced approach to your training becomes even more critical.

Why Balance?

Training for Boston is much like the structure of a table where the four legs provide support for a common platform. In this case, the platform represents the capability to qualify for Boston, and the four legs that carry the weight of the goal represent;

- **speed training**
- **distance training**
- **rest**
- **cross training**

Without all of these legs of balance, your road to Boston may become a much longer one. Without a doubt, cross training is an integral part of training for Boston, but don't find out too late due to injury.

Counting Cross Training as Miles

I recommend counting workout time associated with stationary cycling, elliptical training, and stair climbing as part of your running mileage. The key requirement is that the cross training must be at an exertion level that builds fitness by systematically training at a target percent heart rate. For example, if your heart rate is held at 70 to 80 percent of your maximum for 60 minutes, this could equate to a six-to eight-mile training run. Although these minutes are not actual training miles, you should count this time toward your training as equivalent mileage. This approach will also help you reach your weekly mileage goal, while easing the load on your joints. **Note that the total miles for each week in Table 5.2 include the cross training time as equivalent miles.**

Some running textbooks will preach training time at a specific exertion level and not the specific mileage. Their point is not to focus on speed or distance, but rather the quality of the effort. Cross training falls clearly into this category and is an effective substitute to pounding the pavement when utilized as a supplement to your marathon running training plan.

Chapter 6
Strength Conditioning

"If you train your core, you'll see the results...when you consider the time you spend running, what's a few more minutes... when that time can help your running?"

    - Meb Keflezighi, 2004 Olympic Marathon silver medal (February 2008 *Runner's World*)

Photo 6.1 Muscle tone, not mass, is desired for proper form and speed. A proper balance of weight training and running allows this runner to participate in a lead pace group of a marathon.

Why Strength Train?

For most runners, the answer is not obvious, since the focus is commonly understood as building speed and endurance by running, not by lifting weights. So what does strength training (or weight training) do for a runner?

To be a successful Boston qualifier, you must incorporate speed work, distance runs, and tempo runs into your training plan—all of which we've covered in Chapter Four. These running elements complement each other well and round out your ability as a runner to achieve excellent performance and endurance. However, to achieve the next level of performance, a runner must have balanced strength ...without the excess bulk.

Building muscle tone in the key leg muscle groups—calves, hamstrings and quadriceps— is critical to building speed. Another often-overlooked strength area consists of the abdominal and back muscle groups— also known as the core muscle group. Optimizing the core muscle groups has recently become a focus of many elite runners due to the benefits of stabilizing your torso as you fatigue. A stable torso allows for continued proper form and balance as your body mass shifts during the running motion. With poorly conditioned core muscles, you may find yourself leaning forward as you fatigue, which will result in a slower pace due to the decline in your stride length.

Also, don't overlook shoulder and bicep conditioning. Since arm swing constitutes a natural element of your running form, these muscles serve a critical role for propulsion. As a marathoner, you will be required to hold your forearms up for more than three or four hours, which will easily deplete your body of energy. Stronger bicep muscles, however, will minimize the effort and, ultimately, muscle fatigue.

One key difference between sprinters and distance runners is the need for muscle mass to develop force. Since sprinters focus on acceleration, their force exerted to move forward must be greater than that of a distance runner who focuses on sustaining speed. The equation $f=m*a$, where f(force)= m(mass or body weight)* a (acceleration rate) illustrates the point that a sprinter must have more force to accelerate than the distance runner who runs at zero acceleration (or constant speed). This force is generated through muscle strength. Therefore, a distance runner doesn't require strength to generate force, but can benefit from strength training to sustain strenuous output for extended periods when running at constant speed.

Strength training also promotes stronger bone mass, consequently reducing the risk of injury. In addition, strength training enhances your speed work training (similar to a sprinter) to improve volumetric efficiency (VO2 max). Instead of gaining muscle mass, which hampers distance runners with its undesired added weight, distance runners should focus on toning muscles through high numbers of repetitions, which enable sustained speed or strength for long periods of time.

Figure 6.2 Boston or bulk? Muscle (mass) bulk is not advantageous to a distance runner and will not get you closer to Boston.

Methods of Strength Training

Before we explore the various methods of strength training, it is important to understand a few of the key muscle groups or specific muscles that are most critical to a runner.

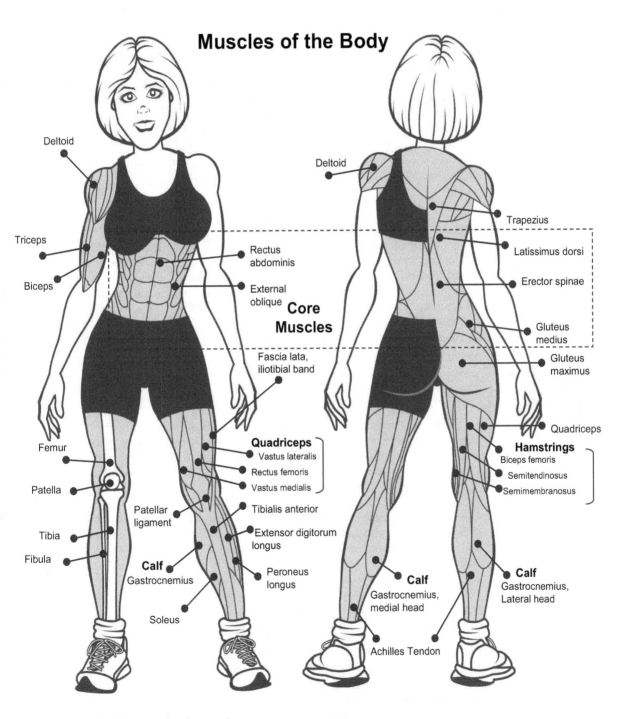

Figure 6.3 Key muscles for running

Hill Repeats

By adding hill work to your training schedule, you will build strength in your quadriceps. A recommended hill workout requires running up an incline at a 10K pace and running back down the decline at a slower pace to recover. Repeat this workout for 40-60 minutes (or 4-6 miles). This will build quadriceps and hamstring strength. I recommend focusing on hills, to build your strength, at least eight weeks prior to your marathon attempt. You can, however, continue to focus on a reduced level of strength training by incorporating hills into your tempo or long runs.

The key to running on hills during a marathon is to maintain your effort going uphill. Do not try to sprint when you ascend the hill, but stay focused on keeping an upright posture and working the muscles, rather than speed. When descending the hill, again, do not sprint, even though momentum will push you to speed up. Instead, try to remain focused on your running posture to keep your balance and stride length in check. When in a qualifying race, descending quickly on hills can be an easy way to make up time. Again, the key is to maintain your exertion level, as a significantly faster descent can actually cause an early fatigue. Even though you may have saved some time in the descent, the total overall time benefit may be negligible. In summary, attack the hills during training, and respect the hills during your qualifying marathon.

Weight Training

As previously mentioned, runners should not seek muscle mass, but rather strength and tone. The best way to accomplish strength and tone is to incorporate sets of repetitions of 15–20 (or more), as opposed to heavier weights at 8–10 repetitions. Unfortunately, for most over 35 years of age and into their 50s, muscle mass will naturally start to diminish unless you incorporate regular strength training into your lifestyle. This focused approach to balanced conditioning can allow runners in these age groups to maintain their competitiveness to go after those 20 to 30-year-old runners. You may not catch them, but at least you'll look good trying. Again, don't focus on gaining weight—*the more, the better* does not apply to a distance runner, but rather balanced strength.

Leg Strength

As illustrated in Figure 6.3, the two major propulsion muscle groups are quadriceps and hamstrings. Running will strengthen both groups. You may find, however, that if you are only running (without weight training), your hamstrings may develop faster than your quadriceps. If so, it is important to focus on bringing balance to your leg structure through weight training. Otherwise you increase risk of injury.

Quadriceps One of the strongest runner's muscle groups, the quads are located on the front of the thigh and are some of the most critical muscles for runners due to their ability to propel you forward. Your quad strength will increase as you continue to run, but exercises will further improve your quad muscle tone and strength.

Squats Typically, a beginning runner's weakest muscles are the quadriceps. Incorporating squats into your workout will strengthen your quadriceps, as well as your glutes (gluteus maximus). You can accelerate the strength gain by focusing on squatting exercises on a weekly basis during the early phases of your training plan, with continued focus as your mileage progresses.

Using the Smith Machine or vertical press (Photo 6.4), as well as a sitting press (Photo 6.5), is an effective method for building the quads, glutes and hamstrings. Focus on three sets with repetitions of 15 to build strength but not bulk. With either exercise, go slowly, and bring your knee bend to a 90 degrees point, push back to a straight leg (180 degrees) and repeat. An optional workout for the sitting press involves using less weight and a shorter distance for the exercise extension while adding more and faster repetitions. Instead of bringing your legs back to a full 90 degrees (as shown in Photo 6.5), stop earlier, with your knees only slightly bent, and focus on a series of repetitions of 50 to 100 for three sets. This exercise will not only build your leg muscles, but also provide somewhat of a cardio burst similar to that of running a hill.

Photo 6.4 Squats at a Smith machine.

Photo 6.5 Leg press with legs at 90 degrees.

The Quads Serve Three Primary Purposes

- **Help absorb the impact of the stride**
- **Propel the runner forward**
- **Maintain a runner's balance during alternating leg strides**

Hamstring curl This exercise (Photo 6.6) effectively builds hamstring strength. The hamstrings, which are located on the backside of your leg opposite the quadriceps, greatly account for your speed and endurance capability. Hamstring curls, like most exercises, should be part of your early training plan and incorporated into a weekly weight session to maintain your leg strength.

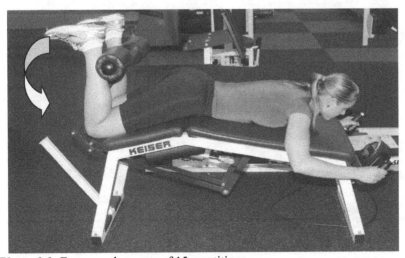

Photo 6.6 Focus on three sets of 15 repetitions.

Calf Raises To help build the calf muscles, use calf raises, in which you lift your heels off the ground while holding weights or a weighted bar across your shoulders. Calf raises can easily be combined with squats. Whichever exercise you chose, calf raises and calf-focused exercises will help improve your speed. You use your calf muscles when pushing off on your power foot; thus, the strength of your calf will influence both your capability to accelerate and maintain speed. Sprinters are known to have large calf muscles and distance runners have well-defined, but not bulky, calf muscles. Photo 6.7 illustrates the use of the Smith Press, where the body is in the upright position, and the calf muscles are extended.

Raise your heels off the ground (Photo 6.8) with slow deliberate movements and descend back down slowly. I suggest using a wood plank or a platform that will support the forefoot and provide maximum movement of the heel. Three sets of 20 per workout should be adequate to build strength in your calves. Be sure to keep your back straight for even pressure along the spine and back muscles.

Photo 6.7   **Photo 6.8**

Lunges The primary focus of lunges is building the glute and quad muscle groups. You can incorporate lunges into your exercise plan through a variety of methods; however, they all have the same basic motion. The critical aspect of lunge-motion is keeping your body's torso perpendicular to the ground, while one leg is extended out at a 90-degree angle, so that the majority of the body weight moves to the forward leg. This motion involves keeping the forward thigh parallel to the ground while alternating legs to this forward position as you stand in place or lunge (move) forward.

Modular stair steps (found in most gyms) can be used to increase the vertical height gain. A Bosu can be used in place of the steps to absorb shock load when using 20- to 30-pound weights in each hand.

Again, three sets of 15 repetitions will typically ensure that you get a good workout.

Photo 6.9 Weights added to lunges are an excellent method of strengthening legs.

Photo 6.10

Balancing leg strength   A commonly overlooked muscle segment is the inner leg and outer leg muscles. As shown in Figure 6.3, the Vastus lateralis combine with the Vastus medialis to support the upper leg muscle group and balance the power of the quadriceps. The quadriceps (rectus) femoris is connected to the knee and kneecap through strong ligaments that influence kneecap movement. Should you focus only on forward and vertical motion training, the quadriceps (rectus femoris) may overpower the Vastus lateralis and Vastus medialis, which may result in a change to your kneecap movement path. This change in movement or tracking of the kneecap combined, with the repetition of running movement, can lead to a condition called runner's knee (chondromalacia patella syndrome). Chapter 9 provides more detail on runner's knee. Balanced leg strength, combined with stretching, can help prevent this injury.

To provide balance in your upper and lower interior and exterior (leg) muscle groups, it is important to add strength/resistance training. As shown Photo 6.11 and 6.12, two methods of exercise can accomplish this: interior leg lifts or resistance exercises. Either approach is effective for balancing muscle mass and/or improving knee stability where you are adding three sets of 15 repetitions for interior and exterior muscle groups. By adding balance to your leg muscle mass, you will also reduce the risk of injury.

Photo 6.11   Add ankle weights for an increased resistance.   **Photo 6.12**

Leg strength through resistance   By adding resistance to your running, you will add difficulty to your strength workout. One simple way to do this is to use a jogging stroller—of course, with a willing toddler included. Even though they (the toddlers) require their own specific level of maintenance, they can provide a very enjoyable addition to your running by keeping you company.

Many times I have "bribed" my daughter to ride in the jogging stroller by offering a trip to the local ice cream shop as a reward for cooperating with the four- to five-mile round trip. A jogging stroller is a vital accessory for any single- or dual-parent family that includes a runner.

If you are really looking for a resistance workout, slightly deflate the stroller tires of some air or pull up the passenger canopy (which is an effective parachute), and you will have a significant challenge on your hands. Strollers are also convenient when going to parks or running on paved trails. You can also use the storage compartments to carry additional clothing, snacks, or sports drinks.

Core Body Strength

Abdominals When running, you continuously use your abdominal muscles, to some extent. Most runners aren't aware, however, that stronger abs and core muscles can help them improve their speed through quicker leg "turnover" through better form. Getting strong abs usually requires a lot of work; unfortunately, most runners easily forget about this muscle group or don't attempt the extra effort in training. However, once you have strong and defined abdominal muscles, you may start to see your times/intervals start to improve.

Numerous exercises focus on building your abs. Find a few exercises that can easily be incorporated into your training routine, and work them on a regular basis to maintain core body strength. Below are examples of leg raises that focus on lower abs. In addition, most gyms have multiple types of abdominal machines to select from, or you can simply do leg lifts or sit-ups in the convenience of your home.

Body balls or stability balls are large rubber balls (approximately 24 inches in diameter), that are highly effective for building abdominal and other core muscle groups. Experiment with various exercises and equipment, select one or two abdominal exercises, and work them at least twice per week to maintain core fitness.

Photo 6.13 Stability ball is excellent for ab exercises.

Photo 6.14

Upper Body Strength

Why discuss upper body strength when it's the legs that provide propulsion? Not only does the added upper body strength reduce fatigue in the late stages of a marathon, it also allows the runner to maintain good upright form late in the race to stay on stride. Runners who lean forward due to weak core and upper back strength will overstress the quad muscles because they (the runners) are essentially running out of balance. In addition, strong arms and shoulders are used to propel runners when accelerating and running uphill.

Shoulders and upper back This frequently overlooked area includes the shoulder and upper back muscles (Trapezius, Deltoid, and Latissimus dorsi). Strong shoulder and back muscles help ensure that you are getting effective power and rhythm out of your arms while running. Sprinters usually build their upper body muscles to ensure that they have the power to shift body weight and build momentum by swinging their arms. Distance runners need strong shoulders for a different reason, simply to keep their arms propelling the body for extended periods of time. It may sound simple, but in reality, you will need to swing your arms and shoulders thousands of times during a marathon, which means that your arms and shoulders will suffer fatigue unless conditioned.

My personal favorite is what I call Runner's Fly, as they work the biceps, shoulders, and upper back muscles such as the Trapezius and Deltoid. By starting with the weights down at your hips (Photo 6.15), with legs slightly bent, bring the weights up to shoulder height with your arms at 90 degrees (Photo 6.16). Repetitions of three sets of 15 will work great. For added focus on balance and core muscles, stand on a Bosu ball while doing this exercise.

Shoulders and Back (Runner's Fly)

Photo 6.15 Starting position   **Photo 6.16** Finishing position

The combination of your back and front core muscles provide the total support required to maintain good running posture. This upright posture ensures optimum stride length and even weight distribution.

Below are two exercises that will help in building core back strength. Photo 6.17 illustrates "Lat pulls," where a dumbbell is used to build the upper back muscles (Trapezius, Deltoid, and Latissimus Dorsi, or "lats"). Starting with your arm extended and perpendicular to your body and keeping your body slightly upright, pull the weight until the dumbbell is even with your chest for three sets of up to 15. Photo 6.18 illustrates Shoulder-Lat pulls, where you start with arms fully extended and pull the bar down to neck level behind your back or to the front of your chest. Both exercises focus on upper back and shoulders. These are excellent exercises to maintain your strength and posture to maximize performance. Again, you are not after bulk, but strength and tone.

Shoulder and Back Strength Exercises

Photo 6.17   **Photo 6.18**

Biceps Similar to shoulders, the bicep muscles work to keep your forearms in the air while running. Weak biceps may cause you to drop your arms during a marathon. Not only does this slightly increase your wind resistance, but more importantly, it also reduces your capability to maintain pace and momentum by swinging your arms. Arm swing plays an important role in maintaining momentum/speed. While distance runners only require a small amount of arm swing, sprinters effectively use their arm muscles for acceleration.

For bicep strength, start with arms down at your side with dumbbell in hand and bring the weight up to your chest where your elbows are bent to 90 degrees or less. If standing, do not rock your body and swing the weight up to your chest, as this will lead to back injury if the weight is excessive. If standing, keep your knees bent slightly to take the stress off of your back.

Photo 6.19 Hand dumbbells or a curl-bar may be used with light weight, three sets of 15.

Advanced Core Strength Training

Using stability (body) balls or specifically the Bosu (dome) for core strength in combination with weight training is a highly effective method of mixing strength training and balance training.

By incorporating a balance dome under your feet while doing arm curls or Runner's Fly, you will work your legs and core muscles, as well as the back and arms for a full-balanced workout. It may take a few weeks to become proficient at balancing the weight, but you will quickly find the benefits to your core muscle groups and the balanced strength focus to your legs and ankles. These half size stability domes are an excellent addition to a weight training regimen for runners.

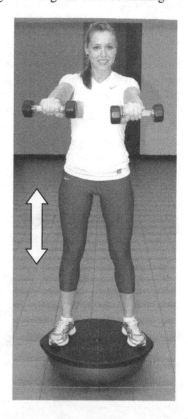

Photo 6.20 Incorporating a balance dome (Bosu) into a strength workout is an excellent method of combining upper body and leg exercises. Advanced forms of Bosu exercises may incorporate squatting movements (while keeping your back upright) or using a single leg for balance while incorporating curls or other upper body exercises.

Strength Training for the Qualifying Run

Within two weeks of your approaching marathon date, you should eliminate any weight/strength training workouts on your legs. Continuation of strength training up to your race date will yield negligible benefits and may actually leave you at a slight performance deficiency. Your muscles require time to recover after strength exercises, and they also deplete the critical glycogen stores you've been building for your marathon. You can, however, continue to tone your upper body muscles, but at a reduced weight and intensity. Even this should be discontinued entirely one week before your marathon.

Closing Comments

Strength training is an often overlooked element in becoming an effective marathon runner and a necessary element for improving your performance and chance for a Boston qualification run.

Strong and toned muscles are advantageous, as they improve running economy, reduce fatigue, and improve speed and stamina. Strong core muscles (abs and back) will allow you to maintain an upright posture, which improves your running efficiency in burning calories.

You will rarely see muscle bulk on an elite runner, but rather, toned and cut muscles. Since running does not require just the leg muscles, a balanced physique is very important. A weakness in any of the areas or muscle groups discussed may negatively impact your marathon performance.

Luckily, a plethora of exercises are available to enhance your balanced strength. I have only listed a few that I practice and have found to be beneficial with respect to running. Remember, bulk does not equate to speed for a distance runner. The weight that you gain from muscle mass must benefit you to move faster and for longer distance. Strength conditioning for a distance runner is about balance of the core muscles and key muscle groups to ensure that you have eliminated weak areas of your body to maximize your running economy and running longevity.

Photo 6.21 Balanced strength is a key to running fast.

Chapter 7
Nutrition and Supplements

"The will to win means nothing without the will to prepare."
- Juma Ikangaa, 1989 New York City Marathon winner (*Runner's World)*

Photo 7.1 Pasta (like this spaghetti) is the primary carbohydrate resource (fuel) for most runners.

The key to good health is simple…eat a good, low-fat, nutritional (balanced) diet and exercise (cardiovascular exercise). Since cardiovascular exercise takes effort, a high number of people will eventually fail unless they incorporate some type of exercise into their daily routine or they establish an achievable goal. Races such as a 5K, half marathon, or even a full marathon are excellent goals to allow you to gradually build your fitness and health while focusing on nutrition.

Does Nutrition Influence Your Boston Qualification?

Without a doubt...**YES**. Proper nutrition is essential for any athlete to ensure optimum performance, and runners are no exception. As a runner, you need to focus your nutritional intake during training to ensure that you are carb'd up for the long training runs and especially for qualifying attempts. Also, you need to ensure that you are consuming the important proteins to rebuild muscles stressed during intense workouts, such as intervals and long runs. If you think about food in a similar approach as fuel for your car, you will enhance your muscles, cardiovascular system, and overall performance by consuming premium fuel of high octane as opposed to regular fuel of lower-energy content. You may still perform acceptably in training or a marathon by eating high-fat cheeseburgers and fries, but proper nutrition may be the difference between a qualifying marathon or just another marathon. Nutrition is one of the top 10 variables (see Chapter 3) that you can control, and you should take advantage of this variable.

For most runners and new marathoners, it is not obvious what your nutritional needs are and when you need to eat specific foods to benefit performance. Avid runners will typically consume 60 percent carbohydrates, 15 percent proteins, and 25 percent fats. Each element is important to your balance of strength, stamina or energy, and recovery. If you aren't one to measure your intake, you should still be aware of what is beneficial to eat and what is not. This chapter is intended to give you some basic facts about nutrition and its importance to the runner.

The Basics

Much like choosing running shorts or shoes, you learn the significance of nutrition once you've stumbled through a few races and can't figure out why you were sluggish. It's important to eat the right food types for training runs, as well as races, during the days, and even weeks, before the event. If you have an important qualifying attempt approaching, you should watch your diet throughout the entire training period or for at least the month prior to the event.

Types of foods to definitely avoid the days before an important running event are fried foods, alcohol, foods of high fat content, exclusively protein meals, and meals with a high percentage of roughage, such as leafy foods or salads. Many runners savor the completion of a marathon by celebrating with beer or wine or that cheeseburger and fries that have been void from their diet for months.

Basics on Nutrition for Training or Preparing for a Marathon

- **Fuel -** Eat carbohydrates when preparing for a long run or race 2 to 3 days in advance. In addition, eat carbs with the meal immediately following a significant run.
- **Recovery -** Eat protein after a hard workout and definitely after a race where you've pushed your ability. Proteins promote quick recovery time for muscles, thus allowing you to reach mileage goals and continue training as quickly as possible.
- **Hydrate -** Drink ample fluids during and after a training run or race to replenish what has been lost. You should hydrate in advance of a marathon, but don't over hydrate.

You need not be concerned with a special diet, but you should eat smart when it counts. If you find you are gaining weight, you are either not putting in enough miles or effort or you are overindulging on carbohydrates or other foods. Carbohydrates are a great source of energy, but you still need balance in your diet. On that same note, you don't want to eat specifically high-protein content food and expect to have sufficient fuel or energy. Carbohydrates aren't bad (contrary to some popular diets), but they're very efficient forms of energy for your body. Carbohydrates are necessary for even the basic functions of your body and even provide fuel for your brain.

What to Eat, Why, and When – Simplified

The importance of what you eat, why, and when is not so obvious to runners and in some cases, even the venues in which we participate don't fully understand. For example, many events hold a pre-race (evening prior) pasta dinner. Typically this is white spaghetti that consists of an excellent carbohydrate content (usually 44-48 carbs per serving of 1-½ cups). This is great energy food, but the catch to this is the low glycemic index (GI) of spaghetti (38 on a scale of 100). Lower GI numbers require more time to digest and convert into energy (or glycogen) required by runners. In some cases, it may take up to 20 hours to fully process into glycogen.

Considering that the marathon will be starting in roughly 10-12 hours from the time you consumed your spaghetti, you only achieve minimal benefits from gorging yourself and thinking that you are fueling up. Foods with higher GIs and high carb content should be consumed the night prior where they don't require much in terms of digestion time to convert into glycogen. Potatoes and white rice are excellent examples of pre-race dinner foods that should be consumed the evening prior, as their GI numbers are high, and they have high carbohydrate content.

The Pre-Race Pasta Dinner: Does It Really Help?

Eating a large complex carbohydrate dinner the night prior (for a morning race) to a marathon is not recommended due to the amount of time it takes to digest and absorb nutrients and process the carbohydrates into glycogen. Since the process to convert these complex carbs can take 20 hours or more, the result is approximately 50% glycogen conversion or useful energy and 50% added weight that will be of future value. A light carbohydrate meal is fine the night prior, just don't gorge yourself with an evening pasta dinner.

In addition, running or exercise that consumes high amounts of glycogen will result in a slowed or stopped digestion/processing of solids. Therefore, the pasta dinner will not be fully converted until some time *after* the marathon. Prior to and during the event, stick with simple carbs, such as sports drinks and energy bars or gel energy packs.

Table 7.2 What to Eat and How Much

What to Eat When: *Training*			
What	**Why**	**When**	**Examples**
Carbohydrates	To charge your body with glycogen at the same level when you were depleting it from long training runs.	Two <u>and</u> three days prior to long runs and specifically during your peak mileage weeks.	Rice, pasta, bread, sweet potatoes, pancakes, mashed potatoes, corn.
Proteins	To repair damaged muscles.	Incorporate into your diet throughout training. Always after strenuous training runs.	Meat, eggs, milk, fish.
Calcium	To enhance bone density and strength.	Incorporate into your diet throughout training.	Milk, cheese, nuts, broccoli, leafy vegetables, supplements.
Fat	For energy storage. Each pound of fat = 3,500 calories of energy.	In moderation. Typically, every runner has ample body fat to support a marathon.	Fried foods, sausages, hamburgers, fatty meats.

Continued

Table 7.2 What to Eat and How Much (Concluded)

What	Why	When	Examples
Carbohydrates	To charge up your body with glycogen at the same level when you were depleting it from long training runs. You will need to store about 1,500 to 2,500 calories of glycogen initially taken in as carbohydrates. (This is about the maximum amount the body can store.)	Entire week prior to event and no less than 24 hrs prior to event. **DO NOT OVERLOAD ON COMPLEX CARBS THE NIGHT PRIOR**	When carb loading, don't try anything new, especially the night prior. Stick with the carbs that you know you can digest. I suggest bread, bananas, and cereal the morning of the race.
Proteins	To repair damaged muscles.	Some proteins the night before, but definitely the evening following your race.	Meat, eggs, milk, fish.
Hydration	To avoid dehydration. Dehydration reduces performance and can lead to a major issue if not treated early. Water will actually help in the conversion of carbohydrates into glycogen.	Begin serious hydration five days before, **but avoid over hydrating** the morning of the event. Otherwise, you will no doubt be in line for the porta-potties much of the pre-race, or you will be fighting off the urge to get rid of fluids during the first miles of the marathon.	Sport drinks, water.

What to Eat When: Preparing for a Marathon — column headers above: What | Why | When | Examples.

The specifics of what to eat and how much will vary by runner, the amount of mileage/week, weight, metabolism rate, etc. Most runners who put in 40- to 50-miles per week are usually entitled to eat just about anything they want. Runners should always ensure that they consume significant (high mass) and protein-rich meals after training, not beforehand. If you eat a significant meal less than one hour before a training run, prepare for some slow times. Digestion takes energy and time, and since the food hasn't been processed, it is just extra weight that you will be carrying. However, if you like bananas or easily digestible foods, you can eat "lightly" prior to a run, as it will provide additional energy toward the end of the run (due to the 30 minutes or more to enter into the bloodstream). From a nutritional standpoint, bananas are loaded with calories and carbohydrates and are easily digested. As such, they are sometimes considered to be a runner's/athlete's best friend.

Why Store Energy for a Marathon?

When running, your body uses a mixture of carbohydrates and fat for energy, both of which get converted into glycogen as a form of energy that the body can use. The higher your rate of consumption (or speed), the more carbohydrates you burn. When jogging at a slow pace (approximately two to three minutes per mile slower than M.P.), more fat is used for fuel than glycogen. This process works great for overweight individuals who want to shed a few pounds, but jogging doesn't do much for a runner to build speed or endurance. Some texts, therefore, have classified these low-intensity jogs as junk miles.

However, there is a one key point to note when running a qualification marathon that supports running a slower-paced first half. You will burn off less stored glycogen and more fat since you are not running at your lactate limits or pushing hard (reference lactate threshold. Chapter 4). The conservation of glycogen, as well as the reduction in buildup of lactate acid, will promote a stronger second half of your marathon.

Unfortunately for marathon runners, fat does not convert to energy as efficiently as carbohydrates. Thus, it is critical that your body has sufficient glycogen stores for energy throughout the marathon. When your body becomes depleted of these glycogen stores that have been building up for days/weeks from carb-loading, your body will slow down and could potentially hit the wall. For any marathon, specifically a qualification attempt, it is essential that you also take in some level of calories and carbohydrates during the race.

Figure 7.3 Eating the right foods will make a difference in your performance, but it can be confusing. Focusing on the right foods at the right time during training will enable you to obtain optimum fitness.

One easy method of taking on energy during the race is to consume gel energy pack(s). GU® and Power Gel® are two brands, and each comes in a variety of flavors. These gel energy packs will help to fill in for the depleted stores of carbohydrates and electrolytes. When taken with sugar-rich energy drinks provided during the run, you should be able to replenish your body with electrolytes for proper muscle function, as well as glucose for energy to fuel the muscles. Because of the gel form, these energy packs are easily absorbed into the body for quick energy. More detail on the importance of these gel energy packs and the appropriate time to take them is contained in Chapter 11.

Most events provide gel energy packs at Mile 17. Unfortunately, Mile 17 may be too late for some runners. If your body can support consuming these gel energy packs while running, I suggest taking them at five-mile intervals starting with the fifth mile. You will want to take in approximately 100 to 250 calories of carbohydrates each hour of the marathon (depending upon your weight). Each gel energy pack typically contains 120 calories, so that works out to about three or four for most marathoners.

When carbing up the night prior to the race (as well as race morning), do not take in an excess of complex carbohydrates. Since the body's digestive process slows during extended exercise such as running, the conversion from complex carbohydrates to glycogen will be slower than normal. Thus, most of this last-minute solid food that you consumed will become additional weight until you slow to a point when oxygen can be redirected to your stomach to support digestion.

Photo 7.4 Spiderman to the rescue with orange slices!

In some cases, spectators or marathon volunteers will provide oranges, bananas, or candy late in the race. Unless you're running at a slow pace, you will most likely see little benefit from these solid foods after Mile 20 or so, due to their moderate GI levels (oranges GI=42, bananas GI=52). However, some candies with high sugar content offer GI values of 70 or more and can provide quick energy. The hard part will be getting children to share the candy.

In summary, if you wait until you've hit the wall, your body will not recover in time to keep you on pace. Energy or fuel deprivation is much like dehydration. You shouldn't wait until you are out of energy to re-stock, nor should you wait until you're thirsty to replenish fluids. Look for these helpers and grab a few snacks early in the race...say Miles 5 through 20. Be selective, and choose the simple carbohydrates with high GI values, as that is where you will get the most benefit. Planning ahead with gel energy packs is the preferred method, so be sure to supplement your stored energy as it gets consumed.

What Is Proper Hydration?

When competing in a marathon, some runners may lose up to five or more pounds of water, depending on the layers of clothing, the temperature, and, of course, the initial weight of the runner. Dehydration will ultimately reduce running performance to varying levels depending upon the hydration deficiency. When a loss of body water is not adequately replenished, a runner may experience a five to six percent performance loss or a complete failure, if the dehydration becomes debilitating. It is expected that a runner will not be able to replenish all fluid that is lost during a marathon, but will be able to offset the effects of dehydration.

The body must have water to survive. Losing even seven pounds of water (approximately one gallon) can create a significant imbalance in your body chemistry, since the body consists of 70 percent water. Water also provides a very important function to a runner by cooling his/her body temperature. Much like the radiator of a car, water circulates through your extremities (in the form of blood and sweat), thus helping to regulate your body temperature, with wind being the cooling source. If you aren't cooling your body due to (low) fluids or you have dressed inappropriately for the temperature, your heart rate will increase the blood flow, or your body temperature will rise, or both. This results in a potentially risky situation, which may lead to heat stroke or exhaustion.

Photo 7.5 The effects of dehydration or heat exhaustion can bring a runner to a dangerous and quick stop. These runners avoid an unfortunate victim to the lack of proper hydration.

Water can be lost through perspiration and breathing during a race. Waiting to drink until you're thirsty on a warm day is too late, because dehydration has already set in. Some runners will pass many of the early fluid stations in a race to save time due to congestion, but they will feel the results of this poor judgment later in the race.

Drink early in the race, but don't overdo it. Drinking excessively a few hours before a marathon will only keep you in the porta-potty lines for most of the time before the race. Drink no more than 12 to 14 ounces of sports drink the morning of the race, along with a breakfast juice of choice.

The International Marathon Medical Directors Association (IMMDA) now recommends that marathoners should consume 13 to 27 ounces of fluid per hour (or four to seven ounces every 15 minutes). This quantity has dropped from higher levels in the past due to the potential exposure to hyponatremia. A sometimes fatal condition, hyponatremia is the result of overhydration, as it impacts the body's electrolyte balance—specifically, sodium deficiency. As you sweat, you lose both water and electrolytes, which can be carried out with sweat. You may witness a salty crust on your skin or clothes after a marathon or long training run. This is sodium or salt. When replenishing lost fluids with only water, your sodium levels drop, and if continued for extended periods, this could lead to hyponatremia.

Photo 7.6 Some runners walk to drink to ensure proper hydration.

Photo 7.7 For faster times you **must** learn to drink on the run.

Why Proteins?

Proteins are the nutrients found in meats, eggs, and dairy products. When consumed, the body converts and uses them in components of the body, such as muscles and bones. Protein provides two key elements to a runner by **building muscle** and **repairing muscle damage** from a training run or strength training, etc.

Protein in your diet is responsible for helping your muscles increase in strength. Protein is not typically recognized as an energy source. It does provide some energy value, but this is negligible when compared to carbohydrates. Runners need a daily supply of protein, which should comprise roughly 20% of their total caloric intake. Since proteins are the key resource for muscle strength and repair, it is critical to eat high protein content meals shortly after strenuous workouts.

Carbohydrates...What Are They?

Carbohydrates (carbs) provide the key energy source for runners. However, the body does not store carbs in their original form as an energy source. First, carbohydrates must be converted into glycogen, which comes in two forms:
- Glucose in the blood
- Glycogen stored in the muscles

During a marathon, the body uses these carbohydrates that have been stored in your muscles as glycogen. As this energy source is depleted, your body then uses the blood glucose (sugar stores). As you consume other carbohydrate-based foods, such as bananas, sugar-based candy, or sports drinks, your blood sugar will continue to provide glucose for energy sources to your muscles.

Storage of glycogen is built up over time as a runner trains. Amazingly, the body learns to store more glycogen when the muscles or blood are depleted of glycogen/glucose after completing long runs. If you eat a huge meal of carbs, a portion will go to glycogen to replenish what has been lost, and the remainder will get converted into fat where it can be used (less efficiently) at a future date. Essentially, the body stores what it needs in the form that best represents what recent usage has been.

Fuel for the Body: Facts

1. The body burns 100 to 120 calories per mile (approximately 3000 calories for a marathon)
2. The body can store approximately 1,500 to 2,500 calories from carbohydrates that are stored as glycogen in muscles or glucose in blood
3. You burn roughly the same amount of calories, whether you run fast or slow—the only variable is your rate of energy consumption
4. Each pound of fat contains 3500 calories
5. Each gram of carbohydrates provides 4 calories
6. Caffeine can enhance performance. However, since it is a diuretic, it can lead to water loss before and during a marathon. Stay away from caffeine products in the days before the race to ensure that you will be able to convert the necessary nutrients your body needs to sustain a qualification run, as well as getting the rest your body will require.
7. Foods with high GI convert carbohydrates into usable energy faster than those which are lower GI values. **Examples of high GI value foods are** white bagel or wheat or white breads (72-80),white rice (86), bran flakes (74), corn flakes (72), sports drinks (89), instant mashed potatoes (97), baked potato (85), pretzels (83)
8. Foods with lower GI levels and high carbohydrate values are excellent forms of energy for distance runners, as the energy conversion to glycogen spans over a longer period of time due to a longer digestion process. **Examples of low GI and high carbohydrate foods are:** noodles (46 GI/40 carb), white spaghetti (38 GI/48 carb), macaroni (47 GI/48 carb), chocolate cake (38 GI/52 carb)

The two forms of carbohydrates are simple and complex, and both are important in balancing your energy needs during a period of extended exercise, such as a marathon or event of greater physical requirement.

Simple carbohydrates are typically foods or drinks with sugar as the primary element. When ingested, these foods provide quick energy. If you've ever seen a four-year-old after eating a bag of cotton candy (100% pure sugar), you will relate to the level of energy that sugar provides. Again, unless you're planning to burn off these simple carbs quickly, they will take the form of fat, unless used. These instant energy foods are typically made with processed sugar and are found in soft drinks, chocolates/sweets, breads, potato chips, and other sugar-coated foods or snacks. Simple carbs, such as sweets and sports drinks, can easily replenish glucose during marathons. These simple carbohydrates typically have a high GI, which indicates they are quickly digested and converted into energy or glycogen.

Complex carbohydrates provide a better and more consistent source of energy for runners than simple carbohydrates. These complex carbohydrates take longer to break down and enter the bloodstream (as glucose) but provide a longer-life energy source, which is most beneficial for distance runners.

For example, think of a **simple** carbohydrate as a 1.5V AA battery and a **complex** carbohydrate as a 1.5V D-Cell battery. They both have the same power level (1.5 volts); however, one type (D or complex carbs) will last much longer. The body stores complex carbohydrates in both the liver and muscles as glycogen. Examples of complex carbohydrates are rice, pasta, potatoes, vegetables, beans, broccoli, and corn. As a runner, these foods are your "friend," and you should start to integrate them into your diet as you are increasing your energy demands.

As indicated, these complex carbohydrates take longer to digest and are measured typically at moderate or low levels of GI. Make sure you are accounting for the slower conversion into energy as you depend upon complex carbohydrates to support your training schedule.

Calories (Stored Energy)

A calorie is the numerical measure of the energy level in food, and in most cases it correlates well to the amount of carbohydrates in food (per 100 grams) at a ratio of four calories per carbohydrate. Table 7.8 provides the correlation of many common energy foods.

Table 7.8 Typical Foods that Runner/Athletes Use for Energy

HIGH CARB LEVEL		
Food Type	Calories (approximate)	Grams Carbohydrates (approximately per 100 grams)
Cereals (bran, corn flakes, rice)	300 - 380	80+
Breads	250 - 280	47 - 56
Crackers (whole wheat)	400	68
Dried pears	268	67
Pretzels	390	76
Prunes	255	67
Raisins	290	77
Pasta	400	76
Doughnuts	390	51
MODERATE CARB LEVEL		
Food Type	Calories (approx)	Grams Carbohydrates (approximately per 100 grams)
Cooked rice (white)	109	24
Corn	83	19
Nuts (peanuts, cashews, etc.), peanut butter	560	20 - 30
Bananas	85	22
Baked potatoes	93	21
Pancakes	231	34
Sweet potatoes	141	32
Sunflower seeds	560	20

When looking at energy intake and specifically carb-loading, you will need to be aware of the amount of the calories you are consuming and watch your weight during your training long runs. If you are gaining weight during your training phase prior to the taper, you may be consuming more calories than you are burning off, and the remainder is going to fat as unused carbohydrates. Just because you are running a marathon does not mean that you can eat as many calories as you want.

How Does Nutrition Reduce Your Susceptibility to "Hitting the Wall?"

Long runs train your body to store glycogen over a series of long runs. As the duration or distance increases, this conditions your body to delay the depletion of glycogen, thus becoming less dependent upon the fat stores, which are less efficient forms of energy. Since glycogen availability depends upon how much you have stored recently, you should start loading carbohydrates two to five days before your race date. Don't be concerned with a slight weight gain, since this is normal, and you will find that you will lose most, if not more than what you gain, due to fluid loss by burning the energy that you have stored.

Some running experts will recommend carbohydrate starvation at four or five days before the event, with carb-loading occurring roughly two days before the run. The body may store more glycogen by using this tactic, but some people may have more success than others. My personal rationale is that if I'm starving my body for nutrients it needs close to an event, I'm not going to risk it (my performance) on only a few days of high-carb consumption, until I see data that proves otherwise. There are too many factors that could limit your ability to focus carb-loading into just a few days (sickness, carb availability, travel, stomach disorders, etc). The conservative approach is to load while you can two to five days prior.

Electrolyte consumption also plays a factor in retaining your energy, as well as muscle functions during a marathon. Be sure to take in electrolytes during the marathon, since these vitamins (chloride, potassium, and sodium) need to be replenished during the race. As discussed in other areas in this chapter, sports drinks and gel energy packs are excellent methods of replenishing lost electrolytes.

Photo 7.9 Runners replenishing electrolytes on their way to a well-earned finish at Boston.

Vitamin Supplements

Runners, doctors, and anyone with an opinion on this subject will debate the value of vitamin supplements and the added benefit to a runner. The body absorbs only so much of specific vitamins and minerals and discards the surplus. Many vitamins provide 100 percent of the recommended daily allowance (RDA) for minerals that the body requires. You should, however, consult your doctor/physician for recommendations as to whether certain vitamin supplements will improve your performance or prevent certain injuries. Therefore, because of the subjectivity regarding the value of vitamins on an individual basis, I have opted not to make specific recommendations, but rather to inform you of the needs that an athlete may encounter. It is up to you to investigate further to determine applicability of your specific needs.

Fe

- **Iron**. Essential in promoting the abundance of red blood cells, which carry oxygen to your muscles. Iron is a critical element that is necessary for runners and athletes.

Ca

- **Calcium**. For healthy bones and the prevention of stress fractures, make sure you're getting an ample supply (one or two glasses of milk each day). I have personally experienced stress fractures and have transitioned from a low-milk diet (due to cholesterol) to a moderate milk diet, primarily to promote the bone density in my legs and feet.

Mg , K

- **Magnesium and potassium**. Both vitamins have a direct impact on muscle response (contractions), and a lack/loss of this mineral can lead to performance loss or cramps where the body is not able to reverse muscle motion or relax (un-contract) the muscles. A magnesium supplement in addition to a potassium-rich banana may help offset leg cramping or muscle cramping in general. Magnesium is available in cereals, nuts, raisins, meats, milk, and legumes. Potassium sources are cereals, fruits, potatoes, and some vegetables. Some Ironman athletes have been known to eat potato chips as potassium supplements to offset leg cramps during the running portion of the event.

Na

- **Sodium**. Sodium is a mineral that the body needs to have replaced during a marathon or prolonged exercise due to its loss associated from perspiration. Sports drinks usually provide ample sodium replenishment. Additional sodium supplements can be considered if repeated cramping occurs during marathons. Some runners may lose five or more pounds of sweat (consisting of water and sodium), which is evident by a crusty salt coating on their face, neck, or shirt. Each individual sweats at different rates. These rates and sodium losses are greatly temperature dependent, where the warmer temperatures require more replenishment. As a marathon runner, you should be aware of the potential benefits of sodium replenishment during a marathon, as water by itself will not be sufficient to sustain your chemical balance.

- **Caffeine**. Although not a true supplement, caffeine acts as an energy booster and is beneficial because it allows you to use more fat while running and less glycogen to extend your more efficient energy resources. Make sure you don't overdo your caffeine intake, as you can become easily dehydrated, due to its diuretic characteristics.

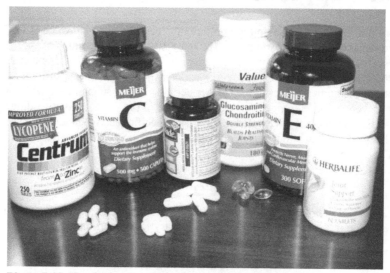

Photo 7.10 Hundreds of supplements are available on the market.

The debate continues about the benefit(s) of many supplements and their impact on improved health and fitness. However, it is now more commonly accepted that runners (or anyone else) can get all of the necessary nutrition from a good balanced diet. Some supplements such, as glucosamine and chondroitin, may provide more tangible results with decreased joint pain when running or walking. Other supplement needs may be adequately provided through a general multi-vitamin. However, as race day approaches, be sure to focus on your electrolyte intake and other nutrients or minerals that address any deficiencies you may have or expect to experience.

Race Day Nutrition

Pre-race nutrition (a typical breakfast)
- Energy bar – 100+calories
- Bagels/bread – high in carbohydrates and easy to eat before a run or race
- Bananas – moderate carb content, easy to eat before a run or race, and provides adequate calories (85-100) and necessary potassium
- Cereals – easy to digest and high in carbs

During-race nutrition. Your race pace strategy should be to run the race at a level in which you burn both fat and glycogen so that you conserve glycogen for later in the race. The speed work, tempo runs, intervals, etc., that you have been doing for the past few months will allow you to run at a lower glycogen burn rate. As a general rule, the higher the rate of exertion, the higher the glycogen burn rate ratio versus fat. In addition, you must be able to replace your lost carbohydrates (glycogen) during the race while you are running. This can be done by consuming sports/energy drinks and combining them with carb/gel energy packs or some candies. One strategy recommendation is to consume 25 grams of carbs every 45 minutes of exercise. This is accomplished by consuming one carb/gel energy pack at the following mile intervals during a marathon: 5, 10, 15, and 20. Gel energy packs are much easier to swallow if taken right before the fluid stations during the race. Once you see the drink station ahead, pull out your energy pack and "enjoy."

You'll notice that elite athletes have their own drinks along the route with their specific fluid mixture of carbs and electrolytes. Some races will allow non-elite runners to utilize these same stops, but you will need to ask. Family and friends are also a great resource if you know exactly where they will be along the course. In fact, you can save time at drink stops by being handed a 12 oz.–16 oz. squeeze bottle that will last four or five miles, depending upon the temperature. However, these bottles can be awkward to hold while running.

Post-race nutrition. Immediately following the race, not only will you need to re-hydrate, you will also need to replenish your carbohydrates and proteins. Most finish areas offer a wide variety of instant carbs, including bananas, chips, cookies, etc., as well as sports drinks. Be sure to use this free food as short-term nourishment for your body, as this will get you through the next hour or so until you are ready to replenish your proteins and complex carbs. This is the time to reward yourself with a steak, seafood, beer, or basically whatever you have avoided in previous weeks. However, be aware that should you have another race in the next few weeks to even a month away. Getting the much-needed proteins back into your muscles will expedite your muscle recovery and allow you to start training sooner than if you skipped on proteins in your post-race meals.

Photo 7.11   A typical post-event reward for a weary runner…bananas.
Photo Courtesy of Big Sur International Marathon, photographer Cath Tendler Valencia

Proper nutrition is definitely a factor that you have control over when seeking a Boston qualification marathon. The months prior, as well as the week prior, to the event are both equally important when considering your nutrition. The fuel(s) you select will prepare you for the demands of training and the critical energy balance when seeking a personal best marathon.

Chapter 8
The Strategic Taper

"Anyone can run 20 miles. It's the next 6 that count."
- Barry Magee, 1960 Olympic Marathon bronze medal

Photo 8.1 Will you have something left after Mile 20?

Although this is one of the shortest chapters of this book, it is by far one of the most important. Some say that a marathon is essentially two races in one: a 20-mile paced run followed by a grueling 10K. The outcome of the race usually depends on how you perform <u>after</u> Mile 20. Your performance is a reflection of both, how hard you have trained, and how effectively you have reduced your intensity and mileage during the final training weeks.

The taper is a gradual reduction of your weekly mileage to rest your body for an upcoming race. It is one of the most critical aspects of your training effort. An improper taper may cause you to fatigue on race day, with the potential result being a missed qualification attempt or injury.

The proper taper is something that can be learned, but better yet, you can follow the guidelines recommended for specific types of venues. For a marathon, you should run your final long (training) run a minimum of three weeks prior to your qualification attempt. If you don't adhere to this minimum guideline, you will learn firsthand what the ramifications may be, just as I did. I have included a personal experience to demonstrate what a deviation from the three-week rule can do to your race performance. I thought I knew myself better than the running experts. In short, I learned...they were right.

How to Use a Taper

All levels of runners will differ regarding the amount of time needed for a proper taper. Even Olympic athletes taper their training between marathons. They usually have a minimum of four months to sometimes more than six months between marathon races. Although they are putting in more mileage than us non-Olympic hopefuls, they, too, must ensure that their muscles are fully recovered to provide optimum performance. Through coaching guidance and experience, they train diligently during the months up to the event, but also still apply a taper prior to any major event.

Wanting to push myself to a Boston Qualification quickly, I elected to use a two-week taper in my first four marathons. I ran my longest training run (approximately 20-22 miles) two weeks prior to each race and found that my legs were fatigued and uncooperative in the final miles. On my fifth marathon, however, I decided to change to the three-week taper, and when miles 22, 23, 24, 25, and even 26 clicked off, I could not believe how fresh I felt. My legs actually had energy. I even managed to hold a strong pace for the last two miles. I finished the race with a negative split (a faster second half marathon) and a P.R.

There is clearly a huge difference between an 8:30min/mile marathoner and a 5:00 min/mile marathoner. However, proper training and taper remain critical for all runners to ensure you are 100% capable of your conditioning level on race day.

Adhering to the three-week taper on future marathons and feeling confident with the approach, I then pushed the envelope about what the long run should entail. In the process, I learned that the three-week rule also depends upon the level of effort exerted. There is a fine line between a training run and pushing yourself too hard on a training run.

Even though you are utilizing a three-week taper, don't think that a marathon (at three weeks) is an appropriate element of your taper regimen. Competitive venues are obviously different than a training run. The mood of the day is competition, and you will end up pushing yourself harder than intended. A mistake during your taper period can cost you a P.R. or, more importantly, a successful qualifying marathon. To reinforce the need to properly taper, I will painfully share a training error I made that resulted in extreme fatigue and a failed attempt for a P.R. My conditioning was exactly where I wanted to be, but my attempt at a proper taper was poorly executed.

My taper mistake. My ninth marathon (a training marathon) was planned just 22 days prior to a serious marathon and P.R. attempt. I planned for this event to serve as my long run, and from what I'd read, three weeks should have been adequate for muscle healing…or so I thought. Even though I held back in my ninth marathon, my time reflected a 94% effort versus my goal M.P. This pace, as I found out three weeks later, was far too aggressive and far too close to a critical race.

I quickly felt the effects of my over exertion early into my tenth marathon. By the time I was midway through, my legs and body were fatigued. I was forced to walk and jog the final eight miles just to finish. At Mile 15, as I watched the 3:00-hour pace group pass me, my only goal then was to "get this thing over with." If I would have run the ninth marathon a minimum of five to seven weeks prior and at a pace of M.P. +30 seconds, I would have been fully recovered. This was a humbling and disappointing experience, but it helped me understand the importance of a proper taper and how it is comprised not only of mileage, but also effort within the three-week (taper) window.

Using a Marathon as Training...Properly

It is possible to use a marathon for training if it is properly placed in your training schedule. Learning from my previous taper experience(s), I ran a full marathon and a half marathon at six weeks and four weeks respectively prior to a qualification attempt. I also moved both my longest run and my most aggressive speed work outside of the three-week (taper) window. The combination of these two changes to my marathon training and taper approach improved my strength and performance, which resulted in my best marathon ever. Specific timing of incorporating marathons outside of the taper period and the suggested training approach is covered in Chapter 4 and also Table 8.2.

Minimum Recovery Rule (marathon)

For recovery from a marathon, you should typically include one day of rest and/or mild training for every mile raced. You should rest for about a month before any significant effort is put into another timed event.

The following chart recommends a proper approach to tapering after your maximum long run and maximum interval training distances. Week three to six can be interchanged between speed-work and/or long runs, depending upon events and schedules. I do not recommend , however, alternating speed work with long runs within three weeks prior to race week. Should you find that your schedule allows no alternative, do not try to make up for it. You simply cannot cram for this test.

Table 8.2 Final Weeks of Training with Application of the Taper

Week(s) Prior	M	T	W	TH	F	S	S	Total Miles	NOTES:
3 Weeks	11 miles at M.P.	60 min bike --or-- 6 miles at M.P.	7 miles at **tempo** + 3 M.P. +30	7 miles at M.P. +30	4 miles at EP	20-22 mile **long run** at M.P.+30 with last 4 miles at M.P. (**NOTE:** if marathon was run at Wk6 or Wk7, reduce mileage to 20 max)	Rest	60-62	**HIGEST MILEAGE WEEK**
			**START OF THE TAPER**						
2 Weeks	5 miles at M.P.	60 min bike --or-- 6 miles at M.P.	7 miles at **tempo** + 3 at M.P.	Rest or 3-5 miles at EP	5 miles at M.P.	8 X 1 mile **Interval** at M.P.– 45sec min/mile	Rest	34-39	Interval run should be even-paced
1 Week	11 miles at M.P.	3 miles at M.P. +30	7 miles at **tempo** + 3 at M.P.+30	7 miles at M.P.	5 miles at EP	12-mile **long run** at M.P.	Rest	48	Eliminate cross training and weight training unless fending off injuries.
Race Week	7 miles at M.P.	5 miles at M.P.	3 miles at EP	Rest	Rest	**Race 26.2 miles**	Rest	41.2	Carbohydrate loading all week

Respecting the Taper

One of the most common mistakes by a runner is to run too fast or too long without allowing for a proper recovery period. Your muscles will break down when training aggressively. Low mileage weeks are vital to ensure that you've allowed your body to heal. You want your body (muscles and glycogen stores) to be fully recovered on race day. This is one of the primary purposes for tapering.

The last few weeks of training are just as critical as the months of training that you have put in prior to the taper.

Figure 8.3 provides an example of an adequate taper for proper recovery time before a qualifying marathon.

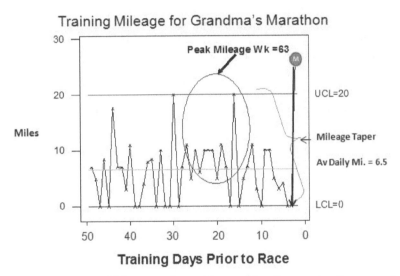

Figure 8.3 Training for a qualifying marathon with transition from peak mileage week to taper. UCL or upper limit in miles is 20 and LCL or lower limit in miles is zero or rest day.

Running Great in the Final 10K

Considering the marathon is actually two races in one, the taper approach is critical to your performance in the final miles. Here are a few key rules to ensure you perform as you intend to in the last 6.2 miles (or 10K) of a qualifying attempt.

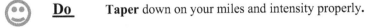

☺ <u>**Do**</u>   **Taper** down on your miles and intensity properly.

☺ <u>**Do**</u>   **Eat right** and carb-load the three weeks prior, and especially during the final week.

☺ <u>**Do**</u>   **Incorporate a long run** of more than the typical 20 miles in your training plan. Place this run three to six weeks prior (depending upon the distance). Training marathons should be kept to six or seven weeks out.

113

🚫 **Do Not** **Run your long runs at goal M.P.** Training is just that— training. It's not racing. Run at M.P. + 30 seconds to M.P. + 45 seconds for the majority of the run. You can mix in running at goal MP in the final 25% of your long runs. For example, on a 16-mile long run, the final 4 may be at goal M.P. to simulate race conditions and build your glycogen storage.

🚫 **Do Not** **Run 26 miles in a training race** less than 6 weeks prior to your qualifying run. You should keep the 20-mile long run at three weeks prior to your event. If you are utilizing a full marathon event as part of your training, run the 20-mile long run 3 weeks prior at M.P. + 30 seconds to M.P. + 45 seconds.

🚫 **Do Not** **Overeat** the day prior by attempting to car- load. Eat a moderate meal of carbs for lunch the day prior and a light carb and protein dinner that evening.

You will find that using a taper before your qualifying attempt will allow you to be well rested and properly conditioned for your marathon run. However, there is no exact, proper taper. It will vary by your weekly mileage, availability to train, illness, age, physical condition, and many other factors. The key is to respect how critical the taper will be to your qualification or marathon run. Don't waste your great training efforts and the sacrifices you've made with a poor taper.

The Race May Start in the First Mile, but the Marathon Starts at Mile 20!

Chapter 9   **Problems, Precautions, and Prevention**

"A time you appreciate running most is when you can't due to injury."
> - David Venable, Boston Marathoner

A number of things can go wrong leading up to or during a marathon. Some things are uncontrollable, like weather or an illness. Injuries or inadequate preparation issues may be avoided with proper attention while training. Unfortunately, most every runner deals with some issues or injury at some point in their running endeavors. Understanding how to avoid an occurrence and how to remedy the issue is a clear step toward maximizing your running time and efforts. Injury prevention is something that is learned as you mature as a runner — and unfortunately, to some novice marathoners (see above quote) it is *not* intuitive.

Photo 9.1 Understanding your physical limits versus the conditions you are competing (such as level of effort, temperature, hydration, etc) are critical factors that you will need to balance when running a personal best. This runner didn't find that balance.

This chapter focuses specifically on identifying a few of the possible running issues that you may encounter and providing you with information about how to avoid them. By minimizing risk or the likelihood of occurrence, you *will* improve your chances for a BQ.

Avoiding Running Injuries

It is very important that you are not injured during your marathon training, especially within the final eight weeks. An injury incurred during the final portion of your training, may jeopardize your BQ performance or limit you from running at all. **During these final training weeks when you are building up mileage and stress on your body, you are most susceptible to injury.** You will need to train smart, stick to the training plan, and take precautions to minimize risk of injury. It is critical in these final weeks that you are utilizing cross training as a regular component of your training plan.

I have experienced a few running injuries or obstacles, as you will read in this chapter, but more importantly, I have learned to understand why they occurred and how to avoid future susceptibility. As a future Boston qualifier, applying preventative approaches to your training should keep you focused on running and improving your performance instead of tending to injuries.

Tight muscles. Typically, tight muscles at the start of a workout are a result of inadequate stretching or warm-up. Tight muscles are not necessarily a problem, but they are an indicator of your limited flexibility. If not remedied by stretching and warm-up, this limited flexibility can increase the risk of ligament and muscle strains or tears when you continue your training effort. Many runners, unfortunately, approach stretching as an item of training that is not critical and can perhaps be cut short to a few minutes. However, as you progress into running more frequently and adding more distance, you need to ensure that you are also spending more time stretching to maintain flexibility. Yoga, Pilates, or similar stretching exercises can help marathoners maintain optimum flexibility.

To avoid tight muscles on a training run, start off the first mile at a warm-up jogging pace. After the first mile, stop to stretch your muscles thoroughly once they've warmed up. See Chapter 4 for recommended stretches. Although stretching prior to your run is important, stretching **after** your first warm-up mile, as well as your cool-down stretching, are most beneficial to improving flexibility. Stretches should be held for at least 30 seconds to achieve optimum benefit. In addition, be sure to stretch prior to any weight training, especially when exercising legs. Injuries to your legs/knees can occur when you are strength training, especially following a strenuous long run in recent days.

Sore muscles. Sore muscles are a result of not allowing adequate recovery between workouts or races. Much like any physical activity, if you train hard and stress your muscles, they will be sore. If you are sore prior to a run, re-evaluate the purpose of the training run for the day. If you are planning intervals or a long run, you should choose a cross training activity and adjust your plan to accommodate a re-schedule for the critical training missed.

Running aggressively on sore and recovering muscles will not allow them to heal properly, and you may be faced with an extended healing time. Sore muscles are a signal that you have increased your strength or endurance by tearing your muscle tissues. This is good. Building strength and endurance is the sole purpose for training, but you must allow your muscles time to recover. As part of that recovery, be sure that you have adequate protein in your diet before and immediately after strenuous workouts. If in doubt, rest your sore muscles and approach the next workout aggressively.

Blisters. These annoyances are caused by friction between your skin and an object, typically a sock or shoe. The blister is the result of the body trying to protect itself from the friction by putting up a shield of fluid.

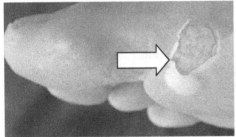

To avoid blisters, ensure that you have good-fitting shoes with ample toe room, but do not allow the foot to slide inside the shoe. Also, be sure there are no pronounced shoe seams that rub the side or top of your foot. The fit should be snug enough that your heel and the sides of your foot do not allow movement while running.

Photo 9.2 A torn blister can be painful.

If you run with a fold in your sock, you are almost assured a blister, especially on a long run. To avoid this, stop, loosen your laces, and adjust your sock to a proper fit. This may take some valuable time, but it will slow you further in a race as the blister becomes more painful.

If you find that you don't have a perfect fit for your shoe or you are getting blisters, socks are available in varying thickness to increase the shock absorption and minimize movement of the foot in the shoe. If you find that a blister occurs frequently in the same location, apply petroleum jelly over the area (especially between toes). You may also use bandages or synthetic protective skins to resist blistering. If you encounter a blister, it is best to let it heal naturally.

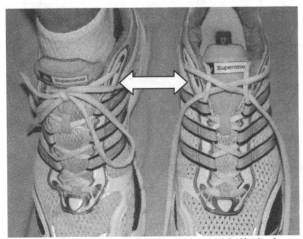

Another option to improve a poor-fitting shoe is to change the lacing path. By changing from traditional cross-lacing to a higher lacing path shown at left (left tied, right un-tied), this configuration yields improved ankle support. The higher tie point specifically leads to a tighter fit at the top of the foot to minimize foot sliding in the shoe.

The lacing configurations possible are numerous, and individual preference will vary. If you experience blisters, a better lacing path may be the remedy.

Photo 9.3 Lacing tie point raised to provide limited movement to the foot while providing ankle support.

Chafing. Most runners will undoubtedly experience chafing from clothing rubbing against the skin. Shorts, sports bras, shirts, jackets, or any garment that causes friction during the running motion is almost assured to cause chafing. Ensure that you are wearing the right type of material (avoid cotton) to minimize susceptibility to chafing. If the clothes don't wick away moisture, the moisture will make the material more abrasive. In some cases, chafing can also result from prolonged skin to skin contact in areas such as the under arm region and the inner thighs. Lubrication, like petroleum jelly, applied to the sensitive area can alleviate the damage caused by friction. You will know where to apply it after about 15 miles.

For males, shirt movement may cause chafing of the nipples. A bloody shirt on race day is easy to avoid. An occurrence will not slow you, but it can sting while you are running and can be a distraction to your rhythm or draw attention from the spectators. Round Band-Aids® are the easiest solution to this problem. The key to avoid chafing is to use your judgment as to what has worked for you on long runs and try not to deviate from that attire for your marathons.

Sunburn. In order to avoid sunburn, wear clothes that cover susceptible areas, as long as the temperature allows. If you are faced with a hot or sunny day, you should apply sunscreen with an SPF of 45 on the neck, face, ears, and all other exposed areas. A hat will offer some sun protection, but if it is a hot day, you don't want a hat to insulate the heat on your head. Visors or thin mesh hats are a better option to keep the sun off of your face on a hot day while keeping your head cool. Runners can be susceptible to skin cancer due to the combination of prolonged sun exposure and sweat-covered skin.

Strains. Defined as a pulled, twisted, or minor muscle tear, strains are often due to improper warm-up, lack of stretching, starting out too fast, and possibly over-stretching tight muscles. Strained muscles often remain sore for days, whereas sprains may hurt for weeks. If you have a strained muscle, the best recommendation is to rest and ice the injured area. Avoid running, and, instead, cross train with an activity that does not require use of the injured muscle.

Sprains. Sprains are a tear in a ligament or muscle fiber when stretched beyond the normal limit of movement. Sprains are typically evident by blood, which moves to the sprained area, discolors the skin, and then swells. The most common sprain for runners is the ankle. Sprains are sometimes a result of being careless, although it is not always easy to watch where you are stepping, especially if around traffic while running at night, or with a group of runners. Aside from the typical obstacles that runners encounter along the road side (parked cars/traffic, rocks, curbs, and even road kill) here are a few things to specifically watch out for:

- Running on uneven surfaces, like curbs to street transitions
- Running over or near potholes or areas with loose gravel
- Running on grass or trails where the terrain is unknown
- Running in unlit areas at night or pre-dawn

Two Important Rules to Stay Safe when Running at Night

1. **Only run where you are familiar with the streets or paths.** You should never try a new route at night that you haven't run during the day.
2. **Always wear a visor hat to block oncoming headlights.** You can easily lose your footing while being blinded by an oncoming motorist.

If you have encountered a sprain, you will most likely need to consult with a doctor. Wrapping the impacted area with a compression bandage and applying ice are typical recovery methods.

Stress fractures. Sometimes difficult to diagnose, stress fractures are a hairline break(s) in the bone that can result in a sharp pain when running. In most cases, you are not able to run without pain, nor should you. If you find that you can run but have a nagging pain that will not go away, you should see a doctor. Typically, a family practitioner will refer to you a specialist for proper diagnosis, including X-rays or an MRI.

Occurring commonly in the feet and weaker leg bones, stress fractures will put a runner out of commission for weeks or even months, depending upon the severity of the injury. Many times stress fractures occur without any warning. Drinking milk and taking vitamin supplements to strengthen bone density can help prevent stress fractures. In addition, the importance of well-cushioned shoes can make a significant difference in stress fracture prevention. If you have the opportunity to run on a trail (dirt, cinder, mulch, or sand,) or even grass a few times a week, the softer and more absorbent surface will significantly reduce the pressure and impact on your bones.

Tendonitis. Tendonitis can be described as a numbing or discomforting feeling that can be difficult to diagnose, especially when it occurs in the feet. There are many forms of tendonitis: they are found in the arch area of your foot, your knee area (iliotibial tendonitis), and also in the ankle (Achilles tendinosis).

Achilles tendinosis is considered one of the most common forms of tendonitis. It occurs in the Achilles tendon, which connects the heel of the foot to the calf muscle. The injury is apparent when discomfort above the heel is experienced when pushing off with your toes. To improve pain or tenderness, avoid running hills, strengthen your calf muscles, and reduce your running weight, if possible. Reduced weight lessens the tension on the tendon when pushing off on your running stride. This discomfort may gradually reduce after exercise or stretching. If the discomfort continues or becomes more painful, consult a physician, as the tendon may be torn, and the injury could easily worsen, if untreated.

If tendonitis in the arch of your foot is encountered, an effective treatment is to use a flexible compression wrap that fastens with Velcro and wraps around the arch area of your foot. It is best wrapped on the outside of your sock, due to the possibility of blistering. This compression wrap effectively supports the arch tendons to alleviate discomfort while running. Rest and icing after exercise will help to reduce inflammation.

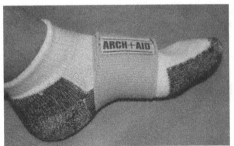

Photo 9.4 An Arch Aid will help in reducing discomfort of tendonitis of the foot/arch.

Various forms of Runner's tendonitis can be brought on by running in the wrong type of shoes, continuous pounding on pavement without mixing the pace or terrain, or rotating shoes. For a diagnosis, seek professional help, and always remember to see a qualified and credible shoe store for proper shoe selection.

Shin splints. This injury will commonly appear as an pain along the length of the tibia (the larger of the two lower leg bones) when you run. Shin splints, also known as Medial Tibial Stress Syndrome (MTSS), most often occur into the first few weeks of a training program or when mileage increases too drastically. Other potential causes of shin splints are tight and un-stretched muscles or improper shoe type, which can lead to imbalanced or strained muscles while running. Shin splints are more common with overpronating runners (inward roll) and may be corrected with motion control shoes and running on softer surfaces.

To avoid shin splints, it is suggested that you first ensure you have the correct type of shoe for your foot and stride type (pronation). You should keep your weekly mileage increase to no more than 10% and stretch your calf muscles prior to, during, and after workouts. You may also try to rotate your shoes or try different shoe brands (while keeping the correct pronation type) to reduce the discomfort. If the pain continues up to two weeks or worsens, you should ice the area after each workout and drop back in mileage.

Leg raises with ankle weights may help in some cases for reducing the discomfort of shin splints. Either seated or lying flat on your back, do leg raises with a five-or ten-pound ankle weight. Perform three sets of ten slowly as this will strengthen the anterior leg muscles.

Runner's knee. Runner's knee (chondromalacia patella syndrome) is a condition where the cartilage of the kneecap becomes worn and rough, resulting in an agitated (sore) and swollen knee. It is a common injury and afflicts most runners that run more mileage than the typical runner (over 30 miles per week).

Runner's knee will not usually go away on its own. You should reduce your mileage or move to cross training until you can run more comfortably. Icing the knee(s) after workouts is highly recommended. Numerous knee supports on the market can support the kneecap while training, like the neoprene wrap. This wrap (supplied with the knee cut-out) helps to stabilize the kneecap motion and keep it tracking correctly as you run. Other wraps, such as a lateral "J" buttress support, actually pull the kneecap (patella) inward to force an improved alignment while walking or running.

Runner's knee is often diagnosed by the pain or stiffness that is felt after an individual has been sitting for a period of time, as well as pain or discomfort when running downhill or walking down stairs. This pain is usually located behind or around the kneecap.

Runner's knee can be caused by shoes that lack support or from weak inner or major thigh muscles. These muscles aid in aligning your kneecap for proper tracking during running. Running will strengthen the hamstrings but may cause an imbalance in the muscles that support the knee. This imbalance may cause the kneecap to track improperly and wear away cartilage. Runner's knee can also be experienced when an individual has increased mileage too aggressively or has been running on uneven surfaces, causing the kneecap to move off track.

Photo 9.5 Knee supports help in alleviating the discomfort of runner's knee.

Wraps are not considered a long-term solution but may allow you to continue to train more comfortably at reduced mileage. Numerous types of knee supports are on the market, and you may need to experiment with various types until you find a match for your injury. Again, the best advice with any injury is to seek professional medical direction. A sports medicine center is highly recommended.

Leg lifts are good exercise for alleviating the discomfort and improving your muscle balance. While laying flat on the ground with feet pointed up, lift each leg up approximately 12 inches at the heel slowly. Do three sets of ten for each leg. For inner thigh muscles (This example is for the right leg) lay on your right side and lift your right leg until your heel is about 12 inches above the ground. Slowly complete three sets of ten. Alternate legs and add five-or ten-pound ankle weights to increase the resistance.

In addition, ensure that you are stretching your calf muscles and hamstrings daily, even when not training. Reducing the tension of tight muscles that support or pull on the kneecap will eventually improve your (patella) tracking.

Knee discomfort/general. As a mid-lifer who struggled with knee pain early in my running efforts, I found a supplement that allowed me to continue to run and build mileage without pain from runner's knee. Glucosamine is an over-the-counter supplement that rebuilds and repairs worn or damaged cartilage. Glucosamine usually becomes effective in just a few weeks. Most doctors will say that you cannot add cartilage, but glucosomine will improve the knee joint's tolerance of running and training. A common product on the market is a mixture of glucosamine and chondroitin. These supplements are expensive, but they are worth the value if you are experiencing sore knees. Other supplements are also on the market to ease knee pain that have been produced to help the elderly with cartilage loss. If you opt to use one of these products and do not see noticeable results within three to four weeks, you should seek professional help.

Iliotibial band syndrome (IBS). IBS is experienced as pain on the outside of the knee and is caused by tightness (inflamation) of the band that joins the pelvis to the shin bone. This band's purpose is to stabilize the knee during movement. IBS is typically the result of irritation due to overuse. Rest, combined with a reduction of miles and application of ice after you run, is the best remedy. Leg raises, which focus on the inner and outer leg and thigh muscles, will help to strengthen muscles. Stronger muscles will reduce the dependency on the band to support the leg and hip muscles. Before and after you run, it is imperative that you stretch properly to reduce the occurrence of IBS.

Plantar fasciitis. Most runners detect this injury when they first step out of bed in the morning and experience piercing pain in their heel. The pain is due to torn or inflamed tendons that connect the heel to the ball of the foot. Plantar fasciitis can be caused by pointing the foot too far inward on your stride and/or running mostly on your toes, where in either case you are stretching the arch tendons beyond their normal range.

Again, ensure that you have been fitted with proper shoes to address the needs of your stride. Should you experience plantar fasciitis, numerous remedies may help. It has been found that massaging the bottom of your foot and wearing wraps that stretch leg, foot muscles, and ligaments when sleeping can improve symptoms. Rolling your foot over a ball or cylinder will help to stretch the muscles and improve flexibility. Icing the foot and a daily massage are suggested methods for healing plantar fasciitis. If your symptoms are persistent, you should seek a diagnosis from a medical professional before continuing with your training.

Bruised bones. Doctors are now finding through more frequent use of MRI scanning that bone bruises are more common among distance runners than initially thought. Bone bruises (contusions) rarely reach the point of pain, due to the body's ability to heal after a marathon or long run. However, over a long and constant running season, the bruise may worsen until your pain threshold is reached. Bone bruises occur in the knee joint, where pounding or running at a constant rate of speed has focused the impact on a specific area.

Similar to a stress fracture, the pain will stop a runner on very short notice. Sometimes changing pace may help temporarily. The pain should quickly fade if you slow to a walk, as you have changed your angle of contact on your knee. A key indicator of a bone bruise can be when pain occurs when walking up steps or a curb as you pass through the sensitive impact point of contact from running.

Doctors cannot predict how long it takes for a bone bruise to heal, and in some cases it may be months or more, depending on the severity of the injury. To remedy the injury, cross training and rest is recommended. You should also seek softer shoes and a very gradual return to running (on soft surfaces), with continued icing on the area after the runs as it heals. Ensure that you are rotating between at least two pairs of shoes during your active training, as in most cases it will take a shoe an extended period of time (about 24 hours) to re-achieve full cushioning. It is suggested to number or label shoes and allow for off-days for your shoes, even when walking or cross training. Surprisingly, the compression on the shoe requires time for recovery, much like a runner does.

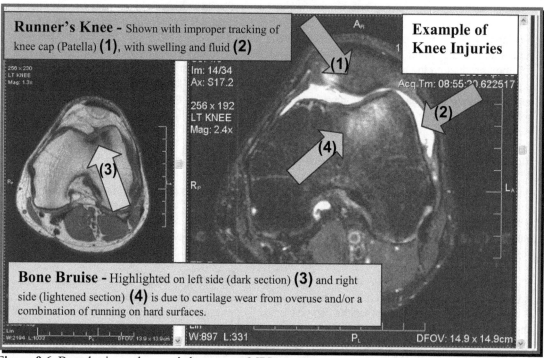

Figure 9.6 Bone bruise and runner's knee on an MRI scan.

Figure 9.6 illustrates two overuse injuries, bone bruise and runner's knee. In some cases, a bone bruise may be the result of worn cartilage that has gone undiagnosed as runner's knee, and continued use may lead to a sudden and painful bruise behind the wear area (see area 3 or 4 in Figure 9.6). These injuries can be avoided by running on a cushioned surface whenever possible and incorporating cross training in to your training plan. Having trained for a January marathon with only an indoor 1/12th -mile cushioned track and elliptical due to cold winter temperatures, I developed a bone bruise a few weeks before my marathon (just after my 20-mile long run of 240 laps). Continuous repetition on an indoor track (even if padded) or treadmill can cause a bone bruise, due to running at a constant angle and speed. Be sure to mix your indoor training with outdoors, when your schedule allows. Always remember to ice the sore knee(s), as swelling and irritation in the knee could exacerbate an issue and lead to increased cartilage wear.

Headaches/general pain. Due to the combination of sunny conditions and raised blood pressure from running, you may experience a headache during a race. It's a good idea to run with a few pain relievers tucked away in a pocket. You may wish to consult with a physician as to what type of pain reliever to take during or prior to a marathon that is safe for your medical condition. I personally recommend that runners stay away from blood thinning pain relievers due to the potential for blood in urine.[1] Acetometophine will not act as blood thinning drug and will provide pain relief similar to ibuprofen. For any pain experienced in the chest area or arms, you should seek immediate medical assistance.

Blood in urine (hematuria). Dr. Tim Noakes M.D., author of *The Lore of Running*, has stated various reasons for blood in urine. During extended periods of exercise, such as long runs and marathons, the blood vessels of the kidney can allow passage of larger blood cells and is termed red cell leakage. In addition, bladder trauma due to running may also cause blood in urine as the bladder becomes bruised and also allows for the passage of red blood cells. According to Dr Noakes, this blood leakage into the urinary tract in both cases can be corrected when exercise stops.

If You Are Injured

Without question, first and foremost seek the proper diagnosis from a medical professional. If you are unable to find a doctor who can diagnose your injury or if a doctor tells you to stop running, you should consult with other runners for professional medical recommendations such as orthopedic specialists or doctors in sports medicine. In some cases it may take a few visits to different doctors or specialists, but finding a doctor who understands the psychosis of a runner/athlete is highly recommended. This type of doctor will understand what it means if they tell you to stop running.

If you experience an injury during a marathon, you should stop and evaluate the consequences of continuing your race. Taking a ride on a medical vehicle to the finish may be the smartest decision a runner can make, but this will be a difficult decision to a marathoner. If an injury occurs, don't compromise your ability to train or run just to say you finished. A runner's pride is sometimes stubborn, but a smart runner knows when to stop.

One of the most difficult aspects of an injury, especially during your marathon training, is accepting that you must take ample time off from running to recover. The healing period is contingent upon many factors. As with any injury or illness, however, you should maintain a positive outlook and train however you can. A good way to maintain your fitness is to cross train by cycling, water training, or fast walking. Try to stay in good cardiovascular shape so that once you start running again, your recovery time to your previous fitness level will be minimized. You should also watch your caloric intake while you are injured. This is an easy time to put on a few pounds that may make recovery even more difficult.

The most important way to reduce injuries is to recognize the early warning signs your body is providing. You may encounter a few minor pains that show up early during a training run, especially within the first half mile. These pains are typically a good indicator that you didn't adequately warm up. When you encounter a new pain in your legs or feet, you should slow down or jog, if it is bearable to do

---

[1] An unexpected injury happened to me while training with a long run of 20 miles. At the conclusion of my run, I experienced blood in my urine and immediately sought professional help. The medical diagnosis was mixing blood-thinning pain killers (taken for foot pain) with an extreme workout where blood pressure and heart rate were elevated. The result was a ruptured blood vessel in my kidney. The corrective action was to move away from ibuprofen when exercising and use acetaminophen for needed pain relief.

so until the pain subsides. If the pain persists after you have slowed to a jog or stopped to stretch, use your judgment to decide if you should continue.

Muscle Cramps and Fatigue

Muscle Cramps

Although muscle cramps are not truly defined as an injury, they are considered a major detriment to your running ability when they occur. My first marathon was unhindered by muscle cramps of any kind. However, as I began to participate in more marathons and push myself harder, I started to experience painful calf and hamstring cramping and began to wonder why they were occurring, as they definitely impacted my finish time.

These muscle cramps (calf and hamstring) soon became my greatest obstacle in running marathons at my goal M.P. I spent a significant amount of time investigating how and why I get them and the potential causes. I uncovered a few credible reasons and concluded there was no single cause, but rather a combination of many factors. In addition, many texts are inconclusive as to the definitive cause(s) of leg cramps, as runners may vary greatly in their susceptibility.

There is one factor, however, that may be a larger contributor to leg cramps than the other issues stated herein: one is not physically conditioned well enough to run at the pace demanded. To quote Dr. Noakes in *Lore of Running* "Exertional cramps tend to occur in people who run farther or faster than the distance or speed to which they are accustomed." Furthermore, Dr. Noakes defines cramps as "spasmodic, painful, involuntary contractions of muscles." I tend to agree with his definition from a doctor's description, but as a runner, they hurt like heck!

Photo 9.7 A runner with quadriceps cramps at Mile 20.

This is typically the distance where they (cramps) may start to occur during marathons. Unfortunately, these painful leg cramps can occur without any advance warning and can stop you in your tracks, causing a loss of precious seconds or minutes. A trigger situation such as an abrupt change in terrain, combined with the added loss of electrolytes, may cause your legs to unexpectedly "lock up." If you sense a cramp is eminent, slow down first before you stop, or walk to save time during a qualifying marathon.

In my first ten marathons (see Table 9.8), I experienced leg cramps in 60% of the races and at various distances during the race. Each time they occurred, my pace slowed or I came to a complete stop due to the pain. My personal experience shows that cramps were encountered after Mile 20 and were brought about by something as simple as a change in posture, terrain change, or a sudden imbalance. However, I also believe that the combination of these factors, as well as your physical condition (training preparation as per Dr. Noakes), or any electrolyte imbalance can exacerbate your fatigued condition and may lead to cramping.

Table 9.8 A History of Leg Cramps During my First Marathons

Venue	Cramps Experienced	Mile	Terrain at Cramp(s)
Indianapolis (IN)	None	-	
Grandma's (MN)	**Yes**	**25**	**After a hill***
Big Sur (CA)	None	-	
Grandma's (MN)	**Yes**	**25**	**After a hill* (same as above)**
Chicago (IL)	**Yes** (Mild Cramps)	**25**	**Slowed at hill***
Disney (FL)	**Yes**	**24-25**	**Flat**
Boston (MA)	**Yes**	**20**	**Top of Heartbreak Hill**
San Diego (CA)	None	-	
USAF, (OH)	None	-	
Chicago (IL)	**Yes**	**25**	**After a hill* (same as above)**

Note: In these venues a hill* was a highway overpass

Causes of muscle cramping – a personal consensus
Muscle cramps
- do not typically occur on a training long run, due to the slower pace and lower level of energy or oxygen consumption.
- will usually occur after Mile 20 in a marathon.
- can occur when not properly trained for the level of energy output.
- can occur when there is a change in terrain (hills) on where balance changes. Leg muscle usage shifts can trigger cramps late in a race.
- can occur with electrolyte imbalance. Electrolyte loss has shown to be a factor in cramping for endurance athletes like runners and tri-athletes.
- can occur due to lack of stored energy. Muscles use carbohydrate stores in the form of glycogen. Glycogen is utilized in muscle contraction as an energy source. Since glycogen is the energy source, it could be a contributor to cramping when energy is reduced.

Preventing muscle camps
1) **Stretch the muscle(s) that predominantly cramp** – If you are on a training run, stop and stretch periodically. The rest will replenish nutrients and oxygen to your tired muscles. If on a qualification run, you may not have the luxury of stopping so frequently. However, thirty seconds spent stretching at Mile 20 may save you three or four minutes over the remaining miles of a marathon.

2) **Train at a speed faster than you plan to run for your M.P.** – This speed work will condition your muscles (and cardiovascular system) for strenuous demands.

3) **Train with distance farther than the "normal" marathon plan of 20 miles** – I've never encountered cramps during a training run and have concluded the amount of effort exerted does have some impact on your susceptibility to cramps. The incorporation of a long run of 26 miles or an actual training marathon at six to eight weeks prior to your marathon will help to improve your resistance to cramps.

4) **If you encounter cramps, change your running style** – Shorten your stride and slow your pace to allow your muscles to recover. Avoid coming to a full stop. This will only cause the muscles to lock-up during the later miles of a marathon. Due to the increased susceptibility of

cramping on hills late in a marathon, a suggested venue would be one that offers a downhill or flat course for the final 6 miles.

5) **Electrolyte imbalance and/or supplements**
- **Magnesium and potassium** – These mineral deficiencies have been proven to impact muscle response. It is recommended on race morning and the two days prior to the marathon that you incorporate two bananas or equivalent source(s) rich in potassium and magnesium into your diet. Also, consume sports drinks as part of your daily intake a few days in advance, and definitely consume sports drinks during your marathon race for these critical electrolytes.
- **Calcium** – Calcium supplements have been known to help ward off muscle seizures. Incorporating milk or a daily calcium component into your diet within a few weeks of the marathon will help to ensure a more proper mineral balance.
- **Sodium** – Experts argue regarding the impact of a loss of sodium leading to cramps. Some runners may lose four to five pounds of sweat (combination of water and sodium) when running a marathon. For this reason, we cannot fully discount sodium loss as a cause of muscle cramping. Sodium supplement(s) may help, but drinking sports drinks during the marathon should replace the majority of sodium loss.
- **Iron** – Blood rich in iron increases the oxygen content of your blood and, thus, will improve your performance. Iron supplements can reduce the possibility of low oxygen levels as a contributor to cramps if your body is iron deficient.

Fatigue

Fatigue and performance. Every individual is different in body chemistry, muscle composition, and their motivation to perform. When fatigued, however, we will all tend to slow. The effects of air travel (delays) or stressful travel the day prior to a marathon may have a negative impact on race day performance. To ensure fatigue is kept to a minimum, I would recommend traveling at least two days prior to the event date to allow for rest and recovery and time zone adjustments. In addition, arriving earlier to a venue allows time to leisurely work through the marathon expo, seek out restaurants of your choice, and enjoy a marathon vacation.

Sleep deprivation and performance. My initial suspicion was that sleep deprivation (the night prior) was a contributor to poor marathon performance. After researching the relationship, however, I found a very low correlation between amount of sleep the night prior to a marathon and the resulting overall time to complete it (Figure 9.9). Statistically, this personal data resulted in a low correlation (20.1% out of a possible 100%) between sleep (hrs) and the resulting finish time (min). This suggests that the amount of sleep the night prior to the event is not critical, but obviously the more sleep you have, the better rested you will be. In each of these events, I had a solid seven to eight hours sleep two nights prior to the marathon. It is therefore suggested that the amount of sleep two nights prior to an event is equally or more so critical to performance.

While it is okay to have some pre-race jitters the night prior to your qualifying attempt, make sure you get as much rest as possible for the two consecutive nights leading up to the race. Noisy hotels or makeshift lodging the night prior to a marathon can be a stressful occurrence to a would-be qualifier. Be sure to pack ear plugs and maybe a travel fan for cooling or perhaps a calming noise. If you are a heavy sleeper, bring two travel alarms so that you rest free of concern. It is important to make sure you eliminate all reasons why you might lose sleep the night(s) prior. As you enter into your evening sleep the night prior, end your thoughts with the reassurance that you did your training well and will run a smart race. This may be a good opportunity to change your focus to develop a mantra for race day such as..."Run smart "..."Nothing left in the tank"..."Don't doubt,...do"...etc.

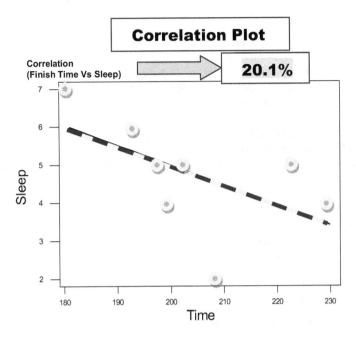

Figure 9.9 A statistical relationship between (hours) sleeping and marathon time (minutes).

Energy Deprivation

Running out of energy (hitting "the wall") after you have trained for months or years for an event can be very disappointing. Fortunately, it can be avoided by ensuring that your body has the appropriate nutrients by stockpiling this energy through focused training and proper nutrition. Your body needs fats, carbohydrates, and proteins to function during the day, as well as during a marathon. The relationship between nutrition and training is a balance that has to be taken seriously, otherwise you may find your first qualifying attempt very challenging.

If you have participated in a marathon or have watched from the sidelines, Miles 20-26 typically show you who has come prepared to run with a balanced approach to tapering, nutrition, and training. Simply eating spaghetti at the pasta dinner the night prior to the race is not the proper nutrition your body needs. As stated in Chapter 7, the pre-race pasta dinner event has limited benefit on race day due to the time required to convert complex carbohydrates into useful energy.

> **The energy content of most foods is defined as the amount of calories that are contained in one serving. The unused energy is converted to fat for future energy needs.**

Carb-Loading Prior to the Race

Beginning three to five days prior to the marathon, you should eat at least one meal per day that is high in carbohydrates. Since you are now running less mileage, or tapering, your body will store more glycogen. This storage of glycogen is due to fact that you are now burning off fewer calories and your body is storing the glycogen at the level it was demanding just days/weeks earlier from the long runs. Rice, pasta, bread, potatoes, pancakes, and corn are all excellent sources of carbohydrates.

Pre-Race Energy

Most marathons typically start in the early morning hours between 6 am and 7 am. It is advisable to eat a light-to average-sized breakfast consisting of juice, breads (bagel), banana, and cereal. Each of these is high in carbohydrates and easily digestible. Do not eat an excessive breakfast because, in most cases, what you are eating will not be processed into energy until after the marathon. In addition, gorging yourself with breakfast can lead to stomach problems along the way.

Before the race, you should consume between 200 and 500 calories of carbohydrates. It is advisable to get this into your body at least two hours before race time. One important element in pre-race eating is not to eat something you don't normally have for breakfast, due to potential indigestion. If a normal start to the day includes coffee, drink coffee.

On the way to the event, it is also advisable to take an energy drink or water with you and an additional energy bar. Most energy bars are quickly absorbed and converted into glycogen before the race. The combination of an energy bar and breakfast should be adequate for pre-race fueling. Many marathoners also consume a gel energy pack in the starting corral to "top off" the electrolytes prior to the start.

Typical Contents of a Pre-Race Energy Bar

Sodium	95 mg
Potassium	200 mg
Carbohydrates	45 gm
Protein	10 gm
Electrolytes	320 mg
Calories	230

During the Race (Energy Re-Fueling)

Some runners mix their own energy drink(s) and strap these small bottles to a running belt. The elite runners have their energy drinks placed at pre-determined tables on the course. The majority of the runners resort to consuming gel energy packs and the race-provided energy drinks to meet their energy (re-fueling) needs during the race. My personal recommendation for fueling during marathons is to carry three or four gel energy packs to provide the added electrolytes and carbohydrates needed. It takes the body only a few minutes to process the gel energy pack into usable glycogen for muscles.

Your body can store as much as 1500 to 2500 calories of glycogen and will require roughly 100 calories per mile during the event. Once you have depleted your glycogen stores, your body starts to consume fat in a much less efficient manner, and this poor fuel source will reduce your speed. It is critical during the race that you replenish your lost calories with gel energy packs or drinks. I personally recommend taking in a gel energy pack at the following mile intervals: **first** at five miles, **second** at 10 miles, **third** at 15 miles, and **fourth** at Mile 20. Most events provide a gel energy pack at Mile 17 if you wish to carry fewer. I've consulted with other runners who take in seven or eight gel energy packs during the race, while others can't digest them or avoid them altogether.

Typical Contents of Gel Energy Packs

Sodium	45 mg
Potassium	45 mg
Carbohydrates	26 gm
Calories	120

Photo 9.10 A sample of the plethora of sports and energy products available. I personally do not use an energy drink that could increase heart rate, especially while running-training. Non-caffeinated sports drinks or water, and gel packs are a better choice for cardio exercising/training.

Consuming more than four gel energy packs may be overkill, and you may wish to start with two or three to see how your stomach reacts to food while running. If it is a cold day, the energy packs may be thick and hard to swallow. If that is the case, take them just prior to the water stop so that they are easier to wash down and swallow.

Race Conditions

Temperature

Weather is always a factor in your performance, due to the body's survival-need to adjust to extremes. Race days that are cold, hot, rainy, too windy, snowy, and even too sunny can all negatively impact your qualification attempt. Ideally, you want an overcast day, no wind, a starting temperature of 48°F-50°F, and a finish temp of 55°F. These conditions represent an ideal situation and should provide an excellent opportunity to set a P.R. to obtain that BQ time.

If it is a cold morning but the temperature will increase significantly as the race progresses, you should dress for the mature race conditions. This means you may be cold at the start and perhaps the first few miles unless you wear clothing that can be discarded along the route. Running in long pants or tights if the temperature is 40°F-45°F at start time will overheat your body later in the race as temperatures rise into the 50°F to 60°F range. The sun will also have a warming effect even if the temperatures stay lower, and the air may feel ten degrees warmer in the sun. For these reasons, wear discardable layers on your chest, gloves on your hands, and a hat for those cold mornings. As the day heats up, you will be glad you have opted for shorts. For higher temperature races, dress at a minimum and definitely stay away from cotton. Always remember to dress for the event at 20°F warmer than race start temperature. For example, if the race start temperature is 50°F when you are running, you should dress for being comfortable at 70°F when you are not running.

Photo 9.11 Women marathoners dressed appropriately for a start in the 40s at the 2008 Olympic Trials in Boston. Sunny conditions and cool temperatures provide a mix in choice of hats, gloves, and light discardable jackets. Note the approach of eventual winner Dena Kastor (#1) to the conditions: shorts, hat, gloves, and sunglasses...Dena knows!

Wind and/or Rain

Encountering wind or rain on race day will definitely have an impact on your results. If you happen to encounter a headwind, it is legal to tuck in behind another runner and draft. You may even choose to find a group of runners to shield the wind. Drafting will save energy and will psychologically keep you motivated to stay on pace with the other runners. Keep in mind that if you are running around a 7:30 min/mi. pace, you are generating an 8 mph (minimum) headwind. When running unshielded (in the open), your running pace is added to the headwind; and even a headwind of five to ten mph can add to your energy consumption. Drafting within your pace group is a smart way to conserve both mental and physical energy.

If rain is encountered or expected during the event, you should try to keep your socks and shoes as dry as possible. Socks will act like a sponge, and the added weight will slow each stride and make your feet more susceptible to blisters. If windy conditions are expected with rain, a very light water-repelling jacket is recommended. Furthermore, a low-cost plastic jacket may be a good compromise to a premium material jacket if you need to discard it later in the run.

Personal Experience: Temperature

Race conditions have both positively and negatively affected my own marathon performance(s). Figure 9.12 illustrates the ambient temperatures during my first eight consecutive marathons. This chart should open your eyes to the impact that ambient temperature has on performance if you haven't already experienced it for yourself during training. Avoid venues that have either high or low ambient temperatures when seriously attempting a qualifying marathon.

Ambient Temperature Vs Completion Time Vs Months in Training

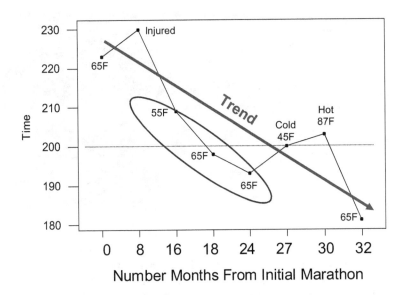

Figure 9.12 Finishing temperatures of 55°F-65°F and starting temperatures of 48°F-55°F offer good temperature range to run a marathon. Keeping your body cool with temperature is much more conducive for a fast time than using your heart/blood and perspiration for cooling.

During my sixth and seventh marathons, the weather was clearly a factor in my performance (see Figure 9.12). Race number six was held with a start temperature of approximately 40°F-45°F, for which I selected long pants, multiple shirts, gloves, and a hat. Although my body temperature was comfortable early on, the ambient and heavier clothing later raised my body temperature. My body was forced to use my heart to cool my body by increasing my heart rate and blood flow. Even though it started as a cool day, the heat (due to improper clothing) negatively impacted my performance.

Conversely, race number seven was my first Boston, and the temperature midway through the race reached 87°F with high humidity. This level of heat was definitely an anomaly for Boston in April. Because of the heat, I had to focus on finishing instead of using it for a qualification run for the following year. The heat affected me, but not as much as the hundreds who required medical attention that day. Some experienced heat exhaustion, vomiting, and other heat- related symptoms.

In contrast to races number six and seven, race number eight in San Diego offered perfect running conditions with, the finish temperature between 60°F-65°F with overcast skies and zero wind. These excellent conditions and my preparation resulted in an unexpected personal best. The variations in my conditioning between the two months was not significant enough to account for a 22-minute differential in time. I attribute a portion of the performance improvement to race time temperature. Again, if the temperature does not allow for a legitimate qualifying attempt, it is better that the runner use that race as a learning or training event and build for the next event.

Hydration

As a runner, it is vital that you are properly hydrated for a marathon prior to, during, and even after your race. Hydration is especially critical in hot and humid conditions. One common mistake for new runners is consuming to much fluid, which typically leads to a relief stop during the race. This may take valuable seconds or even minutes, if you are forced to wait for a portable restroom.

Only through experience did I start to limit my fluid consumption on race morning to approx 12-14 ounces of an energy drink and use of the water stops along the course. If you are able to get four to five ounces of fluid per mile or two, you should be adequately hydrated. If it is a hot day, your consumption should be more. If you find that you are "sloshing" when you run, you are taking in too much water.

Photo 9.13 Most times, there just aren't enough…

You should plan to consume fluids throughout the race to replenish your losses from sweat. Be realistic at the beginning of a race as to what your consumption should be. I once met a runner who consumed over one liter of water just before the start of the race so he didn't have to stop for at least the first five water stops. Not surprisingly, he commented that he tended to "slosh" when he ran for the first few miles. I see a few downfalls to this approach in the added weight and potential discomfort while running.

If you have to slow or walk to drink fluids, you could lose up to ten seconds per stop. This totals about three minutes of stopping time during the race. I highly recommend taking a shortened straw just to ensure that you get enough water into your body without needing to walk. By quickly inserting the straw into the cup and closing off the lid to the cup, you are free to drink when you need to without spilling. When you are finished, simply slide the straw back under your running watch. You may find this hint especially helpful when you are running hard, as that is when it is most difficult to drink.

Hyponatremia (Low Blood Sodium)

A health risk is associated with drinking too much water, or overhydrating. Runners who drink the day prior and stop at every fluid station along the course may risk hyponatremia if they drink more than what they lose through sweat. This condition can lead to nausea, fatigue, vomiting, weakness, sleepiness, and, in severe instances, seizures, coma, or death. To avoid hyponatremia, try not to drink more than you sweat, include bread or pretzels in your pre-race meal, and drink sports drinks instead of water to increase your sodium intake.

According to the American Medical Athletic Association ("The Right Way to Hydrate for Marathons," - Q&A Sheet provided at the 2008 Boston Marathon), exercise-associated hyponatremia (EAH) is more likely to occur when excessive fluid intake is combined with a slow marathon of greater than four hours. EAH can occur with marathoners who maintain or gain weight during a marathon by overdrinking. The AMAA recommends that slower runners should drink when thirsty, and all runners should weigh themselves before and after training runs and marathons. This will assist runners in determining their sweat rates and recommended consumption so as to not drink excess. A 1% to 2% weight loss during a long run **after** running (while replenishing fluids) is typical. Your urine should be pale yellow to reflect normal hydration. Dark yellow urine indicates dehydration, and clear urine (water-like) is indicative of overhydration. This will obviously be difficult to check during a marathon, but you may be able to develop your hydration plan during training runs.

Maintaining Goal Marathon Pace

It wasn't evident to me how critical adherence to a race pace plan actually was until I ran a qualifying marathon where I slowed off of my plan early in the race and paid for it later while trying to make up time. Even though I was using a pace band around my wrist, I didn't know how sluggish I was until Mile three, when I had already settled into a pace that was much slower than desired. I picked up my pace, but by then I was more than 2-1/2 minutes slower than my goal race pace. With this in mind, I ran aggressively in the next 8-9 miles. Once I was back on my pace plan, I settled into my goal pace to qualify. In just a few more miles, my body started to show signs of fatigue. I experienced cramps and tight calf and hamstring muscles at Mile 17. From Miles 18 to 24, my legs were clearly fatigued, and during Miles 24 and 25, I had to come to a full stop on four occasions to walk through leg cramps.

A good approach is to account for a 30 second slower initial mile in your overall planned finish time. As such, you would stay on your goal M.P. for up to 20 miles or so. At Mile 21, determine if you have the energy to pick up the pace, and try to finish strong. Ideally, a flat (even pace splits) or negative split (quicker second half of marathon) is the best approach to a race.

Photo 9.14 Experienced Boston marathoners know the value of staying on pace to have "something left in the tank" at Mile 25.

Not Adhering to a Race Pace Strategy

Starting too slow. If you find you have started out slower than planned for the first few miles, don't panic and attempt to make up the time quickly. If you are expending higher levels of energy to run quicker than planned, it will likely result in physical consequences like muscle cramps and early fatigue. If behind on pace, don't try to make up lost time too quickly. Do the math in your head to spread out the deficit over the next 20 miles or so. Save this precious energy for later in the event. Speeding up by five seconds over an extended distance should be manageable.

Starting too slow can be caused by cold ambient temperatures (30°F-40°F), starting in the dark, too much clothing, congestion, and simply not watching your mile splits. GPS running devices can provide instantaneous speed to keep you on pace, but they also tend to capture too much of your attention. The best way to stay on your pace is to stay focused from the start of the race.

Starting too fast. If you start out too fast with the intent of banking time in the early miles of the race, you will set yourself up for failure. **Banking time does not work!** For example, running the first half of the marathon at or near your half marathon pace (to bank a few minutes) will leave you with lactic acid buildup. This will devastate your finish time.

General Rule: The Theory of Banking Time

For each minute you are faster than goal pace during the first half of the marathon, you will be slower by two minutes in the second half.

On some occasions, you may underestimate your ability when your training has been on plan. Examples may be weather-related, where you have trained in high heat and humidity and your race conditions are much better than training conditions. In such cases, you can actually start out and maintain a pace faster than goal M.P. in an effort to set a P.R. If you need to qualify for Boston, this strategy is not suggested, because of the risk.

A suggested strategy for a P.R. would be to wait until Mile 18-20 to determine if you are still fresh. If so, simply bump it up a gear, but cautiously expend this energy reserve. Passing people at that stage in the race will boost your confidence and give you a rush of adrenaline. With approximately 10K remaining, this is the time the **race** portion of the marathon begins.

Starting at goal pace. Starting at your goal pace and maintaining that throughout the race is the objective, but sometimes the race doesn't end up that way. If you have properly warmed up prior to the start, you should be able to start out on goal pace. **Don't** do an extended warm-up for the start of the marathon. I have seen runners expend far too much energy prior to the start for their warm-up and unknowingly burn off valuable energy reserves. A half mile jog to the start is sufficient.

Time Splits. Time splits can usually indicate if a runner used poor judgment in their race plan execution. When we study these time splits and contrast them with the race profile, we can also speculate what a runner was feeling in the final half of the event. The second half splits are usually good indicators about the runner's conditioning. Runners may have slower second half times if they started too quickly and suffered fatigue in later miles; depleted their energy stores without adding nutrition during the event; were not conditioned; or were over-trained (or applied no taper).

Table 9.15 Race Time Splits at Boston (Actual Examples)

Runner #1

Checkpoints	5k	10k	15k	20k	Half	25k	30k	35k	40k
	0:19:08	0:39:38	1:00:52	1:22:41	**1:27:27**	1:44:56	2:08:24	2:32:15	2:56:24

	Finish	Pace	Projected Time	Official Time	Net Time	Overall	Gender	Division
		0:07:09		3:07:23	**3:07:14**	1040	989	270

Runner #2

Checkpoints	5k	10k	15k	20k	Half	25k	30k	35k	40k
	0:21:15	0:42:29	1:03:21	1:24:44	**1:29:29**	1:46:40	2:09:13	2:32:46	2:56:12

	Finish	Pace	Projected Time	Official Time	Net Time	Overall	Gender	Division
		0:07:09		3:07:26	**3:06:32**	1045	994	271

Runner #3

Checkpoints	5k	10k	15k	20k	Half	25k	30k	35k	40k
	0:22:38	0:43:55	1:05:11	1:26:40	**1:31:14**	1:48:19	2:10:16	2:33:13	2:55:11

	Finish	Pace	Projected Time	Official Time	Net Time	Overall	Gender	Division
		0:07:09		3:07:28	**3:04:53**	1048	997	272

By evaluating the time splits in Table 9.15 and Table 9.16 of three runners (from actual Boston Marathon results), we can determine who best executed a race strategy. Even though runner #3 ran the slowest first half marathon, he finished with the quickest overall time. This runner's time shows us that **running a smart race can actually be worth three to four minutes or more in your overall marathon performance.** Adrenaline from excitement of an attempt can put you into a pace that is quicker than your goal time. Unless you have proven that you can make it 26 miles at this pace, it is best to stay on your game plan and save any additional capacity for the last six miles. Notice the difference in split times for Runner #1 first 5K (19 min) versus the final 5K (24 min). Most runners push hard in the final 5K. This runner had nothing left in the tank and, unfortunately, left it back at the start.

Table 9.16 Analyzing the Results

Runner	First Half M	Second Half M	Differential (first half vs second)	Net Time	Result
Runner #1	**1:27**	1:40	+13 Min	3:07	Time indicates runner "fell apart" due to going out too fast in first half marathon
Runner #2	**1:29**	1:37	+ 8 Min	3:06	Slightly more conservative, but still went out too fast versus split time.
Runner #3	1:31	**1:33**	+ 2 Min	**3:04**	**Ran the best race and started slowest**

Even though it is tempting, **it is not possible to bank time.** The rate of energy release in the first half of the race cannot be recovered in the second half. To maintain your pace, use a pace group (if the event offers this), and stay with them from the start.

Race profile and impact to goal marathon pace. Some courses like Boston offer a fast first half of the course, where a runner is destined to run a positive split because of a downhill starting profile. Again, caution should be exercised as to how much faster the first half of the race can be run without sacrificing energy required for later in the race when the grade changes to an uphill course. The inverse to this would be an uphill first half course, where the runner needs to plan for a slow first half and can pick up the pace in the latter miles of the race. When hills are encountered, the best approach is to maintain a common effort or performance level when both ascending and descending. Your pace will differ, but it is not wise to attack hills to make up time.

All venues will have differences in the course, climate, or other factors that will have some impact on your completion time. A runner who is planning to achieve a qualifying time must study the race profile and modify their pace plan accordingly from the start.

Other Factors

In addition to a focused training effort, you should definitely pay attention to other aspects to your qualification race.

Timing Chip

If the race utilizes timing chips, make sure that the **first thing that you do** when you go through your race packet is **attach it to your shoe!** I've been to many races when runners are in the starting corral when they first notice that they haven't placed the chip on their shoe. At that point, the race becomes a training run. The use of a timing chip can ensure that you have a fair and accurate time for your race.

For un-chipped venues, you can lose valuable minutes from the gun time to when you actually cross the start line. You never get this time back. As a novice runner, you may be content to start behind the perceived faster runners. If you are seriously considering the event as a qualifying race and they do not offer timing chips, be sure that you are near to the front of the starting pack. When starting near the front, however, you may be pushed to run slightly faster than your normal pace. With the adrenaline pumping, you may be inclined to try to keep pace with faster runners which can be a major mistake. As mentioned previously, starting out even 30 seconds/mile faster than your goal pace can be devastating to the latter miles. Start smart, and run your race!

To ensure you are fairly timed, avoid the non-chipped marathon events.

Seeding and Congestion

For events that provide seeding and offer corrals, be sure to bring back-up evidence to the exposition/check-in that you have successfully met the time required for a seeded position at the start. Typically, race entry forms will request verification when corrals are used for seeding, so be sure to provide this to guarantee seeding. Many venues will place runners without proof at the end of the starting line, which can add 10 minutes or more to your qualifying attempt time due to the fact that you must work your way through the slower-paced runners. This is very frustrating and can jeopardize your qualifying attempt.

Photo 9.17 It can become congested at marathons with narrow starting areas. When you encounter congestion, you can easily adjust by moving to the front or to the outside. In such cases, it may take a half mile or more to run unimpeded at your goal pace. *Photo courtesy of Grandma's Marathon.*

To avoid the congestion associated with the first few miles of a race, if seeding corrals are not used, you should move up as far as you feel comfortable when gauging by the pace banners or pace group locations. In many cases, you can ask other runners of their planned pace to get an idea of the quality of runners you will be starting with. Runners of BQ capability are usually in the front 10% of the race entrants or corrals. If unsure, start near the front and move aside if the pace becomes too fast.

Summary

Now that you are aware of some of the many challenges a runner faces on a regular basis, you are better equipped to handle them appropriately. Just being knowledgeable of these potential issues and how they can be solved will give you an advantage in staying healthy towards achieving that BQ.

Unfortunately, you can't measure how many times you **weren't** injured, avoided an issue, or lost time because you **were** properly prepared, but I can guarantee you can count the marathons or races you miss participating in or achieving your goal due to injuries or the issues previously discussed.

Pace with your head and race with your heart…but know your limits.

Every second counts on a qualifying run. A great race plan is worthless if not executed…run smart!

Chapter 10
Qualification

"Pain is temporary. It may last a minute, or an hour, or a day, or a year, but eventually it will subside and something will take its place. If I quit, however, it lasts forever."

- Lance Armstrong, *Author, Cyclist, Marathoner, and Hero to Millions*

Photo 10.1 The start of a qualifying race defines the separation of nervousness and performance.

Ok, you've spent your time training and visualizing your performance for weeks, months, or perhaps years in anticipation of a serious qualifying attempt. **The key point to remember in this chapter is that you don't have to focus on one qualifying attempt.** Rather, if you're looking to qualify during a certain year, it's recommended that you incorporate multiple events throughout the year and train accordingly. I personally recommend at least two events, spacing each event approximately two or three months apart, where you take at least a complete week off after each marathon. This approach has benefits in developing your optimum strength and endurance, but can put you at slight risk of injury if you're not cautious about mileage and training effort. By spacing two or three qualifying attempts throughout the year, you may find that the late winter and early spring events are difficult to train for, due to the weather. Therefore, the first qualifying attempt will be a gauge as to your fitness level, weaknesses, and strengths, and will typically be a good indicator of what you should improve upon for your next attempt.

I highly suggest that your first marathon attempt of the year, if in late winter or early spring, be considered a training run. You should also approach this first attempt with the strategy of running a negative split. By running the first half of the marathon at Goal Marathon Pace (G.M.P.)+30-45 seconds, and the second half at G.M.P., you will have an excellent gauge of how your body will perform when pushed to your desired pace with some reserves of energy to avoid hitting "the wall." If you're doing the math on this, you should finish the "training marathon" at seven to ten minutes slower than your qualifying time.

Some veteran runners consider a marathon to be two races in one, a 20-mile run followed by a punishing 6.2 miles (10K). It is typically in this final 10K where a runner will face the true challenges of the marathon. Therefore, when you are in a qualification race, you definitely don't want to be surprised by signs that indicate you are either underprepared or over trained. By using an early-year marathon as a test, you can experience how to adjust to the hurdles your body will encounter, as well as how to prepare for the event logistics that can contribute to added race time.

Other elements surrounding the qualifying race could be critical to your success in qualifying. For example, going into an event with little or no knowledge of the course, logistics, or average temperature can each pose a risk to your performance. However, as a smart runner, you can select the venue that offers the best opportunity for a P.R. or successful BQ.

Many of the topics in this chapter have been mentioned in previous chapters. I felt it necessary, however, to ensure that each was covered in further detail to provide examples that may be of added benefit toward your successful BQ.

Analyzing Race Course Profiles

The race profile should be a critical factor of a marathoner's race strategy. Simply showing up and asking other runners about the hills is not considered sufficient research. Without strategic preparation, any significant elevation obstacle on the course will slow you down. You need to know what is coming and exactly where on the course to keep your performance at an optimum level. Without knowledge of an overpass, bridge, or major hill, each may cause you to lose valuable seconds where your pace may lapse into a walk due to inadequate preparation, especially late in a marathon.

You've no doubt heard of Heartbreak Hill by now, the final significant hill that occurs around Mile 20 in the Boston Marathon. As an exercise in preparation, think about how you would prepare yourself for that obstacle. One approach may be to run conservatively prior to the hill, then run at a pace of equal effort up the hill. Thus you are going slower up the hill. Other runners, such as the elite runners, may run up the hills at the same pace as on flat ground and possibly start their "kick" with the hills. Some runners don't plan adequately and may end up walking a large part of the hill. Each of these strategies may place you at a different fatigue level to tackle the final 10K. Strategic preparation for these "hurdles within a hurdle" is critical to a successful BQ.

Here are three examples of typical marathon course profiles. Each requires a different pace strategy for an optimum time:
1. A **downhill** first half, with **hills** in the second half
2. A **flat** course or one with few elevation changes
3. An **uphill** first half and **downhill** second half

The key point to make relative to the course profile is to **run a smart race** where you can adjust pace for the variables in elevation and yet stay on your overall pace plan. For instance, in example (1), going out too fast on a downhill course could leave you low on energy to address hills or other hurdles thrown your way in the second half of the course.

A marathon is a runner's test of energy management, and running a smartly paced marathon start to finish can positively impact your final time by 5 to 10 minutes or more. Always study the race profile well in advance of the actual event date, and adjust your training to account for hurdles you will anticipate on race day. This preparation may seem insignificant, but it will pay off in the end and provide you with confidence as you address the challenges.

1) Downhill First Half (Las Vegas): Conducive for a Positive Split

Figure 10.2 is an example of a downhill event. In this case, the marathon drops roughly 800 feet after a slight gain of 200 feet. After the runners pass Mile eight, the course elevation drops off dramatically, and the runner's pace would be expectedly quicker than the average overall pace. Time splits for the first half are expected to be slightly slower than the second half of the course due to the rise and fall of elevation in the early miles. However, estimating a split on this course may be difficult, as fatigue would hit the runner on the flat section after the "easy" downhill running occurred. These are typical factors that a runner will need to consider in their race pace plan. Also, it is a major challenge to be cognizant of where you are during the race and to adjust as needed. For this race profile, using a pace band with even splits would be useless until Mile 18. For this course, a custom pace band could be beneficial.

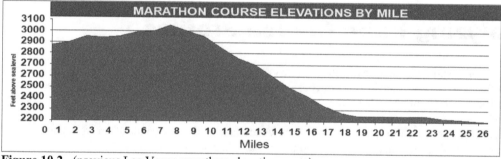

Figure 10.2　(previous Las Vegas marathon elevation route)

2) Flat Course (Chicago): Conductive for an Even Split to Negative Split

Table 10.3

Joe Runner	15K	Half	15M	20M	40K	Pace (min/mile)	Race Time	Chip Time
	1:09:24	**1:37:33**	1:51:24	2:28:31	3:04:25	**7:23**	3:15:04	**3:13:59**

	First Half	Second Half	Total Time
Split times:	1:37:33	1:36:26	3:13:59

The runner in Table 10.3 ran a slightly negative split from a chip time standpoint, but overall it could be considered an even split race pace, due to the one-minute differential. A flat course is very conducive for an even split pace. Staying on pace for the entire race is an excellent and enjoyable way to finish a marathon and provides one with verification that training and preparation went as planned. For the optimum qualification attempt, seek a flat course or one with a continuous gradual downhill elevation.

For the most part, the B.A.A. doesn't discriminate regarding the venue elevation for qualification; it only looks at your time and age as factors. Therefore, a downhill venue should result in a quicker total time than a flat venue such as Chicago. However, the temperature, wind, and many other factors, as indicated in Chapter Three, may give the performance edge to another venue for any given day.

3) Uphill First Half and Downhill Second Half (Big Sur): Conductive for a Negative Split

An elevation gain of significance at the beginning of the race, such as over 500 feet (see Figure 10.4) should be avoided for serious qualifying attempts unless you are limited geographically to a specific opportunity. If this is the case, then you will just have to make the best of it and train accordingly. In a venue such as this, you should add five minutes or more to your expected finish time to account for the elevation challenges. Unless you are experienced in increasing your speed on a downhill grade (Miles 12-15), you may increase the risk of injury or cramping during the rapid descent.

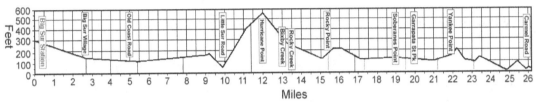

Figure 10.4 *Courtesy of Big Sur International Marathon*

When I ran Big Sur, I fully appreciated the grade challenge and used my energy sparingly for the first nine miles, then ran uphill from Miles 10 to 12 at a slower pace (roughly G.M.P. +90 sec). Once I crested Hurricane Point, I picked up the tempo cautiously on the downhill sections in an attempt to meet my half marathon split goal time. This event was my first attempt of the year (April), and my serious BQ attempt was planned for June. Thus, I approached this venue as a training run and an opportunity to run a negative split, with the bonus of some needed hill work.

An event such as Big Sur should be approached as a training run or for enjoyment and not a BQ attempt. It is great to make a vacation out of a marathon, and many families and individuals do just that. The marathon scenery was the most beautiful I'd ever experienced, which is a key reason why Big Sur has been rated one of the most enjoyable marathons in the world (Photo 10.5). But if you're looking for a serious BQ attempt, you should pick a flat course with predictable, favorable weather.

Photo 10.5 *Photo courtesy of Big Sur International Marathon, photographer Douglas Steakley*

141

Selecting a marathon based upon profile As indicated earlier, the race profile can definitely make or break a qualification attempt, and each venue offers unique challenges at different points during the race (bridges, overpasses, tunnels, steep inclines, or declines). Figure 10.6 shows a typical venue with a few overpasses and bridges, but it is otherwise relatively flat. If you anticipate what challenges lay ahead, you can get yourself mentally focused for them as they arrive. Again, depending upon the challenge, it may be recommended to customize your pace band to adjust mile splits accordingly.

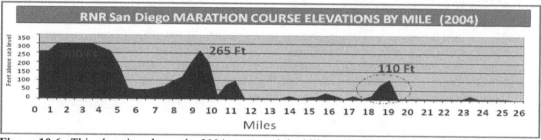

Figure 10.6 This elevation shows the 2004 route, and the hill at Mile 19 was later eliminated, possibly due to difficulty.

The most significant challenge on this course is at Mile 19. Although the hill at Mile 9 is a higher elevation, a runner is much more fatigued at Mile19, and preparation is more critical at that point. How would you prepare for Mile 19 so that it doesn't stop you in your tracks or end up walking up the hill (like I did)? I wasn't mentally or physically prepared for the challenge, and it was a surprise to me. In my case, I was on a P.R. pace, and this overpass knocked me back to reality. I should have slowed prior to this hurdle to gain some energy and loaded up on gels energy packs and electrolytes about 20 minutes earlier. Hurdles such as these can cost you valuable seconds to minutes if you don't properly prepare for them.

I have provided information on only a select few venues to give you some perspective as to how the profile can impact your splits and overall race time. Remember that all venues are different, therefore your race plan and pace plan will be a variable that you control. **Very few venues will offer an opportunity to run an even pace throughout the entire course.**

Positive Split Vs Negative Split

Which is better? Many marathoners have an opinion as to which they prefer, but ultimately it is whichever effort yields the fastest time. For many runners, a negative split is a preferred way to finish a race, and with friends/family at the finish or the numerous spectators in general, you want to finish strong. Conserving energy on the front-end of the race and staying focused on your mile splits is a key enabler to meet your race plan. Managing or conserving energy by pace management must be considered. A race in which you conserve too much energy, however, won't yield your best effort from a total time perspective.

When seeking a P.R. or a qualification time for Boston, feeling fresh for the last two or three miles is good, but it indicates that you haven't pushed yourself to the optimum pace (without exceeding the lactate threshold) for the majority of the race. A slightly positive split (slower second half) may actually be more conducive for a quicker time, as you have expended a level of energy for the first half that you weren't able to match for the second. A very slight positive split to an even split is probably the perfect race, if there is such a term, as you are sure you have given your all. A negative split should be your focus on a training marathon, as it conditions you for the stress that you will put on your body in the actual attempt.

One key factor to your overall performance is the pace you select for your first half of the event. If you select a pace that is even a few minutes too aggressive, you will pay for it in lost time due to fatigue in the second half. The "payback" for running too fast for each aggressive mile (sub-goal pace) in the first half, is that you will see twice as many slower miles in the second half of the marathon. For this reason, it is beneficial to run a training marathon prior to your BQ attempt to gauge your fitness.

Selecting a G.M.P. An approximated guideline for what pace to select as your G.M.P. is based upon your most recent half marathon run at maximum pace and adding five to six percent to your time for each half of the marathon (recent half marathon time X 1.05 = G.M.P. for the marathon).

For example, if your most recent half marathon time is a 1:40, or 100 minutes, your goal time for each half of the marathon should be 105 to 106 minutes, or a 1:45 to 1:46. This is an aggressive approach to the race pace, and you should anticipate a positive split or slightly slower second half. It should give you a good starting point for a G.M.P., however. (See Chapter Four for a comparison of expected marathon times based upon shorter distance performances.)

The Fastest Marathons

The fastest marathon times usually occur at only a few of the hundreds of venues throughout the world, and this isn't by accident. Typically, these venues draw in the world's elite runners, primarily through the offer of substantial prize money and the quest of a world record. Table 10.7 reflects some of the recent top ten marathon times. Since most of the marathons listed are classified as major marathons, they offer the prestige and substantial cash winnings to the fastest time. Not surprisingly, they also usually offer perfect race temperature conditions and are relatively flat courses where the highest continuous elevation gain is less than 60 feet (20m).

If you aren't capable of entering venues such as the London, Berlin, or Chicago marathons, you should select a venue that offers a relatively flat course for your best opportunity at a qualifying time. Another key item to note is that none of the fastest times were recorded during May through August. These summer months are not conducive for optimum running temperatures, due to the heat index (see Chapter 3).

Table 10.7 The World's Fastest Marathon Times

Rank	Time	Runner	Race	Date
1.	2:03:59	Haile Gebrselassie (ETH)	Berlin	09/28/2008
2.	2:04:26	Haile Gebrselassie (ETH)	Berlin	09/30/2007
3.	2:04:53	Haile Gebrselassie (ETH)	Dubai	01/18/2008
4.	2:04:55	Paul Tergat (KEN)	Berlin	09/28/2003
5.	2:04:56	Sammy Korir (KEN)	Berlin	09/28/2003
6.	2:05:15	Martin Lel (KEN)	London	04/13/2008
7.	2:05:24	Samuel Wanjiru (KEN)	London	04/13/2008
8.	2:05:30	Abderrahim Goumri (MAR)	London	04/13/2008
9.	2:05:38	Khalid Khannouchi (USA)	London	04/14/2002
10.	2:05:42	Khalid Khannouchi (MAR)	Chicago	10/24/1999

Selecting the Marathon: Course

The importance of the marathon course elevation profile of your BQ qualifying attempts shouldn't be taken lightly. In fact, as was indicated in Chapter 3, it can result in a substantial difference in your qualifying time. Here are suggestions that will improve your qualifying chances by selecting the right venue:

- **Pick a flat course.** Grandma's (Minnesota), Disney (Florida.), Rock 'n' Roll Arizona, Chicago, and London marathons are excellent examples of flat courses.
- **Pick a course that is close to home** (short driving distance). You may be more relaxed and acclimatized to elevation, humidity, and temperature at the races nearest to home.
- **Pick a course that you have experience with and have possibly run before**. I highly recommend running a course for a second time for your qualifying attempt. You will be familiar with turns, hills, the staging area, and obstacles that await you so that there are no surprises. In addition, you will find that you are much more relaxed for the run itself.
- **Pick a course that doesn't have significant hills, overpasses, or other obstacles in the later miles.** These obstacles can overstress already tired muscles to the point of cramping. Even the slightest change in terrain (concrete to grass, curbs, and gravel) may be enough to cause muscles to cramp. If the venue has hills, ensure that they occur early in the marathon.
- **Drive the course the day before the event.** Familiarizing yourself with landmarks along the way will get you comfortable with the course and areas of concern.
- **Try to avoid courses that are out and back**. You will see the faces of runners ahead and behind you, faces of pain or discomfort, which may be distracting. In addition, many marathons also offer a half marathon that shares a common route. Depending upon your level of focus, it may be easy to get discouraged by the runners who are finishing when you still have 13.1 miles to go. This is the point to stay focused on your goal and your pace.
- **Be aware of shaded areas, windy areas, and tunnels,** where it may require you to wear or keep warmer clothes on slightly longer during the course.
- **Pick a course with great spectator support.** Having run a few marathons where there were virtually no spectators to cheer on runners, it is easy to lose energy and slow. If you need an energy boost, share a few high fives from supportive spectators. Their support, especially late in a marathon, can be a huge lift to tired legs.

The Start Time

The start time is another important aspect of a race, especially if you are looking at a qualifying attempt. Some venues, such as Disney, will start as early as 5:50 am. This will necessitate a wake-up time of at least 4:30 am or the suggested 4 am to allow your breakfast 2 hours to digest. Usually the earlier start times will tend to stress a runner more, since they will need to get to sleep earlier the night prior and will want to make sure they wake up in time. Some runners have nightmares about missing the start of a race, and it does happen. Setting two alarms is helpful for early start times.

Conversely, a later start time such as 9 am or even an afternoon race promotes susceptibility to warmer temperatures, and as a result, the sun will drive up the heat index and will negatively impact your performance. If you have traveled across time zones, such as opposite coasts, or even international travel, you should allow about three days to become acclimated to the time and climate differences. Be sure that your body clock has adjusted to the start time, as you will have invested much into your qualifying attempt. Adding an extra day prior to the race (to be more adjusted to the venue) is time well spent, even if you are only relaxing or sightseeing.

Planning Your Qualifying Calendar

Here is a suggested marathon schedule to use for qualifying attempts over a calendar year. The key with this annual schedule is that you complete an early season marathon perhaps in March or April as part of your training to prepare you for a serious attempt in June. If unsuccessful in June, continue training to improve upon weak areas, such as endurance or speed, and make another serious attempt in the fall. A January through March venue in the United States or northern hemisphere isn't conducive to yielding a best performance, as it is difficult to train due to winter conditions.

Month	Focus
January	Train or early season marathon to build base
February	Train
March	Train, half marathon race
April	**Attempt #1**
May	Maintain fitness, work on speed
June	**Attempt #2**
July	Rest, build on base training
August	Speed work, hills
September	Build on long run
October	**Attempt #3**
November	or **Attempt #3,** but weather may be risky
December	Typical rest month, unless venue in the following January

Table 10.8 illustrates two consecutive years where I incorporated training marathons into my training plan. For these two years, at least one serious attempt at a qualifying run was planned, and the training schedule was built around the attempt. For example, in 2003 the Big Sur Marathon was used as a training run in anticipation of an attempt that was seven to eight weeks later (Grandma's). By building up endurance with an easy-paced marathon and maintaining the normal training focus of intervals and long runs as part of the training plan, the strategy was successful.

The data in Table 10.8 looks fairly predictable where a PR attempt follows a previous marathon at least seven weeks prior. However, one anomaly to that plan was the final marathon of 2004, where I planned to incorporate a training marathon as my long run. The Air Force Marathon in September 2004 was intended to be a training run in preparation for Chicago in early October. Believing that a recovery of three weeks was adequate, I felt that was a safe plan. I was painfully wrong.

The three-week differential and the level of effort during my taper proved disastrous, and I unfortunately learned two valuable lessons that I still practice and coach others to adhere to:

1) A training run IS a training run. Don't push it, even though you may feel great when leading up to a critical marathon.
2) Three weeks recovery isn't adequate time to heal muscles damaged from a marathon, even if run slower than G.M.P. If you decide to incorporate a marathon into your training plan it, should be a minimum of six weeks prior to your BQ run to allow for muscle recovery. I felt great for the Dayton event but as early as three miles into Chicago, just three weeks later, my legs were fatigued and I fell apart. After Mile 20, I walked for much of the final 10K. Had I

planned better, I could have met my goal for a 2:59. This was a valuable lesson learned for a proper taper (see Chapter 8 for more information on a proper taper).

Table 10.8

Year	Venue	Month of	Time	Purpose	Interval (Weeks) from Previous Marathon
2003	Big Sur	April	3:29	Training Run	-
2003	Grandma's	June	3:18	PR attempt	7 wks
2003	Chicago	Oct	3:13	PR attempt	15 wks
2004	Disney	Jan	3:20	Training Run	12 wks
2004	Boston	Apr	3:23	Training Run	13 wks
2004	San Diego	June	3:01	PR attempt	7 wks
2004	USAF Dayton	Sept	3:12	Training Run	11wks
2004	Chicago	Oct	3:06	PR attempt	3 wks*

* A three week venue interval was found to be enough recovery time, as my pace fell off dramatically and in a personal worst positive split differential of 8 minutes.

The Pace Chart

The importance of a pace chart can't be overstated for a BQ attempt. Not only does it establish your goal pace for the attempt, but is also defines much of the rate of speed that you will be running in your training plan for the various types of training runs (i.e., long runs, easy pace, and intervals). For example, if you are a female aged **40-44**, your qualifying time requirement (Ref. Table 10.9) is **3:45:00**. Therefore, this is a pace of **8:35/mile**. When determining your required pace for speed work (intervals) and your long runs, you can incorporate these times into your training plan, as shown in Table 10.10. Just as a note, this pace chart provides the required qualifying times for Boston. (You are advised to check the latest qualification requirements at www.baa.org before you develop your training plan.

Table 10.9   **Boston Marathon Qualification Pace Chart**

Age	Men	Qualifying Pace (M.P.)	Women	Qualifying Pace (M.P.)
18-34	3:05:00	7:04	3:35:00	8:12
35-39	3:10:00	7:15	3:40:00	8:23
40-44	3:15:00	7:26	3:45:00	8:35
45-49	3:25:00	7:49	3:55:00	8:58
50-54	3:30:00	8:00	4:00:00	9:10
55-59	3:40:00	8:23	4:10:00	9:32
60-64	3:55:00	8:58	4:25:00	10:07
65-69	4:10:00	9:32	4:40:00	10:41
70-74	4:25:00	10:07	4:55:00	11:15
75-79	4:40:00	10:41	5:10:00	11:50
80 and over	4:55:00	11:15	5:25:00	12:24

Note: The B.A.A. no longer allows a qualifying time that includes all 59 seconds for the qualifying minute

Table 10.10 Example of Incorporating Your Required Goal Marathon Pace Into Your Training Schedule (for women 40-44)

Weeks Prior	M	T	W	TH	F	S	S	Total Miles	Notes
6 Weeks Prior to Race	7 miles at MP **8:35**	60 min bike or 6 miles at MP **8:35**	7 miles at **Tempo** +3MP **7@ 8:05** **3@ 8:35**	Rest	5 miles at MP **8:35**	10 X 1 mile **Interval** @ MP-1 min/mile **7:35**	8-10 Easy Pace (EP) **9:35**	46-48	Focus on interval run w/ last 4 quickest

(Reference training schedule from Chapter 4 , Table 4.23, to determine M.P., Tempo, Interval, and EP speeds.)

Qualifying Marathons: The Short List

As indicated in the preceding portions of this chapter, picking your qualifying race may be dependent upon budget, geographical location, time of year, and family or job conflicts. The key to get to Boston is that you pick the best races or venues that can provide elements conducive for a quick race. Table 10.11 is a list of some of the marathons available. Obviously, this list will change after published in this text. Periodicals such as *Runner's World* and *Running Times* provide up-to-date venue information. In addition, use a search engine such as Google or Yahoo for marathon listings or local events in your area. Marathonguide.com is an excellent example of a listing of available marathons in your area. Table 10.11 may be of help to guide you towards a venue that meets your criteria.

Table 10.11

Qualifying Marathons Early Year (Training) Marathons			
January	**February**	**March**	**April**
Walt Disney World Marathon (Orlando, FL) *wws.disney.go.com/wideworldof sports/index?id=DWWSHome*	AT&T Austin Marathon (Austin, TX) *www.attaustinmarathon.com*	Rome Marathon (Rome, Italy) *www.maratonadiroma.it*	Boston Marathon (Hopkinton, MA) *www.baa.org*
Houston Marathon (Houston, TX) *www.hphoustonmarathon.com*	Mercedes Marathon (Birmingham, AL) *www.mercedesmarathon.com*	Los Angeles Marathon (Las Angeles, CA) *www.lamarathon.com*	Big Sur International Marathon (Carmel, CA) *www.bsim.org*
ING Miami Marathon (Miami, FL) *www.Ingmiamimarathon.com*	Bank of America Marathon (Tampa, FL) *www.tampabayrun.com*	Sarasota Marathon (Sarasota, FL) *www.sarasotamarathon.com*	Country Music Marathon (Nashville, TN) *www.cmmarathon.com*
San Diego Marathon (San Diego, CA) *www.sdmarathon.com*	Myrtle Beach Marathon (Myrtle Beach, SC) *www.mbmarathon.com*	Valley of the Sun Marathon (Mesa, AZ) *www.valleyofthesunmar athon.com*	Salt Lake City Marathon (Salt Lake City, UT) *www.saltlakecitymarathon.com*
P.F. Chang's Rock 'n' Roll Marathon (Phoenix, Scottsdale, Tempe, AZ) *www.rnraz.com*	A1A Fort Lauderdale Marathon (Ft Lauderdale, FL) *www.a1amarathon.com*	EL Paso Marathon (El Paso, TX) *www.elpasomarathon.org*	London Marathon (London, England) *www.london-marathon.co.uk*
Mississippi Blues Marathon (Jackson, MS) *www.msbluesmarathon.com*	Mardi Gras Marathon (New Orleans, LA) *www.mardigrasmarathon.com*	ING Georgia Marathon (Atlanta, GA) *www.inggeorgiamarathon.com*	Paris Marathon (Paris, France) *www.parismarathon.com*

Continued

Table 10.11 Qualifying Marathons (continued)

SPRING/SUMMER MARATHONS			
May	**June**	**July**	**August**
Vancouver Marathon (Vancouver, BC Canada) *www.bmovanmarathon.ca*	Grandma's Marathon (Duluth, MN) *www.grandmasmarathon.com*	Calgary Marathon (Calgary, Alberta, Canada) *www.calgarymarathon.com*	ING Edmonton Marathon (Edmonton, Alberta, Canada) *edmontonmarathon.ca*
Flying Pig Marathon (Cincinnati, OH) *www.flyingpigmarathon.com*	Rock 'n' Roll Marathon (San Diego, CA) *www.rnrmarathon.com*	Berlin Marathon (Berlin Germany) *www.real-berlin-marathon.com/world/E*	New Mexico Marathon (Albuquerque, NM) *newmexicomarathon.org*
ING Ottawa (Ottawa, Ontario) *info@runottawa.ca*	Mayors' Midnight Sun (Anchorage, AK) *www.mayorsmarathon.com*	Deseret News Marathon (Salt Lake City, UT) *www.desnews.com*	Park City Marathon (Park City, UT) *www.pcmarathon.com*
Cleveland Marathon (Cleveland, OH) *www.clevelandmarathon.com*	Steamboat Marathon (Steamboat Springs, CO) *marathon@steamboatchamber.com*	Nova Scotia Marathon (Barrington, NS Canada) *www.barringtonmuncipality.com*	Pike's Peak Marathon (Colorado Springs, CO) *www.pikespeakmarathon.org*
Madison Marathon (Madison, WI) *www.madisonfestivals.com*	Hatfield-McCoy Marathon (Goody, KY) *www.hatfieldmccoymarathon.com*	San Francisco Marathon (San Francisco, CA) *www.runsfm.com*	SSQ Quebec City Marathon (Quebec City) *www.marathonquebec.com*
Bayshore Marathon (Traverse City, MI) *www.bayshoremarathon.org*	Kona Marathon (Keauhou-Kona, HI) *www.konamarathon.com*		
Green Bay Marathon (Green Bay, WI) *www.cellcomgreenbaymarathon.com*			
Eugene Marathon (Eugene, OR) *www.eugenemarathon.com*			
Buffalo Marathon (Buffalo, NY) *www.buffalomarathon.com*			
Traverse City Bayshore Marathon (Traverse City, MI) *www.bayshoremarathon.org*			
Minneapolis Marathon (Minneapolis, MN) *www.teamortho.us/minneapolis_Marathon*			

Continued

As you will note in this table, in North America, May and October offer the widest selection of marathon venues. These months are most conducive for an optimum temperature, but conditions will vary. Leave your options open an monitor temperatures when focusing on a specific qualifying attempt month. Although it may be costly, entering multiple venues during a "best opportunity" month may provide one opportunity better than another, when considering weather.

Table 10.11 Qualifying Marathons (continued)

FALL/WINTER MARATHONS			
September	**October**	**November**	**December**
Maui Marathon (Maui, HI) *www.mauimarathon.org*	Portland Marathon (Beaverton, OR) *www.potlandmarathon.org*	Athens Marathon (Athens, Greece) *www.athensclassicmarathon.gr*	California International Marathon (Sacramento, CA) *www.runcim.org*
U.S. Air Force Marathon Wright-Patterson AFB, OH *http://afmarathon.wpafb.af.mil*	St. George Marathon (St. George, UT) *www.stgeorgemarathon.com*	Atlanta Marathon (Atlanta, GA) *www.atlantatrackclub.org*	Dallas White Rock Marathon (Grand Prairie, TX) *www.runtherock.com*
Clarence DeMar Marathon (Keene, NH) *www.clarencedemar.com*	The Lasalle Bank Chicago Marathon (Chicago, IL) *www.chicagomarathon.com*	ING New York City Marathon (New York, NY) *www.nycmarathon.org*	Honolulu Marathon (Honolulu, HI) *www.honolulumarathon.org*
Fox City Marathon (Appleton, WI) *www.foxcitiesmarathon.org*	Indianapolis Marathon (Indianapolis, IN) *www.indianapolismarathon.com*	Philadelphia Marathon (Philadelphia, PA) *www.philadelphiamarathon.com*	Rocket City Marathon (Huntsville, AL) *www.huntsvilletrackclub.org*
Newfoundland Marathon (St. John, Newfoundland, Canada) *nlaa.ca/nfmarathon*	Twin Cities Marathon (Minneapolis, MN) *www.mtcmarathon.org*	Seattle Marathon (Seattle, WA) *www.seattlemarathon.org*	Tucson Marathon (Tucson, AZ) *www.tusconmarathon.com*
Erie Marathon (Erie, PA) *www.erie-runnersclub.org*	Columbus Marathon (Columbus, OH) *www.columbusmarathon.com*	Tulsa Marathon (Tulsa, OK) *www.oklahomamarathon.org*	Jacksonville Bank Marathon (Jacksonville, FL) *www.1stplacesports.com/jm.htm*
Quad Cities Marathon (Moline, IL) *www.qcmarathon.org*	Lake Tahoe Marathon (South Lake Tahoe, CA) *www.laketahoemarathon.com*		Las Vegas Marathon (Las Vegas, NV) *www.lvmarathon.com*
	Denver Marathon (Denver, CO) *www.denvermarathon.com*		
	Toronto Marathon (Toronto, Ontario Canada) *www.torontomarathon.com*		
	Marine Corps Marathon (Washington, DC) *www.marinemarathon.com*		
	Detroit Free Press Marathon (Detroit, MI) *www.freep.com/marathon*		
	Venice Marathon (Venice, Italy) *www.venicemarathon.it*		
	Louisville Marathon (Louisville, KY) *www.louisvillemarathon.org*		

Many excellent websites provide marathon venue information on the Internet. The information shown in Table 10.12 from popular websites provides the venue, city, country, and approximate number of participants you can expect.

Table 10.12 Selecting a Qualification Marathon Based on Number of Participants

Marathon Name	City	Country	Approx. # Participants
Coventry Health Care Delaware Marathon	Wilmington, Delaware	USA	550
Rock 'n' Roll Marathon	Phoenix, Arizona	USA	20,000
California International Marathon	Sacramento, California	USA	3000
Los Angeles Marathon	Los Angeles, California	USA	22,000
Napa Valley Marathon	Napa, California	USA	1,000
Big Sur International Marathon	Big Sur, California	USA	4,000
Avenue of the Giants Marathon	Humboldt Redwoods SP, California	USA	500
Rock 'n' Roll Marathon	San Diego, California	USA	20,000
San Francisco Marathon	San Francisco, California	USA	4,000
Continued…			

Example of data available at http://www.races2run.com (see Marathons).

In summary, don't approach the qualifying race without knowing the venue and its challenges before you show up on race day. A little research and preparation will pay dividends. Before you select any of these venues for your qualifying attempt, do your research on the elevation change, temperature, use of timing chips, and other things you have learned to ensure it will be a worthwhile effort.

From my personal experience, selecting the right venue will make a difference in your performance. Some of the performance-impacting factors are out of your control, such as wind or adverse weather. But you can use the venue information to your advantage when selecting your BQ and Training marathons.

Photo 10.13   When running a marathon for the first time in a new city, such as the Marine Corps Marathon in Washington D.C., it is a great idea to arrive a few days early to become familiar with the streets and the route and perhaps jog a few warm-up miles on some of the local running trails.

Many cities, such as Washington D.C., offer outstanding trails with scenic views.

Going to a marathon without understanding the course is like a professional golfer walking up to a ball on the green and just putting towards the hole. They will both miss the target.

Chapter 11
First-Time Marathoners

"Ninety percent of runners go out too quickly... For every minute you go out too fast, you lose 1.5 to 2 times the amount of time you gain early."
    - Bob Kennedy (Two-Time Olympian)

Photo 11.1 Elite runners mentally reviewing race strategy for the marathon that awaits them. They, too, were once first-time marathoners, and preparation cannot be taken lightly, regardless of your experience.

If you've never run a marathon and are considering qualifying for Boston, this chapter will provide you with a few recommendations, as well as areas to avoid when preparing for your first marathon. Much of the content of this chapter has been discussed previously. I have selected a few topics, however, that need to be reiterated specifically for first-time marathoners. It is important to your pursuit of Boston to have a successful **first** marathon to ensure that attempt number two happens, and thus the pursuit continues successfully. Many marathoners, unfortunately, run only one marathon and vow never to run another, due to issues that they encountered. With the proper training, reasonable expectations, a positive approach, and race preparation, this shouldn't happen to you.

The accomplishment of a first marathon is a great achievement and something to truly be proud of as a life goal. However, if you have your sights on Boston, your first marathon helps determine your strengths and weaknesses to prepare you for the qualifying run. Preparing for a first marathon can become intimidating, as you are breaking new ground nearly every training day. For that reason, you need to be aware that the preparation and training for a full marathon with the intent **Just to Finish** versus preparing to **Qualify for Boston** are actually very different approaches.

For example:
- The goal of finishing a first marathon should require focus of the training basics to **complete** the distance.
- The goal of Boston is more of a challenge of **distance and time** in which it is completed. To qualify for Boston, every second counts, and you must have a race plan, confidence, known capabilities, and a focused approach. Again, most of these elements are defined to a level different from that of your first marathon.

The focus of this chapter is to provide some advice to successfully complete your first marathon and build a base of experience to improve your chances to qualify for Boston.

Minimizing Stress

Some of the most significant hurdles a first-time marathoner will encounter are the nervousness and anxiety that accompany the challenges of a marathon. It's important to start off your qualifying attempt day the same as the preceding days, with low stress. You've put in hundreds of hours of training, compromised family time, free time, work time, and perhaps modified your diet. *"Now it all comes down to one morning?"* Not necessarily. If you are concerned with these factors, look at the day as one attempt, but give it your best. It will mentally ease your stress if you plan for another attempt in a few months to alleviate the pressure of *this* attempt. Stress won't help your performance. You should go into the event with the confidence that you've done the best you can with your training and that you will push yourself to a level you can comfortably run for the full distance, even if it involves some walking. Stressing-out at the last minute about your race-readiness is a common anxiety, but stay confident, as confidence will help you in the early miles to stay on pace.

Last-minute travel, rushing to packet pick-up, and even ensuring something as simple as where you will have your race day breakfast can also take a toll on your anxiety level. This anxiety associated with rushing at the last minute can deplete you of valuable stored energy. Keeping your stress low a few days prior to the event will support good sleep and digestion and/or processing of those valuable carbohydrates that you'll need.

Below are a few of the key items you will want to get resolved that could be potential causes of stress. Again, the goal here is to minimize the anxiety of things that you **can** control. These are:

Understand the Course- Drive it, walk it, but at a minimum, review the race profile and anything that describes what you may encounter on race day. Talk to other runners who have run the course. Runners are usually willing to share much about a course ranging from bus pick-up or drop-off locations, challenging hills, or perhaps their race strategy. Just reviewing the race profile will not always prepare you adequately.

Pick Up Your Race Packet Early- If possible, pick up your packet two days before the event, especially if the expo is large and you anticipate that the expo will take a few hours to complete. The expo may have long lines for shirts, jackets, and other notable items, so it may help to get there early. Expos can become mentally and physically draining, as most runners want to see everything, especially all of the latest running paraphernalia.

Most expos position the packet pick-up locations and free shirts near the opposite side of the main entrance so that the runners must shop first before getting where they desire. This is somewhat similar to Las Vegas, where to get anywhere you must first go through a casino.

Be aware of expending unnecessary energy during the expo.

Photo 11.2 *Photo by Zachary Long flickr.com/photos/fenglong*

Organize All of Your Race Day Needs. Lay out all of your race day needs in one location so when race morning arrives, you can easily prepare as needed. Scrambling for your petroleum jelly or gel energy packs at 5 am on race morning through a bag full of expo handouts isn't the way to start a relaxed approach to the day. See the listing below for suggested race day items that you should have organized and ready to go before race day morning.

Race Day/Race Morning Needs

Timing Chip and Bib #	Attach these to your shoe and shirts the night before.
Race Clothes	Review the weather report and dress accordingly. Dress for temps 20°F warmer than race start temperature if conditions will be sunny.
Warm-up Clothes	Wear to the start and put these in your garment check-bag. Don't freeze unnecessarily in the morning by not using the provided garment check services. Staying warm prior to the start will conserve your energy.
Packaged Energy	Pack three or four small gel energy packs that contain the calories and carbs you will need to replenish what you lose during the marathon. Supplements are optional.
Cash for Taxi	To get to the starting line on time, call a taxi if your walk is approaching two miles.
Watch and Pace Band	First-time marathoners should use a pace band and a watch. GPS watches with speed and distance indicators are good for training, but may be distracting on race day, as they can cause you to focus too much on your instantaneous pace. Most venues will provide mile markers to assist with maintaining your pace versus time.
Radio/MP3/Ipod	If you run comfortably with music, take it with you on your first marathon. It can become a distraction if you need to focus on your pace for a qualifying run. Elite runners don't race with music for a reason. Recommendation – leave them at home.
Cell Phone	Leave it at home unless you need to tell someone where you are or you expect to be in need of help along the route.
Sunglasses	Pre-test them on long runs to ensure that they don't fog or sweat up. If they do fog, they will be more of a detriment than a help.
Petroleum Jelly	Apply to friction areas. Some venues provide this on the course, but it is best to plan for providing your own.
Drinking Straw	If you can't drink and run, tuck a five-inch straw under your running watch. You will be amazed how well it works while running at goal pace.

Bandages	Men should use the round bandages to prevent nipple chafing/damage.
Pain Killers	Use only pain killers that do not thin the blood, such as acetaminophen. But don't exceed the recommended dose, even in anticipation of pain.
Pre-Race Food	Bagels/bread, bananas, and power bars.
Water or Sports Drink	Carry these with you to the start.
Sunscreen/Hat	Apply if susceptible to burn or if you expect sunny conditions. Watch that the sunscreen does not get into your eyes if you sweat. A visor/hat may be better option for face protection.
Toilet Paper	Put it in your garment check bag for the start area and don't count on the port-o-potties to be stocked. Also, bring along any necessary hygiene items.
Large Trash Bag(s)	You will find them to be very helpful in cold or rainy conditions. Pack a few for the start, as they are great to sit on if the start is delayed.
Towels or Sleeping Bags	Some venues will bus you out to the start, and you return back to the finish. Usually this travel and subsequent waiting hours prior to the start occur when temperatures are at their coldest and indoor comfort is not available. In such cases, a fleece sleeping bag, large towel, or light blanket can be used to keep you warm at the start, with the ability to pack them into your garment check bag.

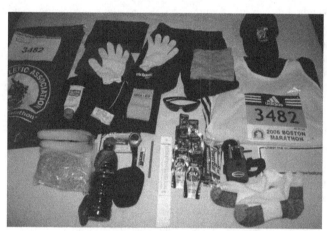

Photo 11.3 Organized race day needs. This is a great way to set your mind at ease the night prior to the marathon, or any race.

- **Understand Your Corral Assignment–** Some venues will require proof of previous race times if you have been placed into a seeded corral. Just in case, bring a previous race printout with your name and the date, if it wasn't provided at the time of registration. If not provided, you may be placed in a corral seeding well below your capabilities. Also, you should get to your corral assignment early for the best opportunity for minimizing congestion along the way.

Photo 11.4 Understand your corral or seeding assignment.

- **Understand How You Will Get to the Start in the Least Energy-Depriving Manner** – A walk of a mile or so, however, can be an excellent way to warm up cold muscles. Definitely don't sprint to the start, unless your alarm clock didn't do the job.

- **Don't Overhydrate Prior to the Race (Race Morning)** – Twelve ounces of energy drink and perhaps a small glass (four to six ounces) of your preferred breakfast juice is sufficient for the morning hours prior to the start. If you drink more, you're likely to need a race relief stop in the early miles of the marathon.

Photo 11.5 The potty lines can be a 30-45 minute wait. If you plan to hydrate race morning, drink about 12 ounces or so within 30 minutes of the start. Don't overhydrate!

- **Be Better Rested** – Take two alarm clocks (battery powered) and ear plugs for noisy hotels.

- **Organize Your Breakfast Meal** – If you are traveling to a venue, you will no doubt need to find your breakfast items, including orange juice, bananas, cereal, bread, doughnuts, or whatever you prefer once you've arrived. A suggestion would be to pack these items away with you even if you are traveling by air, as you may find yourself scrambling for something to eat at 5 am. Finding out that you have nothing to eat when you wake up is not a way to start your day and will undoubtedly put you at a deficit for your caloric intake necessary in the morning. Your pre-race intake should consist of up to 500 calories of carbohydrates consumed two to three hours prior to race time.

- **Use a Mantra** – Change your focus from the things that could be a challenge to the things you will accomplish with this run. A mantra is a great way to reduce your stress by funneling it into a single task. This approach will keep you motivated as you click off the miles more easily, as they now have a purpose. Some suggested mantras are "Run hard," " Let's do this," "This is for mom/dad/or child," "Kick butt," "I am tough," "I want this," and, of course, "Boston or bust."

The preceding suggestions may help to alleviate some of the stress associated with first-time marathons. Again, finding out that you've forgotten something race morning is **not** the time to notice.

Stage 1: Training Suggestions

Carb Day(s) – This term may be confusing for Indy 500 fans (reference to carburetion day), but it is defined as eating high carbohydrate content meals three days and two days prior to race day. The same strategy applies for your long training runs. It takes approximately one full day (24 hours) to fully convert the complex carbohydrates into usable energy. A high carbohydrate dinner the night before will primarily replenish your glycogen stores lost **after** the race and, unfortunately, will provide added weight for most of the marathon. My advice is to eat moderately (not heavily) at the event-sponsored pre-race pasta dinners.

Keep It Together – As an extreme athlete, you may find it best to stay away from pain relievers that thin blood. Ibuprofen may thin your blood, which could lead to minor kidney ruptures. This is due to your body experiencing high blood flow and blood pressure due to the associated heart rate. Acetaminophen may be used, instead of a pain reliever that thins blood.

Cut the Lawn – A good way to cool down (de-lactate) your muscles after a training run is to cut the grass with a push mower while rehydrating.

Brrrrrr – During long training runs on cold windy days, run against the wind as you start out so that on the return, you won't have the cold wind in your face and a chilled body due to perspiration. The same goes for race day. If you will be starting with the wind at your back and turning into a cold wind in later miles, it may be advisable to keep some extra clothing on, even though you may be warm for the first few miles.

Practice Makes Perfect – Prior to running your first marathon, it is highly suggested to run a half marathon to acclimate yourself to the mental drama of a long distance race.

Many first-time marathoners run a half marathon as part of their marathon training plan. For the more seasoned marathoners, a half marathon is an excellent avenue for speed work leading up to a marathon.

Photo 11.6   The look of determination in the final miles of a half marathon.

Slip-Slidin'away – Some runners are more susceptible to injury during cold training runs, as muscles may be tighter than normal, or they haven't taken time to warm up or stretch. Start out slow on the cold days and be cautious. If the road is covered in ice or snow, use your judgment regarding safe running conditions. If you are dressed properly, running in the snow can be very relaxing on a calm day or a snow-lit night.

Baby Steps – Be patient about the time it takes to get into condition to be able to sustain your G.M.P. Your pace will improve, but the conditioning isn't an overnight process. The key to staying motivated is to keep track of personal bests from training runs or races as you approach the physical condition that you need for your G.M.P. Constant effort in training is rewarded by continuous improvement for up to seven years or perhaps more, depending upon the starting age.

Bump in the Night – When doing training runs at night, you should run loops or routes where you are familiar with the streets or paths. Obstacles such as uneven curbs and potholes can easily turn an ankle. As Forrest Gump says, "...it happens!" Just try to make sure you can see your steps at night.

Reward Yourself – Pick something that you like to do as a reward for completing your long runs or interval runs, whichever you find the most challenging. My personal favorite is a cold can of beer in the shower following a difficult training run on a hot day. This breaks the rules on dehydration, as alcohol consumption can exacerbate dehydration. If you have adequately re-hydrated, however, a single beverage is fine.

Involve the Family – Make a vacation out of training/marathon runs, and when possible involve the family by meeting up with them throughout the course for inspiration. They, in turn, will relish in your accomplishment even more so by helping you achieve your goal.

Follow the Plan – Be sure to follow your training plan. Most runners who engage in a marathon training plan for the first time will be setting many new personal bests for distance. You'll find these improvements are the steps that will keep you focused and motivated to the task.

Balance in Training Is Critical – Probably the most important suggestion is to never take your health and fitness for granted. Remember to stretch, replace your shoes, cross train on a regular basis (recommended two times a week), and don't overtrain. Even the slightest injury can impede your qualification attempt, and a major injury may set you back for months or years. An injury attributed to overtraining can be much more detrimental to your marathon performance than undertraining, and could even impact your future running opportunities indefinitely.

In summary, train and race wisely, as there is *no luck involved in qualifying for Boston*. It's your mind and your physical assets against the clock. Health is an immeasurable asset. Don't add on more training miles just because you feel good. Excess does not lead to success... in running.

Stage 2: Race Day Preparation

Be a Neat-Freak Just for a Day –As indicated previously in this chapter, as a method of minimizing stress, laying out your race day items the day prior is recommended. Even if you are not stressed, you should still do this for marathon preparation. You will be sleepy in the morning and perhaps not hitting on all cylinders, so the evening prior is the best time to organize to avoid a missed item.

Make a Fashion Statement – If there is some uncertainty of the starting temperature, bring at least one large trash bag to keep you warm (Photo 11.7). Even though there is usually a clothing check, you will still need to be warm after you have checked your sweatpants and jacket. You won't win a fashion award, but if it starts to rain, you will be the envy of the crowd. If you are more fashion conscious and have a thicker wallet, you may opt for a disposable product that is a plastic sweatsuit with a zipper (Photo 11.8). Trash bags are like gold in a staging corral on a cold or rainy morning. If you happen to be running with friends, take a few extra. Some runners even opt to wear one for the first few miles of the event until they've fully warmed up. If the race day weather anticipates rain, wind, or cool temperatures, it may be advisable to tuck a folded trash bag into a running pouch or pocket, should unseasonable conditions break out during the event.

Photo 11.7 Yet another use for a trash bag.

Photo 11.8 Disposable sweat suit(s).

Cotton Is for Rookies – Don't wear cotton shirts or pants. In fact, specifically, don't wear cotton underwear or shirts. Microfiber materials are used in clothing specifically made for these two areas. Fabrics like Coolmax® will capture moisture/sweat and allow it to evaporate by moving it away from your body. Also, don't use a new shirt on race day unless you are familiar with the material. Cotton shirts will rarely be seen in the first two corrals of a major race. Cotton shirts don't shed water, become too heavy, and also become coarse to the skin when wet.

Disposable Clothes – As the temperature rises during a race from start to finish (up to 20°F) , it is best to use removable clothing layers that can be discarded along the route. A suggested way to cool off as the temperature rises is to first remove gloves or a wool hat, then a long-sleeved shirt. Just make sure your bib number isn't attached to it. You will find that gloves and a hat will do best to regulate your body temperature as approximately 70% of your body heat can be controlled by insulating those areas. Shed these items one at a time so that you can more accurately adjust to the ambient temperature/conditions.

Discount stores will typically sell work gloves and disposable clothes, if you don't already have some collecting dust. These are excellent for wearing and discarding in a marathon. Remember to dress for the race, not for the temperature in the corral.

Check the Weather – Check the weather forecast the days prior to the race **and** race morning! To be prepared for varying conditions, pack extra race clothes that can best be used in rain, wind, or 20°F temperature swings on race day. As you know, forecasts aren't always correct.

Treat the Feet – Buy new socks for race day. Don't deviate from your normal sock brand or selection, but treat your feet to new socks for maximum cushion. Socks are the **only** item in your race bag that could have a price tag on it. Aside from new socks, **don't try anything new** on race day. Even your race shoes should have at least 20 training miles on them, and preferably one long run before race day.

Don't be a Bleeder – Men should use nipple protection, such as petroleum jelly, or better yet, Band-aids. It may sound un-masculine, but after one bloody shirt incident (sounds English, doesn't it?), you will be a believer.

Photo 11.9

Got Cab Fare? – If you have to walk to the start, find a hotel that is close to the start so that you don't use a lot of energy getting there. A hotel location close to the finish is much less critical. In fact, a long walk back to the hotel (post-race) may be a welcome way to cool down and work out the lactic acid-laden muscles.

Top It Off – If you are accustomed to wearing a hat, be aware that it will cause your body temperature to rise, as heat typically escapes through your head. On a warm day, wear a breathable mesh hat, or use a visor to minimize your body temperature increase. On a cold day (45°F and below), a hat will usually be a good choice for body temperature regulation. However, if you choose to wear a hat on race day, please select wisely.

Photo 11.10

Lube Up – Be sure to use petroleum jelly on any moving parts where you will experience friction, including underarms, inner thighs, and even your glute cheeks. You don't want to find out the hard way that you have inadequately prepared for the combination of skin, friction, and moisture, as you'll be sore for days. These friction issues may not be experienced on your long training runs to the extent they will at 26 miles. This is one area where it pays to overcompensate with a lubricant.

More Isn't Better – Don't eat a big breakfast on race morning. Eat the recommended foods, such as bananas, cereal, and bagels, in moderate quantities. Also, drink your favorite sports drink on the way to the starting line, but not more than 12 ounces. Any more than that, and you will be hitting the port-o-potties continuously, especially if it is a cold morning.

Dress for Success – A difficult decision on race day is the strategy for covering your legs and choosing between long pants, tights, or shorts. If you dress appropriately for your torso, with gloves and hat, you should be ok without long pants. Long pants/sweats will be difficult to discard, and you will lose valuable time in the process of shedding them.

Remember your running speed will slow as your core body temperature becomes too high. In addition, long pants and sweats (unless they are a lightweight synthetic material) will limit your motion and potentially hold moisture or add weight. The elite runners know how to dress for success.

As shown in Photo 11.11, when it comes to running fast, the elite runners know, less is best. Stephanie Herbst-Lucke is one of the top elite masters distance runners.

Photo 11.11 Stephanie Herbert-Lucke at the 2008 Olympic Trials with a runner behind benefiting from a draft.

Don't Check the Bags – If you are traveling by air to a venue, put your running clothes and shoes in the carry-on bag, along with fluids, carbohydrates, and your breakfast for race morning. Lost luggage with your running gear is going to be expensive to replace if you have to buy new items at the expo. New shoes will be especially risky to your feet, due to the susceptibility of blisters.

Why Be a Camel? – Don't run a race wearing a fluid pack on your back. They are added weight and unnecessary, just ask the volunteers at the water stops. Water weighs over seven pounds per gallon. Why carry the weight? If you have difficulty drinking on the run, use a straw, but most importantly, don't carry the extra weight. When is the last time you saw an elite runner with this stuff?

Photo 11.12

These runners have the right gear for an Ironman distance triathlon, but carrying this amount of fluid (especially the water pack) is overkill for a marathon, especially when considering fluid stops are offered at every mile.

A runner can get the necessary electrolytes and hydration necessary during the fluid stops in most organized marathons.

160

You Can Do It! – On the evening prior to the race, stay positive, as it is easy to doubt yourself at this point in your preparation. You can lose valuable sleep questioning your fitness when you see other athletes that may appear to be in better shape than yourself. For the majority of us, we are racing a clock for a BQ, not another athlete.

A marathon is a physical and mental event, if you don't think you will do well, you can talk yourself into a poor performance. Marathons require strong mental as well as physical conditioning. Don't forget the hard training runs or intervals that gave you confidence when you finished them. Take that into the run with you, but save that confidence for the second half of the race. Many elite athletes will visualize a successful finish or completion through the difficult parts of the event. Mental conditioning is often an overlooked component of marathon preparation.

Well... Are You Gonna Go for It? – Unless you are superstitious, there is no need to avoid sex the night(s) prior to an event. Coach Mickey from the first *Rocky* movie may disagree, *"Women weaken legs."* It may actually help you to relax if you are stressing about your race day performance. You may be pleasantly surprised to find that no evidence supports that it will hinder performance. Alcohol the night prior isn't recommended, but a small glass of wine may help you to relax. Be reasonable with your intake.

Protect Your Pedals – To prevent blisters, spread petroleum jelly on your feet and toes in areas prone to blisters. Make sure your socks are smooth to the foot inside the shoe when running, or a seam/crease in the sock will cause a blister.

Streeetttch – Stretch and warm up approximately 30 minutes prior to the start. This approach is even more important on cold and early race mornings such as in Photo 11.13.

Remember to walk and jog prior to stretching muscles to avoid stretching cold muscles.

Photo 11.13 Runners select various modes of stretching prior to a race, such as the use of Yoga poses.

Stage 3: The Marathon Start

Save the Banking for Money – You can't bank time in a marathon by starting out fast and holding on. It doesn't work. It is better to plan to start slightly slower for the first mile, then get into your pace around Mile two, but don't wait longer, and don't be off pace too much. Limit yourself to 15 to 30 seconds a mile off during the first two miles, then get back on pace. You can make up the lost seconds over the next few miles by staying on pace and going slightly faster by watching your pace band. **Remember to start slow and finish fast.**

Photo 11.14 Magdalena Lewy-Boulet at the 2008 Women's Olympic Marathon Trials took a risky approach when she sprinted out to a significant lead over the pack early in the race. Later passed by eventual winner Deena Kastor, Lewy-Boulet earned a spot on the team, but her pace was declining due to the early burst.

Look Up in the Sky, It's a Bird, It's a... – Be prepared to see bottles, shirts, gloves, and even trash bags fly through the air just prior to the start of the race. If you do plan to contribute to the mass of discard, don't consider it as littering as the discarded clothes (usually the old sweats, and gloves) are collected and donated to the needy. (Except maybe the hat in Photo 11.10.)

I'm With the Band – Use a pace band for your first marathon if there are no pace groups provided. If you find that you don't like it, or if it isn't helping you stay on pace, you can discard it during the race.

Move to the Front – If you are running in a race that does not use timing chips, work your way to the front for the start. If you are slower than those around you, however, be ready to move to the side to let the quicker runners pass.

Photo 11.15

The first half mile (800m) is usually ample distance to avoid congestion issues with faster runners.

What's That Sloshing Sound? – Don't over drink prior to the start of the race, as you will need to stop to get rid of the excess during the marathon, or face running in discomfort for at least the first few miles. A few minutes or perhaps longer will be lost if you have to stop at a port-o-potties for privacy.

Proper hydration is possible by utilizing the water stops along the course. You don't need to overload prior to the start. A common mistake for new marathoners is overhydrating in the hours prior to the race start.

Watch Your Step – Be prepared to see people finding a convenient spot to relieve themselves prior to the start, especially when there are long lines (and there are always lines) at the port-o-potties. If you are more timid, or if you are faced with a bio-emergency, you may elect to take an oversized trash bag with you to the start for such emergencies. By cutting/tearing out a slot for your head and placing the bag over your body, you can maneuver however you need to in compromising situations, sometimes even undetected. For men, filling an empty energy drink bottle will work fine under the trash bag. Women, however, may find it more challenging to be discreet.

No Cramming – There is no last-minute cramming for a marathon. Either you have trained, or you haven't. If you're undertrained, don't overdo it in the early miles, as the event will go bad for you quickly. Go out at a conservative pace that you can sustain, have fun, and plan for the next event more aggressively.

Stage 4: The Marathon Run

Swallow the Pride – If you are sick or injured, it isn't advisable to run for the experience, as it may make your injury worse. Use good judgment. If you must run, you may opt to run on the shoulder of the road in the gravel or grass (if available) to ease any discomfort or provide added cushion to a minor injury.

Who Said This Was Easy? – If you haven't completed more than 20 miles in your training, be prepared for muscle fatigue, cramps, or other physical hurdles, which may be encountered in the final stages of the marathon. Miles 21 through 25 are the toughest on your body and mentally the most challenging.

Can't Do Math On the Run? Me either. – Use a pace group, as they are a great way to keep you going during the toughest parts of the race. Staying with a group will help you mentally relax as you don't have to focus on time/mile splits. For example, if you need an 8:48 pace for a 3:50 marathon, look for the 3:50 pace group. Usually, the lead runners and individuals in the pace group will be wearing a bib with 3:50 or a runner may be carrying a 3:50 sign for the first part of the race (see Photo 11.16). Running with a pace group is also an excellent way to utilize a draft and save energy for those final miles.

Pace groups are usually on time or a minute or so quicker than the planned time. Also, watch your pace/time time closely, as a pace group (group of runners) may not actually be the pace group. Some runners may look like they are the pace group, however they may have fallen back from the true pace group. I have witnessed multiple pace groups indicating the same finish time separated by five minutes or more. The larger venues usually have someone with a banner or at least a bib on their back that indicates they are the pace leader. Another way to keep you motivated or on pace is to enlist the support of a friend to run with you who can easily achieve your desired pace.

Photo 11.16 The 3:10 Pace Group at PF Chang's Rock 'n' Roll Arizona.

What!...No Time to Stop for a Drink – If you aren't able to drink and run and want to avoid stopping at the water stations, it is suggested to use a straw (cut to five to six inches) for drinking. Use your hand to clasp the top of the cup shut, and you can then drink and run by sucking through the straw. When finished, discard the cup, and slide the straw under your watch. Trust me on this one and try it once. You can save two to three minutes if you have to slow to a walk when drinking.

Also, if you haven't experienced the confusion of water stops during a large running event, you should be prepared for pushing and aggressive behavior to get to the fluids. Watch the runners in front of you and anticipate where they will be going to for their drinks, and then plan for grabbing a drink from the next volunteer. Usually runners will slow to drink along the sides of the route and then move to the center of the street to work their way through the confusion. Unfortunately, when running in larger packs, the etiquette at fluid stations is not the best, so you may need to be politely aggressive to avoid missing a fluid station.

When drinking on the run is required to meet your goal time and you've forgotten your straw, pinch the top of the cup shut, and then use the small opening to drink from. This will minimize the drowning effect you may experience when trying to gulp and run.

Photo 11.17 These two runners show different approaches to drinking while running. The woman on the left has folded the top of the cup, while the man on the right is pinching the cup closed at the top.

Captain, We're Takin' on Water – Taking on water will serve two key purposes: (1) to replenish lost fluids due to evaporation and sweat (2) to cool the body.

A warmer body results in the heart pumping faster to circulate a higher flow of blood for cooling purposes, similar to the coolant in your car engine. In both cases, the car and your body, this effort uses valuable energy. Fluids (water) applied on and in the body for cooling will allow you to conserve your energy. As mentioned earlier, sports drinks, will also replenish the electrolytes that are necessary for proper muscle contraction/functions. Drink the sports drinks and use the water to splash it on your head, neck, and chest. Keeping your head and arms cool with water will most effectively cool the body. Also, don't forget to take on water in the final miles of the race, as at that point you are closest to dehydration.

Photo 11.18   Use water freely on a hot day to keep your body temperature lower.

Get in the Groove –   If you find that your body struggles to find the desired pace and operate effectively for the first few miles, that is to be expected. If you are watching your mile splits you will start to find a rhythm around Mile four, or even up to seven or eight miles. Once you've found your pace, then it's up to you to maintain the running rhythm. Focus on running upright, comfortable, and in your best form during the second half of the race. Running with proper form will help you to conserve energy and maximize your stride.   Once you've run your smart race until Mile 21 or so, then you can push for the finish.

Mind Over Matter – As you approach the final miles, you will start to see people stopping and walking. I guarantee that your first reaction will be, "Wow a rest would feel good right now." Don't do it. Stay focused on meeting your goal. **You'll get all the rest you need after you finish.**

Free Energy – Take in the spectators' energy when you need it. Write your name boldly on the front of your shirt or on your upper arm with permanent marker and enjoy the fan support.

High-fives are a great way to obtain an energy boost from the crowd, and be sure to tell them you appreciate their support.

Photo 11.19 Getting some fan support.

Draft, Definitely Draft! – It works in auto racing, cycling, and definitely works in running. If you have windy conditions on race day, use the draft whenever you can. If you find that you are separated from a group of runners and there are only a few around you, some runners may be willing share the lead responsibilities, but expect you will be up for your turn at some point (see Photo 11.11).

You can often find opportunities to draft behind a group, but on a hot/warm day, you may need the added wind for cooling. Remember that even without a head wind, you are usually generating a seven to nine mph head wind from your speed alone. Drafting is an effective way to conserve energy and eliminate the effects of a self-generated head wind.

Don't Be a Dreamer – For your first marathon, pick a realistic goal for finishing or even finishing with a negative split (second half faster than the first half). This will give you a baseline to work from. Don't attempt your first marathon at your Boston G.M.P. unless you have successfully sustained that pace in a half marathon. You will know by mile 20 if you have paced correctly.

Be Proud – When you are running in the marathon, remember that only a small fraction of the population has attempted or completed a marathon, even though the popularity of marathons continues to increase. And when you qualify for Boston, you will know that you are part of an even smaller percentage of the running community. Take pride in your accomplishment, because so very few have made it to Boston.

And You Thought You Were Done with Geometry – The shortest distance between two points is a straight line. This may sound too obvious, but apply that to a typical marathon course that is strewn with curves and turns, and you will easily lose sight of minimizing the distance run. In some cases, especially on a course with numerous curves, you could run an extra 1/8 mile (200M) or more over the full course just by not watching where you are going. If you are in a groove but staying on one side of the street, you aren't minimizing the distance run. Continuously look ahead at the turns in the course and plan for running the straightest line possible. You will notice that other runners have learned this secret.

Key Strategic Elements of the Marathon

If you've done your training, and all elements within your control are in good shape, then it comes down to (1) your rate of energy consumed or pace, and (2) replenishing energy during the race. So for first time marathoners, these two strategic elements are definitely elements of the race to consider.

Pace Strategy - Rate of Energy Consumption

Finding a comfortable pace can be a challenge sometimes. The first half of the marathon is the time to cruise and put yourself in autopilot to conserve energy (both mentally and physically). The second half of the marathon is the time to focus, as your body will be telling you to stop or slow as you approach the final miles. The final six miles are the most challenging. In fact, Miles 20 to 25 are typically the most difficult, because you don't yet sense the finish, and you are digging deep to push yourself. If you are focusing on a PR or BQ attempt you **must** keep it together during Miles 20-25 and push at a comfortable pace. This is the point your body will tell you to stop and test your mental toughness. You will find that you will be giving all that you have the last two miles.

For first-time marathoners, the critical miles to focus on for mental strength are Miles 20 through 25.

The best tactic for winning a marathon is whatever it takes. The best tactic for every other place is even pace or negative splits. *Running Times* Magazine (June 2008)

Energy Replenishment

To replenish your lost energy during the race, you need to take in additional energy through gel packs. It is best to take these in when you are within sight of the water stops and then have the luxury of washing down the gooey mix with water or sports drinks. My personal recommended intervals for taking the energy packs are at Miles 5, 10, 15, and 20, but other runners take more or less-depending upon their preference. Remember, it takes a few minutes to convert the contents into energy, so any additional energy consumed after Mile 23 or 24 won't be fully used.

You will find spectators are eager to help with bananas and other solid foods, but they don't realize that some of what they are providing may not help the runner in time to make any difference. In the final few miles, or 30 to 40 minutes prior to the finish, these nutrients will be of little help until after you finish, as they can't be digested and converted into glycogen quickly. The body may even shut down or slow digestion to focus energy only on running (depending upon your calorie burn rate). Therefore, nutrients that can be absorbed through the mouth and into the bloodstream quickly are preferred. Sugars taken during exercise (in small amounts) can be converted into glucose and insulin. If you consume more than 250 calories/hour, however, it may result in a negative or negligible effect to even discomfort if in excess. Gummy bears, jelly beans, and most soft candies are examples of high sugar content foods that can be absorbed quickly.

Summary

These suggestions are only a few that would apply to first-time marathoners or even half marathoners. As stated previously, this chapter is focused on ensuring that you successfully make it to, and through, the first marathon and on your way to Boston. Remember, speed and endurance doesn't happen overnight, regardless of how motivated you are. Be patient with your training. Don't shortcut mileage, and the progress will show with your performance(s).

To relish the challenge, you must first be prepared.

A jogger strives to be in shape, a runner drives to become faster, and a marathoner thrives in the challenge itself.

Chapter 12
The Race of a Lifetime

"The most satisfying goals in life were initially thought impossible."
-Confucius

Photo 12.1 The end of a well-earned journey, and the beginning of a new chapter in the lives of these runners.

The desire and vision of running the Boston Marathon loomed over me for years, since the day I realized the race was both challenge and reward. After a successful qualification run, my anticipation became comparable to the excitement of a five-year-old on Christmas Eve. I was absorbed in all that was to be my first Boston.

The eagerly awaited day finally arrived, as my first Boston Marathon was to take place on Monday, April 19, 2004. Traveling with my wife and daughter, we arrived in Boston on April 16. As we exited the aircraft, we were welcomed by race banners hung in the airport terminal and surprised by the numerous sightings of legacy runners wearing vintage Boston jackets from previous years. As we traveled to our Bean Town hotel by subway, the locals greeted us enthusiastically; the whole city seemed to share our excitement, with publicity for the upcoming event.

That evening we ventured into Quincy market and idly chatted with a few local Bostonians while I focused on a carb-loading pasta dinner. In the process, they learned that I was planning to run the marathon (I guess my Boston Marathon attire was the giveaway), and we spoke briefly about the coming event, but quickly focused our discussion on one man who didn't sport the traditional Boston accent. He told us that he was from Ireland, and that he and his family had grown up in Belfast, surrounded by years of violence. He shared unexpected personal accounts of losing two of his brothers to the deadly violence, and he himself had even been shot. Fearing for their lives, his remaining family immigrated to the safety of the United States via Boston. This chance conversation gave me a new perspective of my life, the well-being of my family, and the seemingly insignificance of a marathon. But Boston is not just another marathon. It is celebrated as part of Patriots' Day and is a way for Bostonians to celebrate freedom from tyranny. With this discussion, I was reminded of those who have sacrificed much for the goal of freedom and what it means. I would be mindful on Monday, Patriots Day, that I am free to enjoy the day and run for a finish line, rather than for my life.

I believe most runners who make it to Boston find, as I did, that it is not about the competition, but rather a celebration of the personal achievements that brought you there. The combination of running this event on Patriots' Day and the reward of participating in the most historic marathon makes this one of the most prestigious running events in the world. It is a day when runners, history, freedom, and accomplishments culminate into the event that is…Boston.

Saturday: The Exposition

The expo (Friday-Sunday) was clearly the largest exposition I had ever attended. Shortly after picking up my bib number, runner's pack, and T-shirt, I made my way through congested vendor booths.

By mid-day, the crowd was so thick it was almost impossible to cross some of the hallways. Competitive by nature, many runners don't do well walking in gridlock. Once a gap formed, it was almost comical to watch a runner spring out of the jam to fill it. In this mid-day congestion, it seemed that 20,000 other runners shared a common goal of finally purchasing the coveted race jacket and event shirts.

Photo 12.2 The expo and the rush to buy, buy, buy!

169

The official merchandise vendor area buzzed with excitement resembling that of the New York Stock Exchange. Chatter and commotion filled the area as people tried on jackets and discussed the numerous items for purchase. For me, the wait was worth it, as I finally had the jacket I had desired for years, but if you're not into crowds, you can make purchases online prior to the event. A recommendation would be to venture to the expo when the doors open in the morning and quickly make your purchases before the rush of running shoes.

One last item about the expo and the B.A.A. that can't go unmentioned are the ways they honor the participating runners. Photo 12.3 shows one such method of honor to the runners, as they provided a Wall of Runners. This enormous wall (which spanned the Expo Hall) included every runner's name. I witnessed numerous runners posing next to the wall for pictures. As if that wasn't remarkable enough, the B.A.A. and Adidas (as the sponsor) went beyond expectations in providing runners with a poster that contained all 20,000+ runner names. These amenities made each runner feel a sense of accomplishment even before race day.

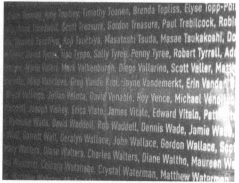

Photo 12.3 The Wall of Runners was an unexpected tribute…and nicely done.

Sunday: Scouting the Course

One day prior to race day, we took the subway (B-line) to its terminus at Boston College. This was the stop closest to the infamous Heartbreak Hill. As a first-time Boston runner, I had to see challenge in person to see if the legend was larger than life. In addition, we wanted to find a location where we could meet me for a few quick photos. We chose the top of Heartbreak Hill.

While studying the course elevation, I began to understand the marathon was actually three distinct sections. Miles 1-15 were downhill, allowing runners to easily meet their goal paces. Miles 16-20 included rolling terrain and Heartbreak Hill. The final six miles provided a gradual decline to just above sea level as you ran into Boston . This mixture would test hamstrings through hilly areas and quadriceps during the last six miles. This sequence in elevation change was something I'd not faced in previous marathons, so I recommend adding hill runs into any training plan in preparation for a strong finish at Boston.

Monday: Race Day Morning

A group of 50 runners watched Boston disappear behind us as we made our way by bus to the starting point in Hopkinton. On the ride, I chatted with three other runners from different parts of the United States. We found that we all shared a common bond in running and discussed the unexpected high temperature forecast. One of the runners, a 24-year-old student, had obviously taken the "stay hydrated" suggestions too seriously, as a few minutes into the 45-minute bus ride, he was ready to burst. Being fellow runners, we understood his issue, but could only offer humor in light of his situation. Finally, at Hopkinton High School, we merged with other runners on the path to the staging area.

Photo 12.4 Runners in line awaiting their bus. The B.A.A. volunteers, staff, and bus drivers do a great job getting the runners to the tents, drinks, and amenities awaiting in Hopkinton.

At this point, the sheer magnitude of the event started to set in. I made my way through the grassy area and walked through thousands of others who had also run their hearts out to make it to this spot. I suddenly realized – I had finally made it!

The Staging Area

I found a spot against a fence to rest and continued carb-snacking. I openly chatted with runners from Pittsburgh, Nova Scotia, and Newfoundland. We exchanged running and qualifying stories, as well as life stories. Everyone I chatted with was an instant friend that day, and the common bond that runners share was proportionally stronger, and spirits were high, as we all shared a common 26.2 miles to Boston.

Photo 12.5 The staging area allows runners to stretch, rest, and continue carb-loading as they listen to pre-race announcements and guest speakers. Tents are provided, but on a warm day, most runners relax on the grass.

Photo 12.6 Runners gradually make their way to the start, while others reflect on the day. Drinks and restrooms are provided, but bring your own snacks and your warm-up bag. It is at least a 2-3 hour wait prior to the start. If the weather is threatening or is cold, be advised to get on an early bus, to secure a place inside a tent.

Departing bus times are assigned by race bib numbers. The lower bib numbers, however, can catch earlier buses.

The highlight for the morning was an inspiring talk by John A. Kelley, two-time winner and host speaker of the 108th Boston Marathon. Amazingly, Kelly ran 61 Boston Marathons between 1928 and 1992, and in those years he also finished in second place seven times. Unfortunately, John died just a few months later, but he clearly left an indelible legacy of achievement for us all. Today a statue of young John and an older Kelley proudly stand together on Heartbreak Hill in Newton as witness of his accomplishments and inspiration to those who pass.

As race time approached, runners dropped of their warm-up clothes/bags and made their way to the staging area corrals. As I walked, I noticed homes along the road where the majority of the elite runners had stayed the previous evening. Some runners were stretching, while others were enveloped in a pre-race prayer for a safe race and most likely a blessing for some extra speed.

The Start: Hopkinton

Once in my corral, pre-race tension started to mount. Added to that was the thunder of an Air Force flyover prior to the start. Runners nervously checked their watches and forced the last few gulps of water to prepare for the already-warm day. I took the moment to reflect on where I was, surrounded by my running peers, spectators, and TV/press. In short, it was a fulfilling and exciting moment.

Since I started with a bib number in the 7000 range, I was out of sight of the starting line. A slight hill spans the first few corrals, and unless you are starting in the first few, you actually won't see the start. I soon heard the starting announcement and the roar coming from up ahead, and it was then evident to me that the 108th Boston Marathon had started. Nearly 5 minutes later, all individuals in my corral (#7) eagerly shuffled our way to the starting line. While approaching the start line, I was amazed by the number of spectators and television cameras that surrounded the area. Proudly I passed over the starting line, started my watch, and waved to the cameras as I also started into a new era of my running endeavors.

With adrenaline pumping and jogging nearly shoulder-to-shoulder with thousands of runners, I made my way down the congested Main Street of Hopkinton.

Photo 12.7 $1600 for family air fare, $700 for hotel, $200 for expenses, the feeling of crossing the start of the Boston Marathon – **priceless.**

Ashland and Framingham: Miles 1-6

As the first few minutes ticked off on my watch, I found that I wasn't paying attention to it, I was enjoying the crowd as I ran. Young and old spectators cheered every runner and visually embraced them as if today they were extended family members.

Photo 12.8   Jubilant runners surrounded by a hometown crowd set out to embark on history.

While making my way past Miles one and two, I was continuously amazed at the spectator excitement and the high-fives that were given freely to the runners as they passed. I also started to realize that due to the sheer congestion, I was already minutes off of my goal pace, and I wouldn't be setting a best time today.

This congestion for the first miles was beneficial for me and perhaps other runners not expecting the ease of running associated with a downhill course. Our pace was slowed to a manageable speed to conserve energy.

As I continued to fuel up on high-fives, the adrenaline boost was unlike any race I'd ever run. It was like being in a parade where the participants are not bands or floats, but runners…20,000 runners.

Photo 12.9 Amazing fan support!

With the excitement of the start of the marathon and the first few miles now behind me, the congestion thinned, and I then re-focused on my pace for the downhill run. On fresh legs, I made my way into the town of Ashland at Mile three. Runners were repeatedly advised to take in fluids at each stop. On this abnormally hot day (87°F by noon), runners took advantage of intermittent stops for water or Gatorade. Since we all got the same hydration message, congestion at the water stops made them very difficult to navigate.

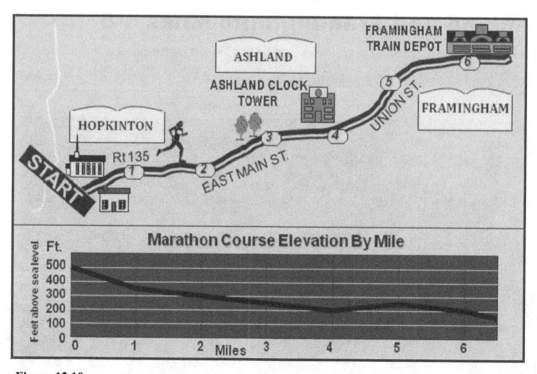

Figure 12.10

As I passed through the town of Ashland at Mile four, I was surprisingly touched by the families and small children that lined up along the road holding up food items for runners as they passed. And, of course, the high-fives continued.

The faces of the children as they proudly held up orange slices, cups of water, bananas, and cookies for runners were heartwarming. I couldn't help but smile as I grabbed an orange slice, thanked them, and watched as they ran back to parents to replenish their stock for other runners. I think many of the tiny ones viewed the thousands of runners as heroes for the day. In my mind, the heroes were the tiny supporters who brought smiles to the faces of many.

Photo 12.11 Tiny "fives"

The logistics at the water stops were starting to improve, as runners were finally spreading out on the course. In the heat, I found myself using both fluid stops for different reasons. The water stop became a grab and splash opportunity to cool off my body, and the Gatorade stop became an opportunity for actually drinking and replenishing electrolytes.

The first 10K of the Boston Marathon included an opportunity to run through the friendly town of Framingham and past the Framingham train depot. This historic depot has been on the route since the race's inception.

Photo 12.12 Runners rounding a corner into friendly Framingham

Photo 12.13 The historic train depot

The most significant experience for me during this first 10K of the marathon was the amazing spectator support. This support reminded me that Boston isn't only a race; it is a celebration of life that involves all communities along the route and runners from across the globe. Every runner I saw appeared to be as excited as I was to be part of this amazing event. Even the initial six miles of downhill running added further enjoyment to the "welcome mat" provided to the visiting runners.

Wellesley College: Miles 7-13

Continuing along Route 135 and passing through Framingham, I bumped into another runner during a water stop. We exchanged apologies, then almost in unison we each said, "Isn't this fun!" As we both agreed, we talked briefly about where we were from (Cleveland and Indianapolis). It became even more apparent that he too, like many other runners, was not after a P.R. on this day, but was out for a 26.2 mile Fun Run. If there is such a thing, it's Boston!

This Fun Run theme for the day was accentuated further as I experienced the girls of Wellesley College firsthand. I had only previously read of the excitement exuded by the students of Wellesley, but text alone could not prepare me for the experience as I approached Mile 12.

As campus came into view, I immediately began to realize that I could I no longer hear the songs on my MP3 player. As I started to run next to the estimated 2000 screaming female students, I was deafened by the cheering and overtaken by their exuberant support for sweaty runners. Some offered hugs, others a kiss, and all offered a friendly high-five accompanied by a cheer.

Photo 12.14   The girls of Wellesley College…my ears are still ringing.

This mass of support instantly gave me another unexpected surge of adrenalin, and my pace increased to boost my half marathon time split. Wellesley was truly a memorable experience, and one of my favorite parts of the race due to the excitement and energy they provide. It is impossible to run the marathon and not notice the most supportive fans in marathon history…the girls of Wellesley College.

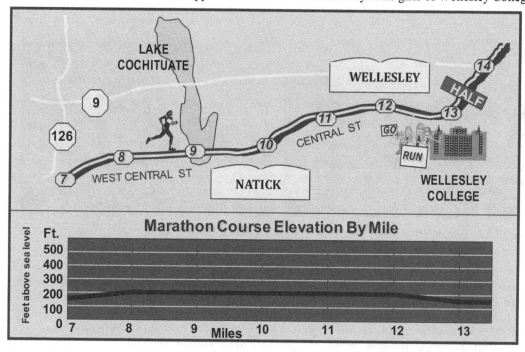

Figure 12.15

Newton and Heartbreak Hill: Miles 14-20

As the race progressed to Mile 16, the downhill portion of the course ended and the second half of the race started. These were Newton's famous hills.

As I made my way along Washington Street and eventually to Commonwealth Avenue, the crowds in Newton continued to show support of the runners. The orange slices, bananas, water cups, and numerous homemade water spray showers continued to keep runners refreshed. Even after hours of continuous support, the residents enthusiastically rallied for runners.

Passing by the famous Newton Fire Station and the town of Newton, runners start to make their way through the undulating hills from Miles 16 to 20.

Photo 12.16   Entering the hills of Newton

At Mile 19, the bottom of Heartbreak Hill, some runners started to walk. I chose to run up the hill with a grimaced face, as I knew my family was waiting for me at the top. As I crested the climb and saw the sign they had made, my shift in balance threw my hamstrings into painful muscle cramps. What I'd expected to be a Kodak moment turned into an anguished break while I worked out my cramps and struggled to hold composure for my three-year-old daughter. I jokingly asked if the Kenyans had passed yet and set off to complete the last portion of the race. Luckily, it was all downhill from here.

If you are planning a meeting location along the route, be aware that the subway access at Boston College gets very congested. Most runners make it to the finish area before their personal fans make it back from their return trip due to holiday/race congestion.

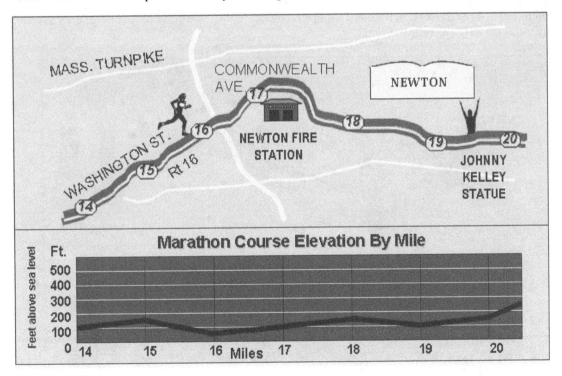

Figure 12.17

The Final Leg: Miles 21-26.2

These miles were easier than in other marathons for two reasons: we had outstanding crowd support, and we were in Boston. I noticed that when runners began dragging due to heat and fatigue, the crowd would not stop chanting their number or name until they started to move forward. As they started to jog or run, the crowd would erupt with support. The Boston College area was exceptionally supportive.

Continuing down Beacon Street through the boroughs of Boston, I sensed I was getting close to the finish. As I passed the well-recognized CITGO sign at Mile 25, I knew I was going to make it, and fans would surely spur me on if I had second thoughts. I made a few short turns, rounded the corner, and the finish line was finally in sight.

Some say that first sight of the finish at Boston gives the novice runner the closest feeling to that of running into the Olympic stadium at the finish. Like most, I will never experience that personally unless I purchase a ticket. The turn onto Boylston, however, was truly inspiring.

Photo 12.18 The CITGO sign is known by all who run Boston as the **only one mile left point**.

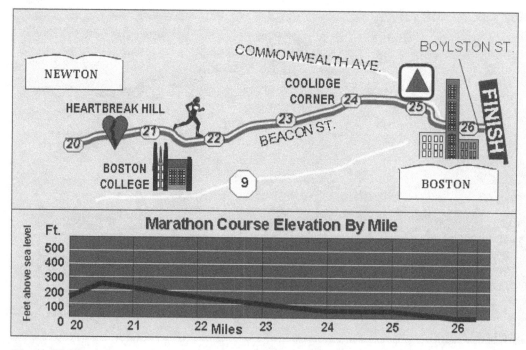

Figure 12.19

The Finish

As I made the final turn, the deafening noise of the crowd rivaled that of the Wellesley ladies. Bleachers lined both sides of Boylston Street, along with television cameras, photographers, and a sea of people. Rather than being hit with emotion, the effect of the crowd gave me an extra boost of energy to lift my legs a little higher. As I stretched toward the finish line, that one moment was worth the 2000 miles I had covered during my year of training in the cold, the dark, and the snow. Those last few strides were an overwhelming experience I'll never forget.

Photo 12.20 The finish line is just in sight after the turn onto Boylston Street and the roar of the crowd welcomes you back to Boston.

After crossing the line, I thought of the running legends who had crossed this exact spot before me – Bill Rogers, Uta Pippig, Joan Benoit-Samuelson, Rosa Mota, Ernst Van Dyk, and countless others. That moment is an awesome and humbling experience for all runners and marathoners from across the globe.

What Is Boston?

In the post-finish area, my thoughts were not my finish time or the fact that I completed the distance. Those thoughts were for the qualifying marathon(s). It was the fact that aside, from the Olympics, I had just competed with the best runners in the most prestigious marathon in the world.

Photo 12.21   The support from the spectators was unmatched and truly makes this a memorable event for all runners.

An unexpected delight was the continuous crowd of supporters. Never before had I experienced an event where spectators and participants acted as one team, seemingly dependent upon each other for success.

Spectators would pick out runners in the pack, leave the curb to run alongside them for a few hundred yards, ask their name, where they were from, how they were enjoying the day, how many "Bostons" this was for them, and then wish them a great race as they departed.

Many of the runners used markers on arms, legs, or shirts to indicate they were running for charity or dedicating their run to a loved one. On my third Boston, I wrote my mother's name on my leg in recognition of her battle with cancer. I hoped she would give me strength from her courage and that I would somehow give her strength from sharing this accomplishment. Many runners seek Boston or any marathon for personal reasons. Even in the worst of running conditions, Boston delivers reward to those who seek it out.

The culminating event for the day was receiving the coveted race medallion. I was surprised that at the time, the medal felt insignificant in contrast to the experience of actually competing. Typically the completion of a marathon brings a huge sense of accomplishment and is signified by the medal. For me, Boston was not about the medal, but was about actually participating and experiencing all that it has to offer. History, tradition, challenge, and excitement; a first Boston is truly a once in a lifetime experience.

Almost as if planned, the reward of Boston came into my life when I most needed illumination and fulfillment. Perhaps that is why Boston is so endearing to me as a runner. Unlike planning for a marathon, challenges in life can hit you when you aren't prepared. Running at Boston helped me keep my focus in life and kept me moving forward. If running is a stress reliever, then Boston is the glue that bonds running and life. To all who compete here, it is also a symbol of achievement, a measure of discipline, and a reward to stepping beyond what is typical.

Closing Comments

I hesitated to write my experience of Boston in first person, but decided to do so because of an article I read a few months before the event. The story was about people and exotic travels. The writer encountered an elderly blind couple who asked her to accompany them on a flight, over the Grand Canyon. She questionably and very hesitantly accepted. During the flight she was careful to describe the contours, vastness, colors, and visible effects of the Colorado River over time. At the conclusion of the trip, she commented she was sorry that they couldn't witness the beauty themselves. Their response was that they **did** experience it to the fullest, by listening to the passion and emotion in her voice as she described the views through her eyes.

Although conveying my experience in written words will not do it justice, I hope it will help inspire you to pursue Boston. If this is your dream, it may take you months or years. But if you are willing and dedicated to get there, you'll find this event is a reward worth pursuing.

Photo 12.22

The finish of Boston has just begun!

Postscript

"Now if you are going to win any battle you have to do one thing. You have to make the mind run the body. Never let the body tell the mind what to do. The body will always give up. It is always tired...But the body is never tired if the mind is not tired."
- George S. Patton

Photo PS.1 Runners that met the challenge and won...time to celebrate!

Motivational Experiences

I've had the privilege to know and even compete with some people who have literally left me humbled from the challenges they've faced or conquered. Perhaps you, too, have met an individual who's faced life challenges, and perhaps they've motivated you, just as the following people inspired me to run that extra interval, set out on a cold windy day, or challenge myself beyond my perceived capabilities.

Along this tangled road of life, I've been privileged to cross paths with a few individuals who, in the face of adversity, have been an inspiration to me as they endured with conviction...regardless of the outcome. The witness of their perseverance has instilled within me the pursuit to accept challenges such as Boston, and has fueled my passion to achieve life goals. To each of these people, thank you for setting the pace for me as a runner. But more importantly, your examples have made me a better person.

Doug Evans

As a 7th grader, Doug Evans was inspired to become a runner by watching Frank Shorter amazingly win the 1972 Olympic marathon. Witnessing this event, Doug was immediately taken with distance running, and wanted to run. Minutes later, he meticulously measured the circumference of his yard with a tape measure. Once the distance was established, Doug ran 100 times around his yard, which he calculated the distance to be 8 miles. To a 7th grader and non-runner, this feat felt insurmountable, but when he finished, he felt like an accomplished runner. Even more importantly, at that point in his life he became a "runner".

He continued his interest in running through high school and into college where he ran daily with a fraternity brother. This focus on distance and speed fueled his desire to qualify for Boston and he did so with a (personal best) 2:50 during his senior year of college. Doug ran his first Boston in 1982 and shared an amazing day in running history with Dick Beardsley and Alberto Salazar (winner) as they competed in their famed "Dual in the Sun", occurring just moments before Doug finished.

Doug vividly recalls numerous locations that played the inspirational song "Chariots of Fire" along the marathon route, as the movie and song were released prior to the '82 Boston. Doug's first Boston was truly memorable and provided fulfillment that only a runner can fully understand. His passion for running and Boston continued and he ran a second Boston to a finish in 1988.

Photo PS.2 Doug Evans

Doug was also driven to help others in need and wanted to give support back into community, and chose to volunteer at suicide hotlines in both Columbus, OH and Indianapolis, IN. This late night support spanned an amazing ten years until 1995. This responsibility was mentally challenging for Doug, but was truly a rewarding experience to help someone in desperate need. In the process of helping others cope with challenges in life, he decided there was another challenge he, too, wanted… the 100th Boston.

Doug's dormant running foundation was quickly awakened as he re-qualified for Boston's centennial celebration. There he joined 38,000 other runners in 1996 as they celebrated the anniversary with the thousands of spectators who lined the streets. Doug, like many others who have crossed the finish line on Boylston Street was again overwhelmed with the experience.

> *"Running is an individual sport, and you clearly get out of it what you put into it- that helps at times when you need to be reminded that you can have impact on the things within your control. Running helps to heal the things not right in your life…it's sort of therapeutic in many ways…"*
>
> - Doug Evans

Doug is a kidney cancer survivor, and while recovering from surgery he had a few months prior, we had the opportunity to jog together in a cancer charity run. As we talked, it was evident that Doug will once again see the final turn onto Boylston Street yet another time. I find a lot of similarities between Doug and myself. Boston is in his heart, and he has a passion for running. It is strange how runners become friends through passion in a common interest. I thank him for the motivation and inspiration he has given me. Doug has completed 12 marathons and has run three Boston's, but there are more roads to conquer yet for Doug.

Terry Molewyk

Without a doubt, my co-worker Terry was my inspiration to run at Boston. I met Terry in his office a few years before I started running. My eyes were drawn to a photograph of him crossing the finish line of a marathon. As we discussed his finishing time, I was humbled by his pace of just over 7 minutes per mile. I thought that I was capable of maybe one mile at eight minutes, but couldn't imagine the combination of 26 miles at that pace. As we talked, the discussion continued to focus on other marathons in which he had participated. Many were abroad, and the one that caught my attention was the Rome Marathon. I listened eagerly as he described the opportunity to run while literally taking a tour through the city with such sites as the Pantheon, the Coliseum, and Vatican City. That discussion opened up my vision of running beyond the streets and sidewalks near my home.

On that same day, we also discussed Boston. He had qualified and run Boston – **Seven Times**! I began to become inspired to run by his success as a runner. In addition, I learned that Terry was also an accomplished cyclist and had even competed in triathlon events. These accomplishments in cycling, triathlons, and running were truly amazing to me, as Terry humbly described them.

A few years after Terry and I met, he was unfortunately severely injured in an automobile accident and sustained massive injuries to both legs. Terry was hospitalized for weeks and had a long road to recovery and rehabilitation. Being such an accomplished athlete, Terry struggled with his injuries and questioned his ability to return competitively. In light of this "mechanical" loss, he was lucky to be alive. He endured 15 surgeries to reconstruct his legs, feet, and ankles, and his body contained enough pins and screws to build a small home. The result of his 35 hours under the knife left Terry with limited range of motion in his left knee (maximum of 90 degrees) and only a third of the range of motion in his right foot. However, once out of the hospital, Terry, an engineer, immediately took a technical approach to modify his road bike to accommodate his range of motion limitations. His adjustments to the crank and pedal geometrically accommodated his new body, and he was on the road again cycling in a few days. Even with the odds against him as a cyclist, Terry would not concede.

A few weeks further into the recovery, Terry demonstrated his unyielding tenacity to compete again as he entered a cycling race. He still had numerous pins in his feet and toes, so he cut away portions of his cycling shoe and left his foot exposed. On that day, he competed very respectfully, but didn't win his heat. Later, others found out that Terry was competing with a severe infection in his foot and fever, which limited his performance. But he kept that to himself until the day was over. In the face of some significant hurdles that day, he clearly won the respect of all who witnessed his sheer determination to compete again.

As a testament to Terry's technical approach to improve and persevere, in the 2006 Ride Across Indiana, or RAIN (a 160-mile cycling race), he came within ten minutes of the course record of 6 hours 35 minutes, which was set by someone nearly two decades his junior. This grueling ride was a personal best for Terry and, again, a testament to his perseverance, focus to training, and overcoming adversity through motivation and technical approach.

Terry's running mobility is still somewhat limiting, but he volunteers his time at many local races in his community and cheers on friends and fellow athletes. His desire to overcome his limitations has refocused Terry to become a better cyclist, perhaps better than he ever was. Terry is truly an inspiration to me personally and to all who meet him, learn his story, or see him compete.

Terry is the reason I pursued Boston and wanted to run a marathon, and for that I will be forever thankful to have met him. His character, humble personality, and pure athletic tenacity are what set him apart and allow him to define what a true competitor should be.

Tom Talbert

When I look at my dictionary for the word perseverance, my dictionary has two words: Tom Talbert. I worked with Tom for years, prior to my venture into running. I knew Tom was a cyclist, but I knew little of his sport and even less about his dedication until one day when I heard that Tom had been hit by a car while cycling. It occurred at the end of an evening ride when Tom and his bike bounced off of the grill of a 1977 Chevy Malibu driven by an inebriated driver who failed to navigate a turn. The impact broke Tom's helmet. He had a concussion, several broken ribs, a dislocated his left shoulder, a collapsed left lung, and a bruised heart, as well as other critical injuries. The responding paramedics and helicopter ride barely saved Tom, who at that time was 45. His sustained injuries put him in the hospital for weeks. Shortly after release from the hospital, he was back in the saddle. An accident such as that may have been enough to stop an average cyclist, but Tom persevered.

A few years later, Tom was participating in his 10th RAIN. During the race, a rider slightly ahead of Tom hit a road hazard and fell from his bike directly in Tom's path. With no time to react, Tom hit this person at 25, mph which subsequently collapsed his front wheel, broke his bike fork, and caused him to accelerate towards the pavement face-first. The impact shattered his helmet. Paramedics assessed his condition as critical due to vital signs and airlifted him by helicopter to a trauma hospital. The severe concussion he sustained kept him hospitalized for a few days. However, the trauma to Tom's head left him with a loss of short-term memory that would last for the better part of a year. Tom was approaching 60 years and at the time of this accident, he was one of the best competitive riders that I knew of any age.

Tom's competitive drive often fueled him to keep pace cyclists 30 years his junior. But this time, it didn't appear that Tom would be able to continue competing, due to the damage his brain had suffered. It was considered by the doctors to be ill advised for him to continue cycling. To the surprise of many, however, Tom persevered in a somewhat limited capacity and continued his cycling as physical therapy. After about a year of recovery, he cautiously ventured back into cycling competitively.

Photo PS.3   A winning triathlon team.

A few years ago, Tom was pulling together a sprint triathlon team, and I was excited when he asked me to run in the event. I had always wanted to compete with Tom, but rarely did our schedules align. Luckily, in this case we could make it work.

With the help of a talented high school swimmer, Tyler Hunter, we won the team event among over twenty teams and did so two years consecutively. With our team ranging from 16 years to Tom's 61 years of age, I was privileged to compete with both Tyler (center) and with Tom (right) and personally witness Tom put in his typical 120% effort on the bike.

With his competitive spirit intermixed with such a helpful and personable demeanor, Tom truly is a delightful person to know and admire. In his retirement, Tom spends a great deal of time doing charity work in Foundation For Youth, but still manages to put in his miles to keep the Gen-X and Baby-boomers in his rear view mirror.

To Tom, I thank him for his friendship and mentorship and for setting an example for perseverance.

Pamela Hutchinson:

I met Pam through a common friend after learning that we had both participated in the same local half marathon. Although her time was not spectacular, it was definitely respectable. But unknown to me at the time, she ran the race with an air cast on her leg due to a recent injury and subsequent surgery. Well, that definitely got my attention. Perhaps there was someone as crazy about running as I was. As we discussed her accomplishment, I learned the history of her injury. After many painful runs, she contacted numerous specialists until she found a surgeon who properly diagnosed her condition as severe medial tibial stress syndrome (SMTSS). Immediate corrective surgery was required.

As I got to know Pam, she shared a passion for running that I've witnessed in very few people. She simply loves running. Acting as the coordinator, Pam frequently runs with a group of runners multiple times during the week. They run irregardless of the weather, and many in the group (like me) are inspired by Pam's enjoyment for running and seek out events to run as a group. Months after her MTSS surgery, the group agreed to enter the Phoenix Rock 'n' Roll Marathon. Just a few months prior to the marathon, she was training on a pavement trail with her dog alongside when it crossed her path, and she tripped. Pam hit the pavement hard, fractured her hip, and sustained additional cuts and bruises. Suddenly her opportunity for a first marathon vanished as she lay on the ground in pain. But she got up, like true runners do. Again, she faced months of physical therapy and slow recovery.

As she began to heal, she accepted the challenge of training for yet another marathon, Rocket City in Alabama. She ran strong, as she and members of the running group finished their first marathon. They all relished in their accomplishment, and rightfully so with Pam as their chief motivator.

Photo PS.4
Our first place 10K sweep, a memorable day.

Pam has an unyielding determination to run, combined with the motivation to improve, and as such she has improved her marathon times and continues to narrow the gap to qualify for Boston. Pam has won my respect many times over from what she has been through just to run. She has completed over 25 half marathon events and three marathons, including the 2008 Athens Greece Marathon. I have no doubt that she will accomplish all that she seeks as a runner and in life.

Pam humbly admits that she doesn't have the natural physique of a runner, but in response, her desire to improve far exceeds any physical limitations she confesses.

A quote from the former head coach of the Indianapolis Colts, Tony Dungee, best describes runners that excel such as Pam. Tony was asked about how he selects the best players for the limited and few positions on the team. (**"I seek out the players that are ordinary players that accomplish extraordinary things through their actions and motivation… and not the extraordinary players that do simple things based upon natural ability."**) Pam would clearly be on *my* team.

Her passion for running is an inspiration to me and all who know her. All that run with Pam become hooked on her exuberant personality. She can turn a miserable day of running into another day to look forward to. To Pam, thanks for keeping me motivated, you are my ambassador of running and an inspiration to all who know you.

Andy Theal "The Competitor"

Few runners can actually say that they know an elite athlete or much less have trained with an elite athlete, but I have been privileged on both accounts. Andy Theal and wife Jean lived in my neighborhood just a few doors down, and nearly every evening after work he would transform himself into a runner. Like clockwork, he would run effortlessly by our house as he set off on an evening training run. Andy is built for running with a 5 foot 9 inch frame and a slight 140 pounds running weight. He had been running for over 20 years when I first met him, and by that time his closets were filled with boxes of running memorabilia, medals, trophies, etc… all that attest to his elite running ability.

One day I invited myself to run with Andy as he stopped for a neighborly chat. After all I thought to myself, I'd jogged a mile or so each week at the YMCA, and the near black outs I'd been experiencing at the conclusion of my runs seemed to have passed. So maybe I was "in shape." Shortly after my self-invitation, I asked what pace we would be running. When I heard the words sub six, I began to quickly think of what injury I could use as an escape from the naivety of my self-invitation. Andy smiled as I backed out, but respected my desire. Content in watching my grass grow from the comfort of a lawn chair, I watched Andy set out and return on many training runs. A few years later I started running, and through continued training, I was finally able to stay with him on a few long runs, where I wouldn't slow him too much. For me, that was a true accomplishment, and as my running times improved, we actually met for a few training runs or grueling cycling rides.

Andy would easily log 80 to 120 miles/week running and another 40 to 80 miles cycling. I soon learned that his goal as a runner far surpassed that of any normal runner, as he wanted to make it to the Olympic Trials.

He trained intensely for this goal and logged in numerous long runs of 28 miles or more. Andy was approaching 40 years and was planning to make it to the trials. This aggressive goal would put him in the Olympic trials as the oldest marathoner to make it. In his prime, Andy had previously run a 1:10 half marathon and was easily capable of a 2:30 marathon; he needed a 2:22 for his level B qualification. After valiant attempts at Columbus and Los Angeles, Andy's best was a disappointing 2:26. But from a normal runner's perspective, a 2:26 is amazing.

Photo PS.5   Andy on his way to a top finish at a half marathon.

Since I have immense respect for Andy's dedication and capability as a runner, I've dreamed of someday competing at Andy's level, but know at the same time that I would struggle to ever beat him. A few years ago, Andy and I started in the same corral of a half marathon, and I knew that would be the last time I saw him after the start. On that day, I finished with a personal best time and was surprised to see Andy just a few feet in front of me as I crossed the finish line. He congratulated me on my time and said that because of his hip injury, he was expecting that he would see me somewhere on the course. Jokingly I confessed that one of my goals was to beat him in a race, and unknowingly, I almost did. I started to become proud of the fact that I nearly beat him after all of my training and continued improvement. Then I was reminded of Andy's competitive nature and in a very non-condescending manner he told me that he "would puke before he would let me pass him." And I knew he was right. Therefore, my goal remains a goal, as someday I hope to see Andy puke (in a friendly way, of course).

For me, Andy is the benchmark of where desire can take you through hard work…without bounds.

My Mother

My third Boston was an emotional run. Just a few weeks earlier in April, my mother Betty was diagnosed with terminal cancer. Understanding that this might be our final Boston to share together, my legs were adorned with her name, and she and my father were in my thoughts.

With a heavy heart, I phoned my parents as I approached the starting corral and described the events as they unfolded on that bittersweet morning. From the start, and through each of the key points in the race, I phoned her and in my best words of description portrayed the race details in an effort for them to experience the day with me.

As I ran past the screaming girls of Wellesley College, I held the phone out for her to hear the roar. Even as I crossed the finish, I shared the moment with them, knowing that her courage and strength was my sole inspiration that day.

My mother passed away a few months after her diagnosis and, as many know, the treatments were nearly as debilitating as the disease. She rarely complained, however, and both she and my father inspired me so much through their strength and faith. You can never thank your parents enough for being good parents, nor do you see the example they've set until you are a parent yourself.

Mom, I know you are running with me...but I still miss you.

My Daughter Casey

My daughter has inspired me since she was an infant to make myself better in many ways, and she has given me inner strength as a runner. She has taught me the responsibilities and privileges of being a good parent, and in the process I have hopefully become a more understanding and forgiving person.

Since she was an infant, each night before she goes to sleep, I've been privileged to tell her a bedtime story. Each night I ask her what kind of story she would like to hear. The topics range from a bird, a bunny, or a princess, to stories about life and experiences. One night, however, she asked me to tell her a story about myself.

I decided to tell her about the time I first qualified for Boston, when she was 2 years old. In detail, I explained to her how the night before the qualifying race I was alone, staying in a college dorm room (at Grandma's Marathon in Duluth, Minnesota), and I was nervous on race day because I had little sleep the night prior. I was very unsure about myself and my preparedness, but told her that I carried a picture of her on my pace band and looked at her picture for inspiration many times during the race.

The pride on her face and the way she held my arm as I told the story was worth every training mile I've ever run. At that point she then realized how much I enjoyed running. When I finished the story, she told me she was proud of me. I couldn't have been prouder as a parent, because she understood her father's passion for running and how she had helped him run. I see in my daughter a passion for competition and perhaps a thrill for running.

Photo PS.6 Casey with her first place finish in the mile and a proud father.

These are a few of the people who have inspired me to run and pursue my running goals. I owe my accomplishments as a Boston Marathoner to them, as well as others not listed. Inspiration is a powerful fuel that comes from others and what they have been through. How you funnel that inspiration is up to you. Find who or what inspires you, and think of that inspiration when you run. The power of inspiration can take you beyond your expectations.

Personal Records (PRs)

As you see from my personal bests (Table PS.7), I am clearly not an elite athlete. Unlike other authors of running texts/publications, I haven't run in the Olympics, haven't set a world record, or haven't won a notable event. I wanted to pursue a dream and searched for a way to achieve it. I credit my improvement over my relatively few years of running to sustained focus on goals, learned training approaches, and remaining relatively injury-free for qualifying attempts.

A few months into pursuit of my goal, my times improved as I learned more about the running "do's and don'ts." As I continued to train, each P.R. I set fueled my motivation to keep going. Realizing that these personal bests were coming, but perhaps not as quickly as desired, I gradually realized that getting to that next level meant that I needed to do something different or in addition to my current training. So I became a sponge for running knowledge and soon found that quality long runs and focused speed work have a direct impact on marathon performance. The more I focused on the quality of training, rather than quantity, the more I saw the improvements to my times again. Soon I was logging nearly 2000 miles/year and modifying my nutrition intake for better energy sources. My training plan now incorporated cross training, intervals, tempo runs, etc…all things I hadn't considered in the months prior.

A word of support for you 35-year "young" and over runners', through continued training and focused effort, you will continue to set personal bests as you improve your physical condition. Sustained training efforts will drop race times at all distances, and you may feel as if you've never been in better shape. Through focused training, a runner should continue to improve for up to 7 years, and then gradually peak. As you can see in Table PS.7, I shaved time at every distance listed in three short years using the principles outlined in this book. The primary reason for showing this table is to illustrate that continued training will improve your performance even at middle age. As you condition your body to the rigors of a marathon and improve its efficiency of utilizing oxygen and stored energy, your personal bests will continue to improve, inversely proportional to your age. Yes, there is one thing that can actually combat age: exercise!

Personal Records

Distance	Initial Times (1st Year of Focused Training)	Age	Personal Records	Age
1 mile	6:55	40	**5:31**	43
5K	23:15	40	**19:07**	43
10K	46:50	40	**40:06**	43
10 Mile	1:16	40	**1:03:58**	43
Half Marathon	1:54	40	**1:25:47**	43
Marathon	3:43:15	40	**3:01:40**	43

According to *Time* magazine, 43% of marathoners in the United States are now over 40 years of age, and in the 2005 Boston Marathon, 20% of the runners who finished were over 50 years. United States marathon participation continues to increase, perhaps due to the growing focus on fitness, needed stress relief, better health/medical services for runners, and desire for a healthier lifestyle. Regardless of the reason, in my opinion running is an age fighter both mentally and physically, which is why it has become an addiction across the United States, and perhaps the globe.

As you start on your quest to become a faster runner, I highly recommend that you track your personal bests as you begin and continue to track your improvements. This positive reinforcement will keep you motivated. You should begin to notice a decrease in times on training runs in just a few short months.

Remember that marathon training at our level (3:00 hour to 5:00 hour marathons) is about racing against three things: your mental state, your physical limitations, and finally, the clock. When you combine the challenge of the clock with that of 26.2 miles (where nothing can go wrong that will cost you time), it becomes an ominous task riddled with opportunities to fail. Thus, the reason I've written this book is to help you accomplish the goal of Boston. So now it's up to you to take that first step.

Beyond Boston: What's Next?

A Goal Completed...Now What?

Once you have witnessed Boston and shared the passion of the event with the half million spectators and 20,000 plus runners, that is a difficult event to follow. Some relish the accomplishment and consider the life goal complete. Others seek the annual event as tradition and continue to run sequential Boston's. The 2008 event had many 25 year plus consecutive Boston runners, with the longest string of consecutive Boston's at 42 by a 61-year-old named Neil Weygandt. Other runners opt to accomplish the goal of running a marathon in each continent or one in every state in the United States. What you do after Boston, is something that only you can decide. I will offer some advice, however.

If you opt to run Boston again, you will not be disappointed. I've run six Boston's as of 2010, and each has provided fulfillment in unique and unexpected ways. Temperatures ranged from low 40s to nearly 90°F, the participants changed, and celebrity runners such as Lance Armstrong brought a new level of anticipation to the event. However, if the increasing expense of travel does not allow, I would suggest two options.

First, seek out a charity to run for, as there are literally hundreds to choose from, and many events assist with travel expense. Charities that support running include local children's hospitals, breast cancer, prostate cancer, the Heart Foundation, Make a Wish Foundation, Relay for Life, American Cancer Society, Team in Training for Leukemia and Lymphoma—and the list is endless.

Your experience as a runner and marathoner can and will benefit others not as fortunate due to loss or illness. You'll find it is truly a humbling experience to have others support you in a cause that is personal to you. When running is no longer for you, but for others and their personal wishes (for ill or lost loved ones), it is much more of a rewarding experience for all involved.

Photo PS.8 Team in Training (the purple shirts) can be seen at nearly every major marathon. They offer opportunities to both coach and participate. www.teamintraining.org

I have personally been part of a team that ran across Death Valley to the top of Mt. Whitney (Whitney Portal) in conjunction with Relay for Life and the American Cancer Society. By becoming part of a team and running for a mutual cause, there are no individual gains. No medals are awarded, but you're left with a greater reward of making a difference in someone's life. I highly recommend running for a charity.

Photo PS.9 Photo of me running along the Badwater course in Death Valley, where temperatures reach over 120°F.

Photo PS.10 Our 2007 Relay for Life Team in Death Valley. Running as a team for a common cause (in our case, the American Cancer Society) provides a unique, rewarding, and emotional experience.

Second, as an experienced runner who has completed Boston, you may be viewed by others as a motivation to begin running. As such, you may be asked for advice or individual coaching to enter a 5K, a half marathon, or even a full marathon. By providing coaching advice, you will be rewarded by helping others achieve their goals and be witness to their successes. This, too, is an unexpected reward to someone with a passion for running who is viewed to be successful or knowledgeable by their running peers.

Sharing your passion for running with others is what makes running endure and grow to the level it has become today, with more marathoners seeking that medal or life goal than at any time in the past. I've been blessed to meet some great people who inspired me to run, guided me towards the marathon, and set excellent examples for me in their compassion for others. Without them to keep me on track, my running accomplishments and this book would not have been possible.

Appendix Glossary, Index, Reference, and Credits

The difference between a jogger and a runner is an entry blank"
- Dr. George Sheehan

Photo A.1 The marathon; all it takes is desire and an entry blank.

Glossary

Aerobic – Exercise with the use of oxygen.

Ambient (temperature) – Typically outside air temperature.

Anaerobic – Exercise where the body is performing at level above the necessary supply of oxygen. Exercising to a higher intensity than normal.

B.A.A. – Boston Athletic Association.

Bib(s) – Bib or Bibs are the numbers pinned to the runner shirt or attire to provide the identification of the runner for official tracking.

BQ – Boston Qualification. Time in minutes required to enter into the Boston Marathon for each specific gender and or category.

Calories – The numerical measure of the energy level in food. In most cases it correlates to the amount of carbohydrates in food (per 100 grams) at a ratio of four calories per carbohydrate.

Carb-loading – Consumption of carbohydrates at a higher than normal level. Takes place over a period of three to five days prior to a race. Replenishes glycogen (energy) stores.

Carbohydrate – Stored energy found in high concentration in foods such as pastas and potatoes. Becomes converted into glycogen and stored in muscles and the liver as an efficient energy source.

Cardiovascular System – The combination of the heart and lungs working together to provide oxygen rich blood through a body's arterial system. The efficiency of the system can be improved through focused (cardio) aerobic exercise.

Chafing – The result of skin rubbing against skin and or clothing where a rash or worn area of skin results.

Constant Pace/Tempo Run – Type of workout used to improve the lactate threshold. Usually consists of a sustained run at a 5K pace+30 seconds. Lasts no more than 30 to 40 minutes.

Cross training – Non-running activities that are helpful in reducing skeletal and muscular stress while building your cardiovascular system. A method of increasing muscle strength and balance while minimizing risk to injury. Examples are swimming, cycling, elliptical, spinning, and water running.

Cushioning – Aspect of a shoe (usually enhanced by the sole or insert) that is focused to reduce the shock or impact on a runners feet. Shoes may be designed primarily for cushioning ability more so than for stability depending upon the characteristics of the runners feet.

Dehydration – Deficiency of fluids in the body due to various causes such as heat, low humidity, breathing, or lack of fluids/intake.

Easy Pace (E.P.) – See Easy Run.

Easy Run – Typically a pace equivalent to Marathon Pace (M.P.) + 60 seconds or more. A pace in which it is easy to talk while running.

Electrolytes – Replaceable minerals that are lost when the body sweats, such as potassium, sodium, and magnesium.

Endorphins – The chemical released into the brain that provides a runner with a "Natural High"; sometimes called "Runner's High."

Fartlek – Slow, even-paced running intermixed with fast running for short distances.

Fast Twitch – Muscles or muscle fibers that are capable of contracting rapidly when needed for propulsion or strength.

Glycemic Index (GI) – Indicates how quickly the carbohydrate content is converted into glycogen. Lower GI numbers require more time to digest and convert into energy (glycogen).

Glycogen – A highly efficient energy source for the body that is derived from digested carbohydrates and stored in the liver, blood, and muscles.

Global Position Satellite (GPS) – A method of utilizing data output from a device worn on the body as a watch or other device that provides instantaneous data of speed, altitude, distance by using one or more satellites.

Goal Marathon Pace (GMP) – The pace you need to achieve for your marathon time goal. See also Marathon Pace.

Heart Rate Monitor (HRM) – A tool used to measure heart rate and specifically used when a person is exerting themselves by physical activity.

Hyponatremia – A health risk associated to low blood sodium which can be due to drinking too much water or over-hydrating. This condition can lead to nausea, fatigue, vomiting, weakness, sleepiness, and in severe instances, seizures, coma, or death.

Intervals – A pre-determined distance (usually 800m or 1600m for distance runners) run at a goal pace with a short break or rest in between intervals. The rest is typically 2-3 minutes at the most. Considered by some to be the most important factor to reducing your marathon time/improving your marathon pace.

5K – The distance (K) refers to kilometers, where 1K =1000m. Each kilometer is equivalent in distance to 0.62 miles or 1000 meters. 5K (3.1 miles), 10K (6.2 miles), 15K (9.3 miles), 42.2K (26.2 miles), etc.

Lactate Threshold – Typically occurs when you exceed 85% of your maximum heart rate. At this point, lactic acid accumulates in the blood faster than it can be removed. When running at this threshold for a sustained distance, a runner will slow due to lactic acid buildup in the muscles. Is not necessarily a point, but rather a gradual event.

Lactic Acid – As the body converts stored glycogen into energy, lactic acid is generated as a by-product in the bloodstream.

Leg Turnover – The speed in which a complete stride is accomplished usually measured in terms of strides per minute.

Marathon – Modern day marathon distance is 26.2 miles (42.2K). Half marathon distance is 13.1 miles (21.1K).

Marathon Pace (M.P.) – This is the running pace that equates the rate of speed (i.e. 8:30 min/mile) necessary to meet your goal time to complete a marathon. Goal M.P. should be about 30-40 seconds slower (per mile) than your tempo runs.

Masters (Category) – Any runner over the age of 40.

Maximum Heart Rate – Measured in the unit of a minute as the highest number of beats obtainable. Typically approximated by the following calculation: 220 - (age of runner) = Maximum Heart Rate.

Mile – 1760 yards, 1609 meters, 1.6 km, Metric Mile = 1500 meters.

Motion Control – Design of a shoe that provides additional stability to control runners with over-pronation or excessive inward roll of the foot when running.

Magnetic Resonance Imaging (MRI) – A process that scans selected areas of the body to provide an image of bone, muscle, tendon and other tissues to detect injuries.

Negative Split – When a second half of the event is run quicker than the first half.

Overpronation – Runners with excessive inward roll of the foot when running (toes pointed in).

Overtraining – When a runner goes beyond planned training efforts in energy expended or duration. The typical result yields sore muscles that take longer than normal to heal, the runner increases susceptibility to injury, and poor performance post training.

Pace – Speed in min/mile that an individual is running. See also Marathon Pace.

Plantar Fasciitis – Small tears in the arch of the foot and detectable when first stepping on your feet in the morning. The torn or inflamed tissue is typically caused by overpronation.

Positive Split – When the first half of the event is run quicker than the second half.

Personal Record (PR) – When a runner completes a training run or event at a best time ever.

Pronation – The inward roll of the foot after the heel contacts the ground and the foot.

Protein – Nutrients found in meats, eggs, dairy products. When consumed, they are converted into components of the body such as muscles and bones. Protein provides two key elements to a runner as it builds muscle, and repairs muscle damage from a run/race.

Recovery Runs – Slower paced run typically used to recover/replenish the body of the necessary elements consumed during a rigorous workout or race.

Runner's High – Term used when the chemical endorphins are released into the brain that provides a runner with a "Natural High."

Runners Knee – (chondromalacia patella syndrome) is a condition where the cartilage of the kneecap softens , and becomes worn and rough, resulting in an agitated (sore) and swollen knee. It is a common injury and afflicts most runners who run more mileage than the typical runner (over 30 miles per week).

Shin Splints – Also known as Medial Tibial Stress Syndrome (MTSS) is a pain that is felt on the inside of the leg or shin bone. Typically caused by running too much too soon or the effects of overpronation, which cause the tendons and muscles supporting the tibia to become irritated due to muscle strain.

Singlet/Tank Top – Type of lightweight shirt worn by runners.

Simple carbohydrates – Instant energy foods are typically made with processed sugar found in soft drinks, chocolates/sweets, breads, potato chips, and other sugar-coated foods or snacks. Simple carbohydrates typically have a high Glycemic Index or (GI) and are quickly converted to energy.

Slow Twitch Muscles – Beneficial for endurance runners, as these muscle fibers are slow to contract, but can outlast Fast Twitch muscles.

Speed Work – Tempo, Interval, and Fartlek are types of speed training where a runner has quick leg turnover to build lactic acid tolerance and improve overall oxygen consumption efficiency.

Sprains – A tear in a ligament where the fibers are stretched beyond their limit. Sprains are more serious than a strain and are typically evident by blood, which moves to the sprained area and discolors the skin.

Stability Shoe – Resists excessive foot movement and usually designed for a neutral (pronation) foot type and a medium arch.

Strains – Designated as a pulled, twisted, or even torn muscle(s). Often due to improper warm-up or stretching of muscles.

Strength Training –The utilization of weights or resistance machines to increase muscular strength through the development muscle tone or density. The intent is to improve an athlete's endurance, strength, or speed.

Taper – A reduction in mileage prior to a race with the primary goal to maximize strength and performance on the event day.

Tempo Runs – An extended constant pace run 15 seconds slower than your 10K pace, and about 30 seconds slower than your 5K pace. Tempo pace is maintained for a recommended of 40 minutes.

Underpronation or supination – The lack of adequate inward motion of the foot during a running stride. In such cases, the running movement requires highly cushioned shoes to account for the improper distribution of weight. (Toes pointed outward during contact portion of stride.)

VO2 max – The maximum volumetric amount of oxygen that can be utilized by the muscles during aerobic activity.

"The Wall" – The condition a runner experiences when the body is depleted of glycogen stores. Usually occurs after the 20 mile mark in a marathon.

Warm-Up – Running at a comfortable and easy pace prior to a workout or race. This loosens up muscles and raises the heart rate. Readies the athlete for a higher level of performance to properly train while minimizing the risk of injury.

Wicking – Clothing that removes moisture from your skin out to the fabric, where it easily evaporates. Wicking clothes are typically worn as the innermost layer of clothing to keep the runner dry.

Index:

Credits and Referenced Readings:

The content of this publication has been compiled from personal knowledge, research from published texts, periodicals, or magazines, and where such direct excerpts or quotations were incorporated, credit for each source(s) has been provided. In addition, in my research I utilized other published readings for reference or clarification of the content herein. Direct reference and credit written or unwritten may be attributable to any of the following publications:

Bibliography

www.baa.org.
Art Liberman, *The Running Book*
Jack Daniels, PhD, *Daniels' Running Formula*
Jeff Galloway, *Galloway's Book on Running*
Tom Derderian, *The Boston Marathon*
Connelly, *26 Miles to Boston*
Balch, *Nutritional Healing*
Noakes, *Lore of Running*
Pfitzinger/Douglas, *Advanced Marathoning*
Gordon Bakoulis Bloch, *How to Train for and Run your Best Marathon*
Finch, *Triathlon Training*
Bruce Fordyce, *Marathon Runner's Handbook*
Rodale Publishing, *Runner's World*
Angus Macaulay, *Running Times*

Photo/Graphic Credits:

Table 2.2	Excerpt from www.BostonMarathon.org.
Table 2.3	Excerpt from www.BostonMarathon.org.
Figure 3.7	Courtesy of BSIM
Figure 3.11	Courtesy of The Weather Channel
Photos 3.14-3.24	Provided by and Copyrighted by ASICS America Corporation
Photo 3.32	Courtesy of Garmin
Figure 3.33	By Tom Steilberg
Figure 4.10A	By Tom Steilberg
Figure 4.10B	By Tom Steilberg
Figure 4.12	By Steve Helming
Table 4.20	Daniels Running Formula
Photo 5.4	Courtesy of Precor Inc. ,*www.precor.com*
Photo 5.8	Courtesy of Precor Inc. ,*www.precor.com*
Figure 6.2	By Steve Helming
Figure 6.3	By Steve Helming
Figure 7.3	By Steve Helming
Photo 7.11	Courtesy of BSIM,Cath Tendler Valencia
Photo 9.17	Courtesy of Grandma's Marathon
Figure 10.4	Courtesy of BSIM
Photo 10.5	Courtesy of BSIM, Douglas Steakley
Photo 11.2	By Zachary Long flickr.com/photos/fenglong
Photo PS.2	Photo by Doug Evans
Photo PS.10	By MarathonFoto.com (Rear Cover)

Special Thanks for support:

- Zsofia Nagy who modeled for the exercise and running photographs
- Tipton Lakes Athletic Club for the use of their facility for photographs
- Steve Helming for graphic drawings used in this publication
- To each of the companies or organizations for the use of copyright material
- To my Father Clinton Venable for continued support with this book
- To Greg Wickliff, PhD. and Isaac Willett for providing editing direction
- To my wife Tracy for understanding my running and writing needs

CONFIRMATION

A confirmation card from the Boston Marathon is now within **your reach**

CPSIA information can be obtained
at www.ICGtesting.com
Printed in the USA
FSHW02n1032101018
52899FS

9 781457 501395